After Year Zero

Fredric Jameson (1934–2024) was distinguished professor of comparative literature at Duke University. Over the course of his life, he developed an influential and richly nuanced understanding of the relationship between culture and political economy. He was a recipient of the Holberg International Memorial Prize and the Modern Language Association's Lifetime Achievement Award. He was the author of many books, including *The Political Unconscious*; *Postmodernism, or, The Cultural Logic of Late Capitalism*; and *Valences of the Dialectic.*

Also by the Author

The Poetics of Social Forms
I. Categories of the Narrative-Historical (forthcoming)
II. Allegory and Ideology
III. The Antinomies of Realism
IV. A Singular Modernity / The Modernist Papers
V. Postmodernism, Or, The Cultural Logic of Late Capitalism
VI. Archaeologies of the Future

Studies
Sartre: The Origins of a Style
Fables of Aggression: Wyndham Lewis, the Modernist as Fascist
Late Marxism: Adorno, Or, The Persistence of the Dialectic
Brecht and Method
The Hegel Variations: On the Phenomenology of the Spirit
Representing Capital: A Reading of Volume One
Chandler: The Detections of Totality
The Benjamin Files

Theory
Marxism and Form: Twentieth-Century Dialectical Theories of Literature
The Prison-House of Language: A Critical Account of Structuralism and Russian Formalism
The Political Unconscious: Narrative as a Socially Symbolic Act
Valences of the Dialectic
An American Utopia: Dual Power and the Universal Army

Film
Signatures of the Visible
The Geopolitical Aesthetic: Cinema and Space in the World System

Essays
The Ideologies of Theory
The Seeds of Time
The Cultural Turn: Selected Writings on the Postmodern, 1983–1998
The Ancients and the Postmoderns: On the Historicity of Forms
Inventions of a Present: The Novel in Its Crisis of Globalization

Seminars
Mimesis, Expression, Construction
The Years of Theory

After Year Zero

On Postwar German Thought

Fredric Jameson

Edited by Carson Welch

VERSO
London • New York

First published by Verso 2026

The manufacturer's authorized representative in the EU for product safety (GPSR) is LOGOS EUROPE, 9 rue Nicolas Poussin, 17000, La Rochelle, France
contact@logoseurope.eu

1 3 5 7 9 10 8 6 4 2

Verso
UK: 6 Meard Street, London W1F 0EG
US: 207 East 32nd Street, New York, NY 10016
versobooks.com

Verso is the imprint of New Left Books

ISBN-13: 978-1-83674-402-3
ISBN-13: 978-1-83674-404-7 (US EBK)
ISBN-13: 978-1-83674-403-0 (UK EBK)

British Library Cataloguing in Publication Data
A catalogue record for this book is available from the British Library

Library of Congress Cataloging-in-Publication Data

Names: Jameson, Fredric author | Welch, Carson editor
Title: After year zero : on postwar German thought / Fredric Jameson ; edited by Carson Welch.
Description: First edition paperback. | London ; New York : Verso, [2026] | Includes bibliographical references and index.
Identifiers: LCCN 2026018467 (print) | LCCN 2026018468 (ebook) | ISBN 9781836744023 paperback | ISBN 9781836744047 ebk
Subjects: LCSH: Philosophy, German—20th century | Critical theory—Germany—History—20th century | Philosophy, German—21st century | Critical theory—Germany—History—21st century
Classification: LCC B3181 .J36 2026 (print) | LCC B3181 (ebook)
LC record available at https://lccn.loc.gov/2026018467
LC ebook record available at https://lccn.loc.gov/2026018468

Typeset in Minion Pro by MJ&N Gavan, Truro, Cornwall
Printed and bound by CPI Group (UK) Ltd, Croydon CR0 4YY

Contents

Editor's Preface

Fredric Jameson delivered the following lectures remotely to graduate students at Duke University in the fall of 2021. Jameson planned the course—and this volume—as a companion to his lectures on postwar French thought, which he delivered the prior semester and published in 2024 as *The Years of Theory*. In the introductory lecture to the present volume, Jameson explains why he titled this course "Modern German Thought," rather than (in parallel to the French lectures) "Modern German Theory." His primary reason is that the term "theory," at least in the US, has come to be associated primarily with French poststructuralism, whereas, in the German context, it often implies the critical tradition of Max Horkheimer, Theodor Adorno, and their Institute for Social Research—often collectively referred to as the Frankfurt School. Jameson played an important role in introducing and critically developing the work of the Frankfurt School and its fellow travelers for a US audience. Here, in some of his last lectures before he passed away on September 22, 2024, he is concerned with a wider range of thinkers, many of whom have received little to no attention in his previous writings. His portraits of these figures add up to a story about the fate of theory, philosophy, or simply "thought" between the postwar division of Germany and its reunification at the end of the Cold War.

As a companion to Jameson's lectures on French theory, the present volume is shaped by a number of resilient Franco-German comparisons. Such comparisons were a staple of the comparative literature discipline when Jameson was studying at Yale in the 1950s, and one can imagine how unavoidable they would have been for a young scholar researching Jean-Paul Sartre while taking classes with the German philologist Erich Auerbach. After publishing his dissertation, Jameson wrote two books—*Marxism and Form* and *The Prisonhouse of Language*—engaging largely with recent developments in German critical theory and French structuralism respectively. These two traditions, often in productive tension throughout the rest of Jameson's work, inspired his ecumenical understanding of "theory" as anything that "prevents the university work of the humanities from deteriorating into a sandbox operation devoted to harmless and decorative eternal values and formalisms."[1] In that spirit, Jameson here asks where this ambitious mode of critique came from and where it might be going.

Despite the global uptake of "theory" as a rubric for critical thought, Jameson found it necessary to organize these late inquiries by national context. In this respect, it is notable that Jameson, in his introduction to *The Years of Theory*, veered from his autobiographical remarks to provide his readers with a survey of French intellectual production in the century following the Revolution. In the Napoleonic period, he argued, France's defeat at the hands of the British issued "for its citizens, consciously or not, a sentence to an essentially superstructural competition, to the exercise of action through language and the elaboration of culture." His story of postwar theory thus begins somewhat earlier, in the high-cultural malaise of the fin de siècle; this transitional moment, Jameson writes, bore "those 'fleurs du mal' which will culminate in the existential and phenomenological philosophies of the immediate postwar period."[2]

The analogous period in Germany is proven somewhat more complicated by the need to account for the emergence of something called "Germany" in the first place. To reckon with Germany's so-called *Sonderweg*, or "special path," to modernity would require a much longer account of the German principalities' attempt to "catch up" (in Jürgen Habermas's idiom) to the rest of Europe after the devastation of the Thirty Years' War, their brief reconstitution as the German Confederation after the Napoleonic Wars, and finally their rallying around Prussia during the

1 Fredric Jameson, "Transformations of the Image in Postmodernity," in *The Cultural Turn: Selected Writings on the Postmodern, 1983–1998* (London: Verso, 1998), p. 117.

2 Fredric Jameson, *The Years of Theory: Postwar French Thought to the Present* (London: Verso, 2024), pp. 6–7.

Franco-Prussian War of 1871, whereafter Germany stood unified for the first time as a constitutional nation-state.[3] But this would be enough to set the stage for the following decades of militarization, industrialization, and imperial competition, all of which came to a head with World War I and, as its conclusion, the Treaty of Versailles, when the Allied powers imposed the war reparations that contributed to the hyperinflation crisis of the early Weimar period, a national humiliation which Hitler and the Nazis readily exploited with a rhetoric of vengeance.

As in France, Jameson notes, the official intellectual scene in Germany at the end of the Second World War was still dominated by phenomenology and existentialism. To be sure, the political associations could not have been more different: Whereas in France these "philosophies of the subject" evolved through the leftist humanism of Jean-Paul Sartre, Simone de Beauvoir, and Frantz Fanon, existentialism in Germany had the particular challenge of its most prominent exponent, Martin Heidegger, having been a card-carrying Nazi.[4] But the common French and German existential background here proves more significant than their respective political

3 Anxieties surrounding German "backwardness" were predictably stoked by France's revolutionary leap into political modernity. Marx put it this way: "If I negate the German conditions of 1843, I am according to French chronology barely in the year 1789, and still less at the center of the present day." Karl Marx, *Critique of Hegel's "Philosophy of Right,"* trans. Annette Jolin and Joseph O'Malley (Cambridge: Cambridge University Press, 1970), p. 132.

4 Assessing the legacy of existentialism for Western Marxism and for the student movement, Hans-Jürgen Krahl summarized the differences in the two national traditions: "French existentialism, mediated through a specific reception of Hegel—essentially limited to the stage of self-consciousness and its forms—had from the very beginning a more intensive contact with philosophical Marxism than did German existential ontology, which, for reasons that were by no means accidental, entered into an alliance with Fascism and sank to the level of an official educative philosophy during and after the so-called *Kehre* [turn] in Heidegger's thought. Likewise, it is by no means merely superficial to the purely transcendental analysis of *Dasein* in *Being and Time* that Herbert Marcuse's attempt to establish a genuine and immanent relationship to historical materialism, in contrast to analogous French attempts such as Kojève's interpretation of Hegel, remained academically inconsequential, although Marcuse explicitly recognizes Marxism in its existential-ontological form as the 'theory of the proletarian revolution and the revolutionary critique of bourgeois society' and seeks to justify it explicatively, which is to say, not like the anthropological reception of Marx linked to Heidegger in West Germany after 1945, which practically defuses Marxist theory and seeks to reduce it to the philosophical elements that it contains." Hans-Jürgen Krahl, *Konstitution und Klassenkampf: Zur historischen Dialektik von bürgerlicher Emanzipation und proletarischer Revolution* (Frankfurt am Main: Verlag Neue Kritik, 1971), p. 101.

connotations. By beginning both series of lectures with a moment in which existentialism was the order of the day, only then to describe its passing or its vigorous critique at the hands of many mid-century theorists, Jameson is not so much recuperating or condemning the familiar existential salvos ("existence precedes essence") as situating them historically. That is to say, he asks why existentialism's central questions—questions about nothing less than the meaning of being, about justifying one's existence, questions which were once so pressing to many of Europe's philosophers—could suddenly be shrugged off in France as a *philosophie de papa* and consigned in Germany to an unusable past.

In doing so, Jameson follows an argument that Hegel, in a quite different context, used to justify the seemingly untimely project of a metaphysical logic. "Remarkable as it is," Hegel writes, "if a people has become indifferent, for instance, to its constitutional law, to its convictions, its moral customs and virtues, just as remarkable it is when a people loses its metaphysics—when the spirit engaged with its pure essence no longer has any real presence in its life."[5] With a similar intention of shifting the emphasis from the question to the possibility of asking it, Jameson once noted how "remarkable" it is that the most deep-seated convictions about what life is and how it should be lived, about meaning and meaninglessness, can be abolished by something as banal and seemingly abstract as the "service economy." But along with the expansion of the service economy comes a vast "dream world of artificial stimuli and televised experience," which constitutes the background for one of Jameson's grander claims: "never in any previous civilization have the great metaphysical preoccupations, the fundamental questions of being and of the meaning of life, seemed so utterly remote and pointless."[6] Such questions can then be assigned their local validity within what Jameson, borrowing from Sartre, called the "untranscendable horizon" of history.

This approach to the history of ideas as a series of questions rather than answers means that the first step when encountering an idea cannot be to rush to decide whether one agrees with it. Jameson will certainly take positions on the ideas surveyed in these lectures, but those positions are only reached via the awkward realization, as he puts it at one point, that

5 G. W. F. Hegel, *The Science of Logic*, trans. George di Giovanni (Cambridge: Cambridge University Press, 2010), p. 7.

6 Fredric Jameson, *Marxism and Form* (Princeton, NJ: Princeton University Press, 1971), pp. xvii–xviii.

no one has ever *had* an idea and that what needs to be explained, first of all, is the appearance of ideas as something one can possess, exchange and so on. To account for what nonetheless appear as ideas, to grapple with the preponderance of the objective situation to which they are responses, will involve more than simply checking them against one's own preexisting beliefs. In this sense, with a nod to Adorno's notion of "truth content," he encourages his students to struggle against that rigidification of thinking which obscures the reasons why an idea, whether or not it grasped something about its world, *seemed* like it could, at least to someone at some moment in time. As Jameson put it in *The Years of Theory*:

> In the normal scientific view, and the view, for example, of Anglo-American philosophy, at least some of it, the past is just worthless. If it's all mistakes, just throw it out, start again, begin afresh. An opposite view—that could be a Hegelian one—is that you have to work through error to get to truth. [...] You have to work your way through [...] the limits of that paradigm, and then you can see why it had to be changed, and why we have to go into a new one.[7]

Even the untruthfulness of an idea can therefore express something truthful if it is reformulated as an expression of the reasons why it could not be true. Likewise, if an idea is an answer to an implicit historical question, then evaluating that idea will involve figuring out in what ways the question to which it was originally an answer is still our own.

In keeping with his career-long reflections on narrativity, Jameson structures these lectures as a historical narrative unfolding on multiple levels at once. The story begins with an opposition between Adornian critical theory and Heideggerian existentialism, which present themselves as alternatives for a wide range of thinkers who are all engaged, whether they know it or not, in the rebuilding of a national culture in the wake of the war. To be sure, such disparate thinkers as Adorno, Alfred Sohn-Rethel, and Niklas Luhmann do not easily fit together under the heading of "critical theory," and much the same could be said of Hans-Georg Gadamer, Karl Heinz Bohrer, and others who are made to stand as latter-day Heideggerians. If there is any pretension to a definition of critical theory here, it would likely involve these thinkers' shared vigilance

7 Jameson, *The Years of Theory*, p. 79.

in keeping critique and negativity alive, so as to avoid ceding any ground to the postwar consumer society's delusions of ultimate satisfaction. But in Jameson's narrative, the lineage of critical theory is defined primarily by its opposition to the other, Heideggerian camp (Jameson's own comparisons between the two notwithstanding). This distinction grows fuzzier after reunification, but until then, as Jameson sees it, the question of national rebuilding shapes what both tendencies would consider a worthwhile intellectual pursuit after *Stunde Null*, the "zero hour" of Nazi capitulation (which Jameson names with reference to Roberto Rossellini's 1948 neo-realist film, *Germany, Year Zero*).

Jameson's "year zero" concept is double-sided: It captures the moment's contradictory sense of possibility (a fresh start à la the new calendar of the French Revolution) and of paralysis in the aftermath of such immense violence and destruction. In particular, both East and West Germany rebuilt under the shadow of what Karl Jaspers called the "guilt question" concerning collective responsibility for the Holocaust. West German historians and politicians engaged in a project of *Vergangenheitsbewältigung* (sometimes rendered as "past-coping"), a term that implies the aim of confronting and overcoming national traumas. Adorno characterized this "working through" (*Aufarbeitung*) of national history as a facile imitation of Freud's therapeutic "working through" (*Durcharbeitung*) of one's personal past, further still from a more emphatic concept of "working upon" (*Verarbeitung*) that past. Adorno's use of *Aufarbeitung* conveys the sense that the academics and politicians who preached the need to confront the Holocaust in fact viewed this task as little more than an "unpleasant obligation," as Henry Pickford puts it, not unlike the need to "clear one's desk."[8] Such superficial reckonings with the legacy of National Socialism and anti-Semitism, per Adorno, were bound to fail so long as "the objective conditions of society that engendered fascism continue to exist."[9]

East Germany undertook a more concerted denazification program, though this did little to convince Adorno—or the other "Western Marxists" returning from exile after the war—that the Soviet model taking root in the East under Walter Ulbricht had done much to eradicate these "objective conditions" either. Many of the Frankfurt School theorists maintained that Soviet-style state planning and US-style monopoly capitalism had

8 Henry Pickford, "Translator's Notes," in Theodor Adorno, *Critical Models: Interventions and Catchwords* (New York: Columbia University Press, 2005), p. 337.

9 Adorno, *Critical Models*, p. 98.

"converged" in their total organization of social relations. For these theorists, the merging of communist and social-democratic parties in the Socialist Unity Party, staged as a famous handshake between the party leaders, never had any hope of reinvigorating the united front, long since put to rest in Germany by the tragedy of the Spartacist uprising and the murder of Rosa Luxemburg and Karl Liebknecht. Well before the Berlin Wall was erected in 1961, many leftists in the West were dismayed by the quashed revolt of 1953 and the subsequent failed attempts at reform in the East. Jameson himself, having traveled to East Germany in the '50s (where he recalls encountering a copy of Marx's *Grundrisse*, which remained unpublished in the West until the '60s) refuses to present the DDR according to "the sterile alternative of apologia or strident anti-Communism."[10] Although West Germany takes up the bulk of these lectures, several dissident works from the DDR are discussed with an eye toward their continuing relevance—not only Ernst Bloch's writings on utopia, staples of Jameson's earlier work, but also Rudolf Bahro's sui generis political text, translated as *The Alternative in Eastern Europe*. (Bahro's original title had a bit more force: *Die Alternative*.)

The search for political alternatives was felt just as strongly in the West, where the hollow victory of the postwar *Wirtschaftswunder*, or "economic miracle," could not be officially opposed by a Communist Party (banned since 1956) and was confronted instead by a new extraparliamentary opposition (APO). It was at this point, during the student uprisings of the '60s, that the Frankfurt School was met with the fruits of its labor, as many of Adorno's own students, inspired by his critiques of "administered society," turned their movement against the university—and against Adorno himself. As attested in a series of letters to Marcuse, Adorno was greatly dismayed by the students' disruptions of his lectures at the University of Frankfurt, even defending Habermas's declaration that the

10 Fredric Jameson, "Introduction," in Peter Weiss, *The Aesthetics of Resistance, Volume 1*, trans. Joachim Neugroschel (Durham, NC: Duke University Press, 2010), p. ix. Like the *Grundrisse*, the first edition of *Capital* was little known in the West until the 1960s; when Hans-Georg Backhaus happened across a copy in the early '60s, he began a more extensive investigation of Marx's elaboration of the value-form, particularly through an attention to the differences between the first and second editions, which continues in a range of more recent work, notably that of Michael Heinrich. In addition to my brief comments on Backhaus and value-form theory below, see Jan Hoff, *Marx Worldwide: On the Development of the International Discourse on Marx since 1965*, trans. Nicholas Gray (Leiden: Brill, 2016), p. 79 ff.

movement was in danger of flipping over into a "left fascism" ("*contradictio in adjecto*!" Marcuse objects).[11] Where Adorno saw the student movement as an abstract negation of existing society, having no regard for the particular form of what it rejects, Marcuse was more enthusiastic about the movement's political energies. In his responses to Adorno, he chastises the doyen of critical theory for failing even to consider the students' motives.

In Germany, as elsewhere, those motives were largely internationalist in orientation, though the meaning of that internationalism remains debated. The Vietnam War, the Six Day War and the war in Palestine, and decolonization movements across the world were often, though usually only symbolically, at the forefront of their struggles. In 1967, for instance, after the police murder of student-activist Benno Ohnesorg during a demonstration against the shah of Iran's visit to West Berlin, leaders of the SDS in Frankfurt such as Hans-Jürgen Krahl and Rudi Dutschke gave speeches denouncing the police and the state as protectors of capital, but they did so as the flag of the Vietcong flew overhead. The APO's international outlook, internally fragmented as it was, took shape amid an influx of "guest workers" from Turkey and students from across the Global South. As in his essay "Periodizing the Sixties," Jameson frames the rise of '60s internationalism in part through these contemporaneous political events and struggles.[12] While the limitations of the survey course prevent him from expounding on the work of the student movement or its feminist critics, he emphasizes the reverberations of the APO's politics across a broader rebellion which soon flared up in Paris, Prague, Mexico City, and elsewhere across the long, hot summer of '68.[13]

As the '70s rolled in, the student movement and broader APO dissolved,

---

11 Theodor Adorno and Herbert Marcuse, "Correspondence on the German Student Movement," trans. Esther Leslie, *New Left Review* I/233 (Jan./Feb., 1999), pp. 125, 128.

12 Fredric Jameson, "Periodizing the 60s," in *The Ideologies of Theory* (London: Verso, 2008), p. 511.

13 The survey course—and its instantiation in the form of the syllabus—is a recurring pedagogical concern for Jameson. His syllabi were constantly under revision, and he was liable to quote from and extensively discuss works that were not assigned, opening up a vast informal syllabus beyond the "official" one. This is one reason why he decided not to include syllabi in these volumes. All assigned works, however, are cited in the footnotes, in addition to occasional nonassigned works that are quoted or require further bibliographical information. The only work that was assigned but not footnoted is a film on the Leipzig-born painter Neo Rauch titled *Neo Rauch: Ein deutscher Mahler* (*Neo Rauch: A German Painter*), dir. Rudij Bergmann (Germany, 2007). The film was screened on the

and there arose a number of isolated militant groups, the most famous of which was the Baader-Meinhof Group or Red Army Faction. The 1972 Anti-Radical Decree, known as the *Berufsverbot*, or "profession ban," prevented anyone affiliated with such groups from becoming a professor or civil servant, marking the beginning of a new phase of counterrevolution in the university. At the same time, plenty of non-violent movements persisted through "the red decade,"t including the women's movement, which achieved a "*successful defeat*," as Frigga Haug later put it, securing better protections for women at the cost of further absorption into the wage relation.[14] This moment also saw a return to Marx for a number of Adorno's former students, including the loose tendency identified as Neue Marx-Lectüre, whose works have become central to a recent revival of "value-form theory."[15] Although these works receive comparatively little attention in Jameson's lectures, his preference for them over the "official" Frankfurt School lineage represented by Habermas is clear enough, especially in those moments when Habermas's account of critical theory is called upon as a foil to Jameson's own.

Meanwhile, the Heideggerian legacy continued in a number of sometimes incompatible ways. Despite having been banned from teaching and publishing for several years, Heidegger remained influential in Germany after the war, though his major influence was routed through a lively

---

last day of the course. Shortly after the course ended, Jameson published an article about Rauch titled "Reunified German Images," *Granta* 165 (2023).

14 Frigga Haug, *Beyond Female Masochism: Memory-Work and Politics*, trans. Rodney Livingstone (London: Verso, 1992), p. 185.

15 One might expect the loose tradition known as value-form theory or *Wertkritik* to receive more attention in these lectures, given Jameson's interest in the new readings of Marx that emerged across other European countries in the '60s (especially Althusserianism in France, but also *operaismo* in Italy). Compared to these other rereadings, the return to Marx in West Germany was far more focused on the internal dynamics of the commodity form in the opening chapters of *Capital*. This reprioritization of the question of value has led in a number of radically different political directions, most notoriously that of the Antideutsch circles, whose structural critique of anti-Semitism is accompanied by a staunch support of the Israeli state. Most of these offshoots of *Wertkritik* lie outside the ambit of Jameson's narrative. For a useful overview, see Frank Engster's review of the first English-language collection of the writings of Krisis group, a *Wertkritik* circle founded in 1986: "Krisis, What's Krisis?," *Radical Philosophy* 195 (Jan./Feb., 2016), pp. 48–51. For Jameson's early comments on the "Capitalogic" of Backhaus and Reichelt, see *The Political Unconscious* (Ithaca: Cornell University Press, 1981), p. 93, fn. 71. On the more recent "Marx revival," see Fredric Jameson, "Sandblasting Marx," *New Left Review* 55 (Jan./Feb., 2009), pp. 134–42.

reception in France, primarily in the work of Jacques Derrida. As for Heidegger's students, some of the most famous—Marcuse, Hannah Arendt, Gunther Anders—did not return to Germany. Though many of their writings are also aimed at the specificity of the German postwar situation, they fall outside the scope of Jameson's survey (with the exception of Marcuse). Jameson instead picks up the Heideggerian thread in Gadamer's hermeneutics, which offers a different set of methods and techniques for "working through" the past. The difference with the Frankfurt School's approach to history resurfaces again here, where the hermeneutic method struggles to find common ground with the aesthetically oriented reconstructions and pedagogies such as one finds in the "rhizomatic" work of Oskar Negt and Alexander Kluge.

With that Deleuzo-Guattarian word, a French influence begins to make itself felt. Jameson waits until his discussion of Friedrich Kittler's media theory to mark the moment of a more self-conscious interaction and cross-referencing between the two national traditions, but he notes that a new, shared international situation made their mutual turns to questions of technology and communication urgent. In a strange turn of events, Habermas—in many ways the antithesis of poststructuralist skepticism about the possibility of communicative meaning—suddenly appears to be of a piece with this broader turn to communication as an encompassing and powerful category for social theory. In his capacity as the representative philosopher of the German welfare state, as Jameson deems him, Habermas thus engaged with the French theorists of language in terms that amounted to "a prolongation of ... the older geopolitical relationships."[16] Appropriately enough, his symbolic reconciliation with Derrida then took the form of a shared celebration of the new "European public sphere."[17]

With the Treaty of Maastricht, the new Germany entered the EU as its largest member, announcing that Europe's "unification," like Germany's "reunification," had definitively eliminated all alternatives to market liberalization (reunification, Jameson adds, was in truth the annexation of one Germany by the other). There is therefore a great irony, in Jameson's view, that certain strains of critical theory seek desperately to reassure themselves of a new democratic cosmopolitanism at the very moment the

16 See page 247

17 Jürgen Habermas and Jacques Derrida, "February 15, or What Binds Europeans Together: A Plea for a Common Foreign Policy, Beginning in the Core of Europe," trans. Max Pensky, *Constellations* 10, no. 3 (2003), p. 291.

European nations are sacrificing any semblance of popular sovereignty to the gods of budgetary austerity, as a condition of their admittance into the "European public sphere." At the same time, Jameson finds that one of the organizing forms of his own geopolitical history of ideas, the nation-state, has been dramatically displaced. The former nation states, as he puts it, were condemned to join the human animal itself in seeking "'meaningful' activity beyond social reproduction as its justification for being."[18] By contrast, the "member-states" of the European Union represent a distinct shift in the role of national collectivity, even as the rise of various fascisms across the world now make it impossible to doubt that the nation-state remains a distinctive parameter of struggle.

In 1972, Jameson wrote that "anyone presenting German and French dialectical literature is forced—either implicitly or explicitly—to take yet a third national tradition into account, I mean our own: that mixture of political liberalism, empiricism, and logical positivism" of the Anglo-American tradition which everywhere stands opposed to dialectical thought.[19] Over fifty years later, Jameson accounts for the retreat of dialectical thought in the same geopolitical terms, though the third national tradition, Jameson's own, is accounted for most often implicitly. On a superficial level, English-language sources "colonize" the footnotes of German social theorists, as he puts it; on a deeper level, the export of the English language marks the ascension of a US-American common sense that attributes every social problem to incomplete privatization. Jameson's lectures thus leave us with the question of how these geopolitical-intellectual relationships are shifting today, at a moment when it is becoming increasingly difficult for anyone to believe that fascism was eliminated as an alternative in the postwar period.

Is it time then to reach for another Jamesonian concept and practice—periodization—to identify this moment as the end of something, even without being able to say exactly what has ended or what comes next? In an intellectual context, Jameson's own death has already been used to mark the end of a certain intellectual moment—the moment of "theory"—which coincided with the postwar expansion of the university system. To be sure, what Jameson once said of Hegel would also hold for Jameson himself: His thought cautions against marking the end of a period too

18 Jameson, *The Years of Theory*, p. 7.
19 Jameson, *Marxism and Form*, p. x.

hastily, and certainly against marking the end of that period with the death of one of its "master-thinkers."[20] Yet one cannot help but feel that something at once less and more than a historical period has passed with Jameson. The bookending dates of his life, coinciding with the momentous historical transformations of the postwar world; the "accident" of his fluency in French and German, the languages of tremendous invention in those decades; his skeptical but generous temperament; his simultaneous disgust and fascination with the oddities of capitalist culture: Just as remarkable as the period itself is the fact that such a mind existed to bear witness to it, to make it visible to us in rich colors of joy and misery. And if we think of Jameson as a period of his own, we should remember that periodization was always also a call to action, a way of saying that the times have changed and that something new is required of us, or rather that we require something new of ourselves.

Jameson has often been praised as a figure who kept dialectical thought alive in the US over the long neoliberal years. It should be added that he did so not by faithfully following or uncritically celebrating the work of its major figures, but rather by transforming and reinventing that work in light of changing historical circumstances. Likewise, in his teaching, Jameson never wanted his students to reproduce his own ideas or anyone else's. Much like Brecht, Kluge, and others who reflected on the difficulty of instructing a national public against fascism, he recognized that merely transmitting knowledge or performing some rote pedagogical function would do little to bring about the kind of intellectual culture that he desired. Jameson's writing and teaching attest to something more powerful than knowledge or discipline at the center of a revolutionary pedagogy. *Is there any feeling stronger than love?* asks one of Thomas Mann's characters in a passage Jameson was fond of quoting. *Yes*, the other responds. *Interest*.

20 Jameson, *The Years of Theory*, p. 5.

1

Introduction

I want to tell you a little bit about what this course will be like. I should say that every course is an investigation into what a course should be. This is not exactly a history course, although it is a course about history, inasmuch as the thought it surveys will often concern history itself. In the case of cultures or ideas, there are really two histories: There is a social history, or the history of events, and then there is an intrinsic, autonomous history of art, culture, or thought. Those two histories are running concurrently, but they are not necessarily the same. Last semester, I taught a course on French theory since World War II, which some of you may have taken. It will sometimes be useful for us to differentiate the content of this course from the contemporaneous French situation. This course is called "Postwar German Thought." Why this change in terminology, from French "theory" to German "thought"? The word "theory" is going to mean something else in Germany. Actually, it will mean exactly the same as it meant last semester: It means French theory. At the same time, when you say "critical theory," then at once, you mean the Frankfurt School and a variety of German thought. This is not a course on the Frankfurt School per se, but certainly much of what we will discuss comes out of the tradition of the Frankfurt School. This is not a course in philosophy either, because the critical theory from which so much of this course's content derives is, in some sense, anti-philosophical, or at least it entertains a complicated relationship with the philosophical tradition as a discipline.

The course will cover four periods. The first extends from the end of the war to the 1960s. In this period of postwar German history, the exiles are returning. But who remained? The official philosophers who remained are mostly not affiliated with the Nazis, but there is Heidegger, who continues to exert a considerable influence in postwar philosophy. I've imagined this first section as a contrast between the first-generation Frankfurt School and Heidegger.

The second period—you could say it comes out of the Frankfurt School, though it ends up being very different—is what we call the '60s, except in Germany the '60s run until about 1977, which is the year of the Red Army Faction. There is not really any art or literature in the reading materials of this course, but I begin the '60s with a unique German artist, Joseph Beuys, who was also a political figure, one of the founders of the Green Party. Beuys will set the stage for the '60s student movement. This period concludes in 1977 with a moment of so-called terrorism and the Red Army Faction, and we will mark its end with an interesting anthology film about that year, as much as anything else, titled *Germany in Autumn*, or *Deutschland im Herbst*, by a number of German filmmakers. So that is a second period, and it will involve the revival of Marxism in a very special way. It will also more explicitly involve the German Democratic Republic, that is, East Germany, and two of its writers: Rudolf Bahro, the most original thinker in the East, and a much older figure, Ernst Bloch, who settled in the East and only went to the West at the end of his life and whose *Principle of Hope* has one foot in Weimar, even pre-Weimar, if you like, and another one in a very different, more utopian place.

In the period beginning in the 1980s, Germany is engaged, in one way or another, in the formation of Europe, and while that does not sound like a philosophical or cultural topic, it has a profound effect on the intellectual production of the period. I was tempted to call this period what the Russians call the Brezhnev period: the years of stagnation. Brezhnev reigned, so to speak, from 1964 to 1982, almost twenty years. The history of East Germany is a little bit different, obviously, and it begins in earnest with the immediate postwar and the Wall in 1961 but largely after Walter Ulbricht, in the '70s. Erich Honecker's regime forms a pendant to the years of stagnation.

From the end of the '60s to the beginning of the '80s is also, by the way, the period of neoliberalism: Reagan in the United States, Mrs. Thatcher in England, and Helmut Kohl in West Germany. Kohl is the figure responsible both for reunification and for the other major event of the era, with which I will date the last of my four periods, the period that begins around 1990 with the Yugoslav civil war, the most atrocious war that took place in Europe after World War II. Kohl was at least partly responsible, since he was the first to recognize Slovenia as an independent republic. But then you could also say it is an era of Islam in Europe, the era of immigration, borders, Brexit, and so forth. A somewhat different period begins there.

Can we cover all of those periods in a semester? I'm not sure, but that is the general framework in which I want to look at our topic. This survey will, obviously, go very fast, but it will also be very uneven in the sense that you will get, in a way, the most important and most difficult readings of the whole course at the very beginning. You're getting *Dialectic of Enlightenment*, a very difficult book, and Heidegger, a very difficult figure, certainly a difficult writer to translate. So, there is something disproportionate in this first period with respect to the others. But these are long years, and we're talking about roughly seventy of them. It is important that you try to invent or retain some sense of the passage of time, and to note, especially in Germany, how very different the situation becomes as we go along. How can we feel that?

It is important also to note that we will not be going back in any nostalgic way to Weimar, to say nothing of the Third Reich. These are both very interesting moments in history, but I think we have to understand that, with 1945, something absolutely new begins, or attempts to begin, with the famous "year zero." It is a moment when Germany has been completely reduced to rubble, when there really is no way of beginning again. I mentioned the French course I taught last year. The end of the war for France—and it ends really with the liberation of Paris, rather than the withdrawal of all forces from France—is a revolutionary moment. It is a moment when a whole new generation, who have not been in the army, but who have been fighting, many of them, in the Resistance, come to an awareness—more than of renovation—of revolution, of total systemic change. Change of that kind will of course not happen, but they don't know that yet in August 1944. In the case of Germany, there is nothing like this feeling of openness. I think what is going on currently in Afghanistan gives you an idea of what this is like. First of all, the exodus. In a panic, thousands and thousands of Germans flee from East to West, fearing the Red Army (and this fear is, if you like, justified, given what the Germans did to the Soviet Union).

Meanwhile, the cities are reduced to rubble. The doctrine of carpet-bombing, the complete destruction of the cities, we owe to Sir Arthur Harris. You probably read about the bombing of Dresden in Vonnegut's novel *Slaughterhouse-Five*, but Dresden wasn't the only city to have been destroyed. There was, for instance, a firebombing of Hamburg. And, indeed, the whole point of the British doctrine of firebombing was to destroy all of the German cities as a way of winning the war, which was something that the British, obviously, could not do with their limited troops. The Americans, when they entered the scene, had a somewhat different view. But there was a successful destruction of these cities in Germany. Clearly, this strategy is not the primary reason Germany lost the war. Some historians have speculated that Germany lost the war at the moment they ran out of oil. This is the reason for Stalingrad. Hitler's move into the southeast is dictated by the search for oil, by the movement towards Baku and into the Middle East. At the same time, the firebombings have not really destroyed the factories and German production, which is able to continue underground, benefitting from forced labor from the occupied countries.

So, it was a very brutal strategy, which was not ultimately successful. It leaves the entire country without … anything. This is not helped by the fact that the Soviets—who have no plans, at this point, for rebuilding Germany, who simply want to destroy it—remove everything they can find, from light fixtures to telephones, until the entire area of the Soviet-occupied zone is completely stripped of any kind of technology; in the US and British zones, it isn't much better, though this is not carried out as a systematic policy. The occupation by the three powers—later they add France—functions more or less until the Berlin blockade. The Berlin blockade, during which the Allies were able to bring one plane every ninety seconds into Tempelhof Airport, is one of the most remarkable technological feats of the era. The airlifts are another useful analogy to the Afghan situation, which can help one imagine this moment of complete desolation in Germany. After the war, the Americans devise plans to make postwar Germany a purely agricultural country. Stalin and the Soviets have no particular plan for any German socialism at this stage; they want a buffer zone between Germany and the Soviet Union. This doesn't come to a head until the Berlin blockade.

Sometimes I will use the German names for these states. The BRD is the Bundesrepublik Deutschlands, that is to say, the Federal Republic of Germany, since the individual states have a certain autonomy. East Germany is the Deutsche Demokratische Republik, or the German Democratic Republic, which is also referred to as the DDR or the GDR. Those states will only really emerge after the Berlin blockade, but what precedes it is very interesting: the decision in the West to reform the currency and to create the deutsche mark. In the days following the announcement of the currency reform on June 18, 1948, the full blockade of Berlin begins. This separation of currency, which facilitates the so-called *Wirtschaftswunder*, or "economic miracle," of postwar West Germany, triggers the whole Berlin blockade, which lasts until May 12, 1949. Immediately after the end of the Berlin blockade, on May 23, the West German Federal Republic is founded and given a *Grundgesetz*, or "basic law," which is its constitution, and which will be important when we look at Jürgen Habermas. Meanwhile, the DDR is officially founded in October of the same year, though it had already been functioning as such.

Those are the crucial moments around the time of this year zero, but what follows it? There isn't any sense of revolution. The problem of the Left in West Germany is the existence of East Germany. Western Marxists don't necessarily want to be associated with the East. What are they going to be associated with? Where is Marxism to take place? These questions only become more pressing in 1959, when the Social Democratic Party of West Germany—the Communist Party has already been outlawed—renounces Marx in the Godesberg Program. The other socialist parties of Europe, of course, follow suit. So, there is no Marxist party in West Germany; the student movement will later take its place, and then, in a sense, after the Red Army Faction, the Greens will come into being as another (albeit non-Marxist) counterweight.

So, where is Marxist theory to go? The Marxist theory of the period will largely emerge from the Frankfurt School, even though, as we will see, Horkheimer did not really wish to acknowledge this progeny, these children or grandchildren of Adorno, if you like. This tradition of Marxist thought will persist in what is analogous to the fall of Napoleon, which was followed, of course, by the Restoration. The Adenauer government, which takes over in West Germany, is a restoration, in some sense. Many former Nazi officials are in the government again. Thinkers who were associated with or at least taught during the Hitler regime, even if they weren't officially Nazis, are still in place. So, the task facing the Western Marxists does not seem to be a question of revolution, but it could be a question of reconstruction. Habermas has a marvelous word for this: *Nachholen*, the "catching up" of revolution. For roughly twelve years, Germany had been out of the world of art and philosophy. There is no great German music from the Nazi period. There is no great art. What Habermas is saying—because he thinks of this period in terms of modernity and modernization—is that the National Socialist regime was an exit from modernity. Now, in 1945, the Germans must go back and catch up with what was happening when Weimar collapsed. Obviously, that can't happen. You can't catch up with music, or even with philosophy like that—these are not the kinds of things one simply "catches up" to—but it gives you an idea of the way in which people conceived this program.

Another way these intellectuals thought of their program—and I think you can find this theme in almost all of the texts we will read—is in terms of pedagogy. If the Nazi regime is the result of a certain kind of subjective formation and if the West, as it is for some of these thinkers, is not much better—some members of the Frankfurt School propose a convergence theory, that is, the idea that there is an economic convergence between capitalism and fascism or that fascism is itself a form of late capitalism—if that is so, then some other kind of subjectivity will have to be created. So, the problem of the formation of the subject, of a new subject, plays its part in much of the thought from this period, particularly in the work of Oskar Negt and Alexander Kluge, who are, unfortunately, still not terribly well known in this country.

But what about what went before? What about Weimar? What about the Nazi years? After all, many people continued to live in that period in an ordinary way, as amazing as that may seem. In my initial suggestions for this course, I recommended that you see not only Fassbinder's allegory of the postwar, *The Marriage of Maria Braun*, which is quite a wonderful film—and you'll see Fassbinder, physically, in *Germany in Autumn*—but also Edgar Reitz's *Heimat*. It runs from the end of World War I, the return of a soldier to his village in the Rhineland in 1919, and beyond the end of World War II. You get a sense of the passage of time in that period. For example, one of the most striking aspects of the series is that it isn't until the Nazi period that electricity comes to the village. The Nazi regime electrifies Germany just as it builds the autobahns, the VWs, and television. There is a very funny scene in a science fiction film when they pick up the first signals from outer space; suddenly there materializes on the screen a swastika, and everybody is stunned. That's because the first television broadcasts were from the 1936 Olympics in Berlin; the waves went into outer space and then were reflected back and picked up. This is just to say that the Nazis' relationship to modernity may have been very specific, but they certainly understood and pioneered a lot of technology, not only warlike technology, though in general technological advances can be said to be a byproduct of war; that was part of Hitler's program. The Nazi pursuit of technological advancement will inspire much suspicion of technology in the postwar period. Part of the politics of the 1960s is anti-rearmament politics, the protest against the atom bomb, and these politics involve philosophical questions about the role of science. Brecht's Galileo play is very much thought of as—or at least it was advertised in East Berlin as—a dramatization of the agonies undergone by scientists like Oppenheimer in building the atomic bomb. Galileo becomes a figure for raising these problems about science itself. (Incidentally, we're not going to read anything of Brecht's. He arrived in East Berlin a little before Horkheimer and Adorno arrived in the West. But what I would suggest you read is Brecht's journals. He kept journals from the '30s until his death in '56, and the entries during his period in the East are very interesting.)[1]

The question of time and history: Isn't the present of postwar German history rooted in its past? Don't we have to go back to the uniqueness of German history in the first place? I suppose so, and one of the things we would have to do is stop thinking of Germany as a Western country. Germany never thought of itself as "the West," like France and England. But it isn't the East either. It is central Europe. And there is always the question of "catching up" in these various Germanies of the past, catching up with the West. "Catching up" sometimes means superiority. When the Germans industrialize in the late nineteenth century, when they modernize, in the technological sense, they immediately leap over everything in England, France, and the United States, in part because they don't have all that old baggage of antiquated machinery to deal with. They leap at once into the most advanced technology. Of course, this holds for postwar Germany as well. Later on, people will say Germany and Japan really won the war, because under the terms of the surrenders, they don't rearm. They have no armies for a long time, until they're drawn into the Cold War, and therefore their whole economic output can be devoted to production. In

1 Bertolt Brecht, *Journals, 1934–1955*, trans. Hugh Rorrison (New York: Routledge, 1994).

that sense, too, there is a way in which catching up can be an advantage, or at least a unique situation with opportunities of its own. Much of German history has been a catching up after Napoleon, a catching up by Prussia after the Thirty Years' War, which was, before World War II, the most terrible slaughter on European soil. If you go to a city like Magdeburg and you talk about "the war," they're not quite sure whether you mean World War II or the Thirty Years' War, because both were moments of enormous devastation. And you have to remember that foreign troops did not invade Germany in World War I; the surrender came on economic grounds long before the Americans entered, so Germany had not been occupied in modern times.

After World War II, as I mentioned, the exiles come back. Heidegger is still in Germany. Many of the younger Germans, as well as the older ones, are schooled by Heidegger. Hannah Arendt was not only a student of Heidegger but his lover for a time. Marcuse was a student of Heidegger, and this is one of the reasons why his relations with the Frankfurt School were unique; Horkheimer was rather suspicious of Marcuse's formation under Heidegger. Hans Magnus Enzensberger said that, after the war, Germans were always asked two questions by foreigners: How old were you in 1933 (that is to say, what were you doing in the Nazi takeover) and how old were you in 1945? If you ask these questions of the thinkers we're considering here, you'll see that Horkheimer and Adorno's students were of a particular generation. Habermas was born in 1929, so he was sixteen when the Nazi regime fell. And you know that, in Hitler's final defenses, children were drafted; twelve-year-old soldiers were rounded up to defend the fatherland. Habermas says that the SS came to draft him on a night when he wasn't home, by some lucky chance, and the Americans arrived the next day. In Günter Grass's autobiography, he describes being drafted into the SS and spending the last days of the war trying to find his regiment, because all of Europe was in chaos.[2] He was scarcely a soldier, but, of course, he had to get rid of his uniform in anticipation of the Red Army.

In this course, we're talking about what confronts the younger generation beginning in 1945. Habermas is not a bad example, because he's still around! He is the most famous philosopher of Germany. Somebody said that even his fame is famous. No other philosopher in any other country is as famous as Habermas. This is certainly not going to be a

---

2 Günter Grass, *Peeling the Onion*, trans. Michael Henry Heim (Boston: Harcourt, 2007).

Habermasian course, but we will read some Habermas, and his life and work pose interesting questions about the period. Where does a young sixteen-year-old student go, for example, if his formation and sympathies had been, for the most part, with Heidegger, who was at that point the only interesting well-known German philosopher? Well, he goes to study with Horkheimer and Adorno. There are other people—Gadamer, for example—who carry on under Heidegger's influence, and they will be of some importance. But this whole generation is, in one way or another, affected by the Frankfurt School.

What comes of the Frankfurt School in this zero-point of German history and thought? Let me, in that spirit, say something about the Frankfurt School in preparation for moving on to *Dialectic of Enlightenment.* I have separated the various chapters. We'll look at Horkheimer's contributions, that is, the opening chapter and the chapter on Kant and Sade. This may recall a famous essay by Lacan, but the comparison was first Horkheimer's.[3] Both those cases will have to do with Sade as an Enlightenment thinker, as a thinker of reason, in some sense. Then we'll look at one of Adorno's most brilliant chapters, the one on the *Odyssey.* I assume everybody has read the *Odyssey* once, but I'm giving you the relevant chapters in Fitzgerald's translation—I think it's the best one—in which Odysseus tells his story to the court before he is sent back to Ithaca. What Adorno does with this chapter is absolutely stunning. After that, we will turn to two very important chapters, one on mass culture and one on anti-Semitism, which are both descriptions of the social world, in a sense. Because Horkheimer and Adorno are writing this in the United States, these chapters, particularly the one on mass culture, belong to the genre of European books about the peculiarities of the United States, like Tocqueville or Dickens. As for the anti-Semitism chapter, it is the first significant notion of the subject as the Frankfurt School developed it, which is rather different from anything else. The Frankfurt School can be seen as attempting to synthesize Marx and Freud, and the anti-Semitism chapter is a part of a larger view of what the subjectivities of capitalism are, both in the fascist regimes and in the West more broadly.

I suggested that you begin by looking at Horkheimer's program essay, "Traditional and Critical Theory," because it gives you an idea of the program, as turgid as it may be, that Horkheimer brought to the Frankfurt

3 Jacques Lacan, "Kant with Sade," in *Écrits*, trans. Bruce Fink (New York: W. W. Norton, 2006), pp. 645–68.

School.[4] What was the Frankfurt School in the first place? There was a wealthy industrialist—I think he dealt in grains—and his son, Felix Weil, was a very ardent leftist in the Weimar period. The son persuaded his father, who had moved his whole operation to Argentina, to endow the University of Frankfurt with a department or an institute that would be focused on the left. If you're going to explain this department to people, presumably the faculty of the University of Frankfurt, you would say something innocuous like "studies in labor" or "social research." So that's what he called it. And the University of Frankfurt, which was, despite the age of Frankfurt itself, one of the newer universities and one of the most modern, accepted an endowment from the Weil family for an Institute for Social Research. Its first leader was precisely a specialist in labor. After him there was another, a sociologist who was ill and didn't last in the position. So this young adjunct professor of political philosophy was able somehow to take over this institute. That's Max Horkheimer.

There are various reasons to be against Horkheimer. You should know that he turned down Walter Benjamin's book on German tragedy, which Benjamin was trying to submit for an academic degree. He also refused Adorno's first attempts. But he had a very specific program in mind, and it was a Marxist program. The problem with Horkheimer was that he was so well attuned to the problems of getting an operation like this going and funded that he was very worried about using Marxist terminology. This is especially the case when they get to the United States, because the climate of anti-communism—and this is not even in the McCarthy period yet—is not exactly propitious. Instead, like Gramsci's various transliterations of Marxism into the philosophy of praxis and hegemony, he called it "critical theory." Critical theory was his phrase for Marxism in this period.

If you are an orthodox Marxist or Leninist, do you consider this work to be Marxist? We can have a discussion about that question, but the Frankfurt School's critical theory was certainly an academic operation, the production of intellectuals. It involved a new way of thinking about the division of labor of the disciplines, which Horkheimer, quite rightly, felt was a bourgeois convention. And, despite the academic nature of this whole enterprise, Horkheimer nonetheless held very strong political convictions. Obviously, there is a big difference in this period between

4 Max Horkheimer, "Traditional and Critical Theory," in *Critical Theory: Selected Essays*, trans. Matthew J. O'Connell (New York: Continuum, 2002), pp. 188–252. This essay was the only reading that Jameson assigned for the first lecture.

an industrial working class and the often wealthy students and sons of businesspeople, which is what Horkheimer was. Indeed, a secret history of the Frankfurt School could be told as the revolt against the father and the paternal authority, authority and the authoritarian personality being, for the Frankfurt School, a phenomenon of Nazism, fascism, and anti-Semitism. Horkheimer was far more political, I think, than most of the people he surrounded himself with, but it wasn't a politics that he always articulated in terms of the working class; he preferred instead to speak in terms of the poor, the oppressed, and so on. And I think we must credit him with a very strong sense of this kind of politics and with an alertness to figures of domination. This will involve a kind of feminism, the rejection of the domination of women as well as the domination of nature. These themes come out much more after the war, but they are there in the early Frankfurt School.

Horkheimer also had extensive philosophical ambitions. He wanted to rewrite Hegel's *Logic* using new categories. But he suffered from writer's block, and he had a great difficulty in producing any writing at all. So, what we have from Horkheimer, besides his collaborations with Adorno, are a few articles—one on authority and the family, one on critical theory—but they don't amount to a whole lot. Horkheimer was, however, a great entrepreneur, let's say. He understood very quickly that there was going to be no place under a Hitlerian regime for something like the institute, so he transferred the funds, first to Amsterdam, then to Switzerland, and then to the United States. He was able to get a lot of people out of Germany. And he tried to reconstitute the group affiliated with the institute in New York. This didn't really work, so he moved to California. At that point, it becomes clear that the real center of the so-called Frankfurt School in the '30s is the journal, *Zeitschrift für Sozialforschung*, or *The Journal for Social Research*, which included a number of articles laying out a Marxist-Freudian framework and very strong reviews of all the work coming out in the social field. This is not, Horkheimer said, sociology; this is an acknowledgement of the way in which each of these disciplines is produced and appears autonomous by virtue of a certain contradiction in the totality of the social order. Critical theory wished to be a totalizing operation in the spirit of Marxism itself, and in that sense, it also wished to be a mode of critical thought which included the future, which included the possibility of change, and which had a utopian impulse. Was it a revolutionary project? Probably not. Horkheimer became more and more conservative later in his life. When he went back to Germany, he returned as the rector of the University of Frankfurt, a government position. This is an extraordinary position of power in the European countries, especially for an exile and a Jew in Germany, and in a sense, that probably gave Horkheimer an advantage, because it was to the credit of the Adenauer regime to have appointed a Jewish intellectual to this position of such importance. But it also gave Horkheimer another reason to watch his step, to withdraw his early writings, to keep copies locked up in the cellar of the new institute, and to issue expurgated editions, in which everything that looked Marxist was removed.

We therefore have two editions of *Dialectic of Enlightenment*: the revised one and the original one, now issued from Stanford University Press, which has essays on the book's publication history and which gives you everything that had been suppressed in the revised version. Where the original version says "capitalism," the revised version will simply say "economic society." The other word they use is "monopoly." Horkheimer was influenced by his good friend, another central figure in the Frankfurt School, an economist named Friedrich Pollock, who had a theory of what he called "state capitalism." His idea was that the period of market capitalism, of competition, was over, its place having been taken by the great monopolies—in Germany that would be Krupp above all—and that, as a consequence, market psychology was gone. In that sense, the society of planning that Lenin institutes in the Soviet Union is not so different from the kind of monopoly capitalism that you find in the United States. This is a part of the so-called convergence theory. In any case, you can see in this new edition of *Dialectic of Enlightenment* where Horkheimer has also replaced the word "monopoly," which was the signal for a kind of Marxist reading.

I want you to realize that this first Frankfurt School was quite different from what we tend to associate with it. I suppose by now, since Horkheimer didn't write much at all, the Frankfurt School is reduced in its reputation to the work of Adorno, and maybe in its American version to Marcuse. But the people who officially formed the inner circle of the initial Frankfurt School were Pollock, Erich Fromm, and a few others who aren't very well known anymore. Marcuse's relationship wasn't established until later, and Adorno certainly did not figure in this first moment. Benjamin was never an official member of the Frankfurt School but was supported by checks from Horkheimer's bank account, supported in desperate circumstances in Paris; he was also published by the *Zeitschrift*. So, the contemporary notion of the Frankfurt School, centering on Adorno and, maybe in some posthumous way, Benjamin, would not have been obvious to people immediately after the war. We will look at some work of Benjamin's that was very important for the student movement, but Benjamin didn't really exist for the broader public until Adorno published some selected essays in the '60s, quite late.

The first thrust of the Frankfurt School is, on the one hand, a collaboration with Fromm and psychoanalysis, and on the other hand, the engagement with social theory, primarily Max Weber and Weberian sociology. Weber is famous for the notion of rationalization—an "iron cage" is coming down over mankind, he said, the iron cage of rationalization —and *die Entzauberung der Welt*, the disenchantment of the world, that is, the removal of magic from the world of capitalist society.[5] Both of these Weberian themes will be very important for the Frankfurt School. What happens in a world which is entirely governed by reason, in the sense of what the Frankfurt School will call "instrumental reason," a reason of means rather than the substantive reason of ends?

After a while, the initial Frankfurt School's work is superseded by Habermas in what are really attacks on the Frankfurt School's theory of the modern. I have assigned, after *Dialectic of Enlightenment* and Heidegger, Habermas's historical take on this moment in *The Philosophical Discourse of Modernity*, because I think it is interesting to see how he tells this story of the emergence of the Frankfurt School. It is not absolutely correct, and I think his critique of the Frankfurt School turns the whole thing around. But you have to remember that Habermas is the philosopher of the welfare state. That is both his greatness and his limit. We'll see those limits later, when we look at some of his debates. You will also see that our starting place, this opposition between Heidegger and the Frankfurt School, leads in many different directions.

Well, I think that's enough for today. Thanks for your patience. We'll try to get this going properly on Thursday.

August 24, 2021

5 Max Weber, *The Protestant Ethic and the Spirit of Capitalism*, trans. Talcott Parsons (London: Routledge, 1992), p. 123.

2

Horkheimer and Adorno (I)

Today I want to get into *Dialectic of Enlightenment* with as few extras, generalities, and descriptions of the historical context as possible. We'll come back to all that, but we do have to say a few things at the beginning. We won't go into the history of this text, except to point out that it has not two authors but three. This is also the moment to say that I regret not to have included many women writers in this survey, and I realize that I have omitted one particularly important German thinker from the postwar period, Hannah Arendt. I associate her more with America, and she is not really in the tradition of the Frankfurt School any more than Habermas is. I think she has had less impact on the German postwar scene than another exile, Herbert Marcuse, but her one bombshell for Germany was *Eichmann in Jerusalem*, on the Eichmann trial. However, I did want to draw your attention to the fact that there was a woman involved in the making of *Dialectic of Enlightenment*, and I think she should be counted as one of the authors. That is Adorno's spouse, Gretel Adorno, Gretel Karplus. She was in contact with all of these people; she had an extensive correspondence with Benjamin, as well as with many members of the Frankfurt School, and she was an influential thinker in her own right. This book came about as a result of discussions between Horkheimer and Adorno, which she took down and wrote up. I suspect that much of the organization of this work is owed to her and that she must really be assigned a third position in the writing and the thinking of the book. The three of them did write it in their American exile, so it was published in a limited edition in Europe after the war and only became a fundamental work when it was republished in the '50s. But that is already getting into the history of this book, which, as I say, we can come back to later.

Today, I'd like to do something of a close reading. In the European seminars, they make fun of us. I remember a seminar in France on Camus's *L'Étranger*, a very short book; it lasted two or three years. If a German philosopher is doing a seminar on Spinoza, you can be sure it will not be over in a semester. We don't quite work that way—we can't, really—so this will not, unfortunately, be a line-by-line reading, but I will try to make it possible for your own readings to have some of those characteristics by at least pointing out some of the themes that might, under other circumstances, require a semester or more to address fully.

We're going to be talking about the meaning of the word "reason." Habermas's notion of reason is just that: "giving reasons," as we say in English, a play of words which you can't do in German. For Habermas, reason is arguing with people by giving reasons for holding one position rather than another. But there would be other ways of talking about reason, and Horkheimer and Adorno will not be presenting an argument of the sort that gives reasons. They do not provide a set of historical proofs of anything, although they draw on some of the histories of the period, as we'll see. What this means for the writing is that each sentence stands all by itself. Each of these sentences is historical in the sense that it is a sentence about becoming. In each sentence, something becomes something else. Each sentence is the statement of a process, rather than the affirmation of a fact or the advancement of an argument. Here is a characteristic sentence: "Science in its neo-positivist interpretation becomes aestheticism, a system of isolated signs."[1] And this becoming, as you understand, will also be a degradation. The whole point of this book is that what is considered progress is also degradation. This is a reverse history of ideas; it is a history of how the notions of progress, civilization, modernization, reason, all come into being, but at each step of their coming into being are accompanied by a degradation of life, and this double movement is the secret of Horkheimer and Adorno's paradoxical style. Each advance of reason is also a destruction of reason, and the sentences that we read will be consequences of this contradiction.

1 Max Horkheimer and Theodor Adorno, *Dialectic of Enlightenment*, trans. Edmund Jephcott (Stanford, CA: Stanford University Press, 2002), p. 13.

I said that Horkheimer's program for the Institute, for these people who are to work together in the Institute, who all come out of different disciplines, is to overcome the division of labor of the disciplines. The disciplines come out of a division of labor, and of course the ultimate division of labor is that between intellectual and manual labor; this is the great discovery of Alfred Sohn-Rethel, whom we will come to later on. At the very base of all divisions of labor is the division between intellectual and manual labor. There may be other versions of this division, which may be the same or may not, including that of the sexes, or that of the human being and nature itself. But the very existence of the division of labor itself cannot be affected by the division of labor; that is, to discuss the division of labor and to criticize it, one should be able to talk about everything, to show how the division of labor affects everything—and particularly in their situation, it is the division of labor between intellectuals in the university and working-class people, the poor, which is the issue. In order to reunify these groups, Horkheimer will argue against the division of labor itself and the mode of social organization which creates the difference between each of these realities: Sociology deals with society, literary studies with literature, psychology with the individual mind, and so on. By attacking those differences in reality and in thought, he is showing how they obfuscate some more fundamental unity of all these sectors. This is why, as you read this text, you find yourself moving back and forth between a range of different topics. What is to be affirmed is not only that whatever is happening in sociological thought, for example, corresponds to something happening in society but also that the very ability to conceive a sociological concept is rooted in a certain moment in the history of what it is now able to recognize as "society," such that sociology itself can be specified as a viable discipline and way of thinking. And what is true in the discipline of sociology is also true in psychology, the arts, economics, and so on.

So it would be against their program for us to specify what its topics of investigation are. Horkheimer tries to make a preliminary program in the essay titled "Traditional and Critical Theory," but what makes his task more difficult is that, in a sense, in each of the moments of that essay, which is far more logically divided than *Dialectic of Enlightenment*, he must argue against himself. In *Dialectic of Enlightenment*, there isn't the same pressure to specify its topics of investigation. It is a self-defeating project, because what they are criticizing in modern society, at least at this point in their work, is identity itself. But, certainly, what runs through this work is the notion that modern society—fascist Germany, the so-called democratic United States, the socialist Soviet Union—proceeds towards the self-same, or repetition, which is the result of (but can also only be subjected to critique by way of) enlightenment reason. As Adorno and Horkheimer develop their critique of this process of reason, they are obliged to mirror modern society's tendency toward the self-same in their own writing by making all topics and disciplines, in some sense, the same. So, we have a difficult feedback loop here in which it is their own system that they must attack. This is, in another sense, obvious. If you reach this ultimate point of reason, where reason is able to criticize itself, will you not have to reproduce all the elements of reason that you set out to criticize? This is another problem that we face as readers.

The general movement of this first chapter seems to start from a definition of reason. In German, there are two words for "reason": *Verstand* and *Vernunft. Verstand* is often translated as "understanding." Understanding is composed of the categories that we need to operate in the physical world. Beyond understanding, there is reason in the sense of *Vernunft*, the realm of ends, purposes, and values; it is the analysis of the categories themselves. In the empirical descriptions of Kant, the possibility of scientific understanding is proven by way of the categories. That would be a gross vulgarization of Kant, but a lot of our readings are going to come back to him, so I have to lay some preliminary picture of his idea of reason in place now.

This division between two kinds of reason is already at work in the philosophical tradition. It is an inner opposition within reason. For Weber, as reason develops its methods of understanding, its capacity to pursue values and ends is diminished. Weber was not a democratic thinker; he was a nationalist. Who knows what he would have become? He died prematurely during the great influenza pandemic at the end of World War I, a little like our own pandemic, and it was thought at the time that his prestige was such that he probably would have become the first president of the Weimar Republic. There is a whole alternate history to be imagined. But Weber's notion of rationalization involves the gradual replacement of ends, of values, by the proliferation of means, the "iron cage" of reason. We'll see this taking place even in music, because, when we come back to Adorno on music, there will be a question of Western tonality, which is a rationalization. Western tonality in music is not a natural thing; it is a construct. Weber's little book on the subject tries to show that the process of constructing tonality is yet another example of European rationalization, this realm of means overtaking ends.[2] That will be continued in a very interesting way by Schoenberg and Adorno, so we'll come back to it as another episode in the dialectic of enlightenment, that of Western music in its movement from *The Well-Tempered Clavier* to the twelve-tone system of Schoenberg and atonality.

So the opposition of *Verstand* and *Vernunft* is one starting point. Another one might be the opposition in the West in general—and it becomes a German thematic in particular—between culture and civilization. One of the books that stands behind *Dialectic of Enlightenment* is Freud's *Civilization and Its Discontents*, in which Freud affirms that civilization—the gradual mastery of technologies, work, the division of labor, and so on—is dependent on the repression of instincts. Civilization, that is to say, increases psychic misery. To understand this title, *Civilization and Its Discontents*, or *Das Unbehagen in der Kultur*, we should take note of an opposition in German between "culture," as a mode of life with ends and values, and "civilization," *Zivilisation*, which they see as technology, work, science, and so on. This would be a slightly different starting point for reading *Dialectic of Enlightenment* than the distinction between *Verstand* and *Vernunft*. I happen to think that reason is no longer an adequate way of talking about the historical process they are trying to describe, and I have a question—we all have a question—about what this "reason" really is. Is all of human history a conquest of reason? Or is it to be identified with modernity? If this is a book about—or one might say, in some sense, against—modernity, does that mean it is also a book about or against capitalism? I think we can't decide in advance what reason *is*. It can be used in ways that accord with each of these readings. There are several readings possible, but we have to be aware of the different consequences that would come from these initial identifications and definitions of concepts.

Whether or not reason is no longer useful as a diagnostic category will depend on how it is related to its opposite, irrationality. Today, the irrational occupies the center that also has been colonized. If you say somebody's behavior is irrational, you say it is the expression of a pathology; you

2 Max Weber, *Rational and Social Foundations of Music* (Carbondale, IL: Southern Illinois University Press, 1958).

consult this huge manual of psychiatric terms in order to find out exactly what this pathology is. The unknown has become a known unknown. Even if it is irrational, we have found it and given it a name. It seems to me that, if irrationality were, in the beginning, simply nature, then irrationality has joined nature itself in being reduced, reexplored, named, processed, categorized, explained, until it isn't there anymore. I like the word "colonization," because it implies the appropriation of a terrain. You have a terrain, like Africa for the Europeans in the nineteenth century. Their map of the continent is largely blank, and they colonize it, name it, explore it. Stanley's horrible expedition crosses over Africa, and now there is a map. Medical science colonizes the body by naming its parts, functions, illnesses, treatments, just as psychiatry names everything in the mind, and the terrain is gradually occupied.

What is reason pushing out of the terrain of irrationality? Well, to anticipate, for Adorno, it is negativity. A colonized terrain is a positive terrain. This is the meaning of positivism: to replace the irrational, to replace superstition and religion and so on by rationality. In this philosophical period, people use the word "affirmative" for this positivism. That is to say, you are to use fewer and fewer negative statements. You are to affirm. Affirmation is the mode of pronouncing the existence of a fact. There is a great book by Mary Poovey called *A History of the Modern Fact.* This is part of the dialectic of enlightenment: the establishment of facts. Does a paranoid person not do such-and-such? Is it not a fact that people who have such an end in life or hold such values are in fact such-and-such? And so on. These are all parts of the naming process, which is transforming things into positive statements, positive propositions, affirmative statements, and, finally, facts.

For Adorno, this process will mean the gradual extinction of thought—speaking in this sense as a good Hegelian, though he wasn't really a good Hegelian all the time—and the negative. When you talk about critical theory, you must talk about Hegelian negativity. Hegel describes history, and therefore reason, as the labor and the suffering of the negative. Horkheimer and Adorno often talk about the law of noncontradiction. To say that something is or is not a part of logic, by measuring it against the law of noncontradiction, is to reduce and push the negative moment out of thinking. What is invented to overcome this deficiency of enlightenment is, of course, the dialectic, which says that something is and is not at the same time.

How do Horkheimer and Adorno begin? I think they have to begin with the negative, in some sense, because the power of reason is a negative power. They have to begin back in a period about which nothing can be said: prehistory. In prehistory, human beings are simply in the power of a hostile nature. This is the moment of animism, and, at this point, I think we're going to see that Horkheimer and Adorno, writing in the 1940s, thinking in the 1930s, are going to be relying on an anthropology of the period and on a view of things from the period, which is very much, if not that of James George Frazer's *The Golden Bough*, then at least that of Lucien Lévy-Bruhl's *Primitive Mentality* or the Cambridge School of myth and ritual. They rely on a picture of the emergence of so-called primitive societies and of human beings from whatever they were in nature, from their state as hominids. The Marxists at the time take as their pattern the great work of Lewis H. Morgan's *Ancient Society*, which proposes a progression from savagery to barbarism to civilization. Savagery is a period of human life which, as Lévi-Strauss will say, does not yet know the incest taboo, a period of abomination. For Lévi-Strauss, the law of the incest taboo, the institution of a kinship system, is the beginning of real social life. Morgan is also reflected in Deleuze and Guattari's marvelous chapter in the *Anti-Oedipus* that I will sometimes refer to here.[3] Barbarism would be the moment of the description of the Iroquois and of military democracies, the high point of Morgan's view of civilization, and of Engels's as well, as presented in a book called *The Origin of the Family, Private Property, and the State*. Finally, civilization, for Morgan, is writing, but of course for the others it is capitalism, and there would be other modes of production inserted here as well.

So it is important to know that they are relying on what looks to us like an old-fashioned model of anthropology. Why is it old-fashioned? Well, because I don't think people ask these kinds of questions anymore. There used to be a mode of linguistics, for example, in which people tried to think: What was the first language? When did people start to speak in what we would recognize as a language? Does it come from grunts? Does it come from gestures? Kant proved in the antinomies that there is no way of talking about beginnings and endings. The arguments for talking about beginnings and endings are just as strong as the arguments for not

3 Gilles Deleuze and Félix Guattari, "Savages, Barbarians, and Civilized Men," *Anti-Oedipus: Capitalism and Schizophrenia* (New York: Penguin, 2009).

being able to talk about beginnings and endings. With Kant, there begins a supersession of the diachronic by the synchronic. We can't talk diachronically about origins or the changes that follow. Let's find everything in the situation itself. Eventually we stop asking questions about the origins of language, much less society.

Horkheimer and Adorno will take this anthropology for granted, and, as I say, it is important to them because it allows them to say that the first form of human life is animism. In animism, they explain, nature is worshipped as an entity, and the various phenomena of nature are assigned certain powers. Most importantly, you try to shield yourself from them. What characterizes that first movement against the powers of nature, which is, for them, the beginning of what we call reason? Well, you get it in the first sentence of this book: "Enlightenment, understood in the widest sense as the advance of thought, has always aimed at liberating human beings from fear and installing them as masters."[4] Self-preservation and domination: In order to liberate yourself from the fear of nature, you have to dominate it. This is the primal ambiguity of the function of reason as such. Spinoza says that self-preservation—*conatus*—is the very form of human existence itself, of individual life. Your first duty is to stay alive. I think he might have added that nature's purpose in self-preservation is to perpetuate the species. The concern with self-preservation runs through the work of the Frankfurt School, in one way or another, and it is one of the preoccupations that would lead you to say that this isn't exactly a Marxist work, that it isn't exactly a critique of capitalism in particular, that it is a work about human history itself, the history of human self-preservation.

The idea of self-preservation makes its way into everything they write, including Adorno's aesthetics. How does he define music? The purpose of music is *ohne Angst leben*: "to live without fear."[5] The real utopia would be one in which we have forgotten fear as the compulsion of self-preservation. What does he mean by that? We don't care whether we live or die? We don't care about keeping ourselves alive? Yes, I think it is partly a freedom from the fear of death, but that entails the possibility of a society which guarantees our self-preservation. Self-preservation, of course, operates by fear. Hobbes said that his whole life is dominated by the single principle

4 Horkheimer and Adorno, *Dialectic of Enlightenment*, p. 1.

5 Theodor Adorno, *In Search of Wagner*, trans. Rodney Livingstone (London: Verso, 2005), p. 145.

of fear. Now, remember that Hobbes lived through the English revolution in the seventeenth century and had to flee to France, and his political thought comes out of this experience of desperation in the middle of an immense historical turning point. Here, the principle of fear begins to play an interesting role in political philosophy: What is the relationship between fear and self-preservation? The consequence of accepting fear as a principle is that it comes with domination. And Adorno understood very well why political philosophy turned around the idea that you can't liberate yourself from the fear of nature unless you can dominate it.

What happens after the stage of animism? At that point, obviously, the most natural impulse will be to use your vision of nature and of animism in order to protect yourself from it, and, therefore, you will develop myths. The stage of myth is the crucial one here, because myth will be a kind of magic whereby you control nature. So, even though the function of reason in our societies is to demythologize, to rid ourselves of the traces of irrational thinking, myth is itself the first form of reason, as is magic. If you perform a ritual, you make nature obey you. You capture the powers of nature so that they're not destructive, and you protect yourself by conquering nature, by dominating it.

So magic and myth are forms of the domination of nature, and it is very interesting that this domination involves sacrifice. Sacrifice is substituting one thing for another. First, you have human sacrifice, then animal sacrifice substitutes the animal for the human. After that, maybe there would be a more perfunctory ritual. The Greeks, as you well know, very intelligently decided to cheat the gods: When they sacrificed the great animals that you find in Homer, the steers and the lambs, they gave the gods the skin and some of the fat but kept the meat for themselves. The gods were tricked into thinking that they were getting the whole animal. That is a very reasonable calculation. Reason is calculating. Can we propitiate the gods by fooling them and keeping our part, the meat, separate from the skin and bones and fat? Will the gods still do what we want? Of course, sometimes the gods do what you want and sometimes they don't.

These are speculative stages in the evolution of a kind of thinking which is able to achieve self-preservation by controlling nature, and the control of nature will require the control of other people, because it becomes clear that, in order to preserve yourself, you have to figure out, for example, how to build walls—to keep yourself safe from floods, as in the present—and how to get other people to do it for you. Therefore, conquering nature requires conquering other people, whom you make work for you. Domination in society will come out of this self-preservation.

So the purpose of reason is not only to preserve yourself by dominating nature, but also to dominate nature by dominating others. For this purpose, a kind of thought is invented which demythologizes. For your thought to be efficient, for your manipulations of nature to have some effect, you have to get rid of what is anthropomorphic in it. You have to get rid of animism and myth. This will be the case all the way up to the French Revolution, when religion is identified as something to be overcome and this new philosophy called positivism emerges. Positivism would be the very spirit of reason, in this sense, because it removes from thinking everything which is mythic. And what happens as a result is very instructive: Positivism becomes a myth. Positivism wishes itself to become a religion and therefore must itself be overruled by reason and criticized as a myth. In itself, before and after its purification by Auguste Comte, it remains amazingly mythical and irrational. There is a whole cult of positivism. Here, you get the beginnings of a kind of thought—the French will explore it in their own way—which produces the notion of a residue or a remainder. When I submit an object to reason and I demythologize it, I can't demythologize everything, so there is a remainder or a residue. And will that residue take the form of new kinds of myth or irrationality? For example, anti-Semitism? In a way, the Nazi movement was absolutely opposed to religion. Hitler worked with the Catholic church, as we now know, and he told his people to leave the Catholics alone, to wait to deal with them after *Endsieg*, after victory. Indeed, you can almost say that anti-Semitism was the religion of the Third Reich, that it is something like a religious belief in its own right. So, there is always this excess; that is, ends and values will still be there no matter how completely you evacuate them, no matter how completely the iron cage has come down around us and turned everything into means and manipulation.

Horkheimer and Adorno are going to follow the emergence of the kind of thinking that corresponds to demythologization. That kind of thinking will be reason, if you like, but first and foremost, abstraction. You will see that their philosophy, their theory, has several enemies. One of them, as we know, is positivism. Another is empiricism. Of course, all of German philosophy is directed against the empiricism of the British and Scottish eighteenth century, because empirical thought is very close to a nominalism, a religion of the facts: All abstractions are bad, all the way up to Wittgenstein, if you like, so we have to get rid of the abstractions and concentrate on what is empirically true. Therefore, the process whereby empiricism comes into being can be identified with the process of reason as such, and there will be sections of *Dialectic of Enlightenment* in which they talk about how logic, abstraction itself, is a process in which it would seem as if to turn the world into a concept is to seize it. "The concept," as Hegel calls it, *Begriff*, is from the word *greifen*, to seize and hold something, which is still an anthropomorphic notion.

Each stage in the formation of reason and logic will be an advance on the older one. Reason develops by condemning its own past—not just forgetting it but positively getting rid of it. Chemistry, for example. There is such a thing as the attempt to understand the world in terms of an element called "phlogiston," which is in the voids of the heavens. Well, the next stage of science says phlogiston is a myth; there is no such thing, and now we develop a more scientific concept. Newton seems to be the pinnacle of science at a certain moment. I'm not saying that Einstein declares Newton to be mythological but, certainly, it would be better to say that Einstein is an *Aufhebung* of Newton, in that he says Newton is still valuable in scientific thought but only within a certain area, and the rest of that area is covered by relativity. When quantum physics comes along, then Einstein becomes mythological. He didn't like that and protested against it. "God doesn't play dice with the universe," he said.

You can see how the progress of reason is a self-canceling process. Reason is constantly denouncing itself. It's Baron Munchausen picking himself up by his own hair. Science is becoming more scientific by attacking its previous avatar, which is now pronounced to be unscientific. It is discarding meaning, they say. Well, was all that older stuff simply metaphysics? Yes. Modern philosophers, from Heidegger to Derrida, wish to show that all previous philosophies have been metaphysical or mythologizing. The attack on metaphysics is part of this process, and it involves the attack on anthropomorphism.

Halfway through *Dialectic of Enlightenment*, there is an *Umschlag*, a turn in which we now see reason not as a positive development, not as progress, but as a negative development, as a process that gradually undermines everything. This is, if you like, also the moment of capitalism. In what way does this new reason, this final scientific reason, become unsafe? The first thing that is denounced is mathematics, measurement. The older notion of *Verstand* was the notion of measurement, matter, the objective world.

Galileo says the universe is a book written in numbers. Older sciences, until the modern period, were not mathematical. If you read Lucretius or the Stoics, they talk about movement, drift, clinamen, changes in movement, and so on. In modern science, all of this has to correspond to a mathematical equation. As we're moving today into other kinds of science, like advertising, things have to be characterized by axioms, just as, in the sense of colonization, gradually conquering everything, mathematics as a science of measurement has gradually conquered and meanwhile displaced thought and action itself. So, the mathematization of thinking is an important part of this movement of reason.

They pick out two features of this movement. One is unity, because just as philosophy and an older science wished to project a picture of the unification of the world, so also modern science wants to create a theory of everything, the unification of all the forces of nature, and to seek a unified science of the world. So also in the academic world of the division of labor, or specialization, there is a kind of countermovement or dedifferentiation. For example, in the structuralist movement everything is now to be rewritten in terms of signs. I would venture to say that computerization is a similar process as well, a process whereby different fields are unified insofar as they are all turned into the objects of a single kind of operation, an operation which will also then involve the matter of equivalence. Equivalence is sameness, the fact of equation, but also exchange. The market itself is based on equivalence, and presumably for non-Marxists, it is the place where the fair price exists, where your labor is valued justly at a certain price, and your products, your objects of sale, your automobiles, books, lamps, and all the rest of them, all have their proper place. The establishment of that system of equivalence is the exchange process, which makes everything the same, or at least tries to, and therefore tends to produce self-sameness, which is sometimes called the commodity world.

With equivalence, we touch on Marx. Remember that Marx's *Capital* begins by saying there are two kinds of value—use-value and exchange-value—and, after the first page, he would not be saying much about use-value. He would be dealing almost exclusively with exchange-value. Marx has his own reasons for this, but with Horkheimer and Adorno, we can go back to Kant's categories: Use-value is a matter of quality, while exchange-value is a matter of quantity. Quantity is the mark of modern reason. Quality is something that you can't measure, that you can't even name: tastes and so forth and meanings themselves, all of those things are qualities. Modernity, in all of its forms, replaces quality with quantity, use with exchange. For example, capitalist theoreticians of ecology will say that in order to do anything about climate change, we have to set a price for water and for clean air; if we don't do that, we can't possibly know how to control these variables. Even the qualitative nature of the elements is replaced by their value in terms of money, since money is the supreme symbol and medium of equivalence itself, at least it is supposed to be, because we must remember that this process can never be complete. It can never be total, because we're still alive and we have values and qualities. But the qualities themselves could be quite different. If you want clean air in Los Angeles, you have to live up on a hill somewhere above the smog, and you have to pay for it. So, there really is a way of quantifying quality.

The point here is that objectivity, the separation of the subject and the object, which is part of the whole nature of the sciences and of reason, is going to require a preliminary step, which is the distance from things. The separation of subject from object, which is implicit in language (to talk about a thing I have to stand back and give it a name) that distance will be—and this is the biggest leap of all and one of the climaxes of the first chapter—as Horkheimer and Adorno write, "founded on the distance from things which the ruler attains by means of the ruled."[6] The distance from objective things is also a hierarchy. It is also the distance between the upper class and the lower class, the rulers and the ruled.

Suddenly this whole operation becomes political. Reason is a politics. Domination is not just domination by somebody finding the right kind of vaccine for a virus. It's not something purely scientific. It's the invention of a state, which can control people, and an economic system in which there is a hierarchy. I mentioned that Horkheimer's politics was always one of oppression rather than one of exploitation, and when you see his moments of political pathos, they will involve the underclasses—the oppressed, women, slaves—and not specifically the proletariat. This position comes from the analysis of reason as a form of domination. As for economics, as I say, the market system will be replaced—according to their theory, their economic underpinnings of Pollock's theory of state capitalism—by monopoly, self-sameness. The thirty brands of toothpaste that you hesitate over in the supermarket are all produced by one company.

6 Horkheimer and Adorno, *Dialectic of Enlightenment*, p. 9.

Self-sameness, repetition, becomes the law of this whole process. And, indeed, the division of labor, the specialization of the sciences, seem to be based on difference, but a difference which is also sameness, and that is why the dialectic is the only kind of thought that can deal with this problem. There is a way of thinking which allows us to recognize how identity becomes difference and difference becomes identity, whereas traditional logic, now reduced to mythology, if you like, is confined by a law of noncontradiction: Something has to be or not be its predicate.

At the end of this chapter are, then, questions about what can be done about the problems it identifies. The missing word is "revolution," of course, although they do write about the revolutionary imagination, and what they are talking about is the ability to think change itself. "Each advance of civilization has renewed not only mastery but the prospect of its alleviation. However, while real history is woven from real suffering, which certainly doesn't increase in proportion to the means of abolishing it, the fulfillment of that prospect depends on the concept."[7] So, there's a way in which Adorno and Horkheimer are really repositioning the critique of reason as the revolutionary center of change, not the abolition of reason but its reconstruction. They are placing theory, in some sense, in this crucial position. "Today when Bacon's utopia, in which 'we should command nature and action,' has been fulfilled on a telluric scale, the essence of the compulsion which he ascribed to unmastered nature is becoming apparent. It was power itself. Knowledge, in which for Bacon 'the sovereignty of man' unquestionably lay hidden, can now devote itself to dissolving that power."[8] That is, the final moment of enlightenment will be—"from the power of things they finally learn to forgo power"—its own self-abolition.[9] "Enlightenment in the service of the present is turning itself into an outright deception of the masses."[10]

Okay, I think that will be it for today. We will go on to the *Odyssey* section next time.

August 26, 2021

7 Ibid., p. 32.
8 Ibid., pp. 33–4.
9 Ibid., p. 33.
10 Ibid., p. 34.

3

Horkheimer and Adorno (II)

Today I just want to get the general sense of this text, which is thought to be the central statement of the Frankfurt School, though their central statement was constantly evolving. As I mentioned, in the Frankfurt School, but also in French theory, to an extent, the enemies are positivism, empiricism, and Anglo-American thinking. I hate to say so, but all this stuff is profoundly anti-American. They were very worried about the House Un-American Activities Committee, by the way—they were in Hollywood, after all—which had condemned the Hollywood Ten and blacklisted others. Many people refused to testify. Brecht testified. They asked him, "Did you write poems arousing the people to attack their government?" "Oh," he says, "but those were German workers, and the government was Hitler." He went on fiddling with all their questions, until, finally, they got exasperated and let him go. He flew to Europe the next day. Horkheimer was very worried about these trials and the anticommunist climate in America, so this is another reason why the first edition is very cautious. And if we jump ahead briefly to Habermas, I won't say that Habermas has been colonized by the Americans, but, if you look at the footnotes and you see the wealth of references to American sources, Germany seems more like a colonized country, with these being the references of the occupiers.

Let's find an even easier way of talking about the Enlightenment. Many of you chose to write about the expression "demythologization," which is, of course, a term that Horkheimer and Adorno use. I think you have to understand the Enlightenment in the most traditional way, as it was in the eighteenth century. Maybe it's shocking: This is against religion! Religion is the crucial thing. Voltaire said *écrasez l'infâme*, destroy this infamous thing which is the church. Religion is the source of superstition, and the Enlightenment was the destruction of superstition. That's what "enlightenment" means. *Lumière*, light. *Aufklärung*, the German term, is also the opening up of light onto the shadows of superstition. The Enlightenment initiates a search-and-destroy mission against traces of religion. Those traces will also no doubt involve myth, because religion is a form of myth. They will involve theology. And they will involve picture-thinking, since picture-thinking is the earliest form of myth.

This critique is not new with the Frankfurt School. The French are undertaking similar critiques, as is their enemy Heidegger, with his attack on metaphysics. He doesn't call it deconstruction; he calls it *Destruktion*, a foreign word in German, the destruction of metaphysics. Metaphysics, for the positivists, for Auguste de Comte, is one of the late forms of religion, disguised religion. It says what life and the universe means. Metaphysics answers two questions: Why is there something rather than nothing at all? And: Why am I here rather than not here? That is to say, metaphysics gives meanings. Well, that is what religion always promised to do. Weber said that if the state has the monopoly on violence, religion has the monopoly on consolation. So, religion is always there to console people for death—I would say also for poverty, for sickness, and so on—but the form of religion would be in the metaphysical stories that it tells, the answers that it gives to the metaphysical questions. That is why Heidegger ends up with Being. Once you tear away everything metaphysical, what do you end up with? Well, it would be too easy to say nothing, because, for Hegel, the two are the same: Being *is* nothing, because it is an empty concept, though as an emptiness it also *is*. For Heidegger, that is not quite true, but, for him, too, the metaphysical question is: Why is there something rather than nothing at all?[1] It is the question, Heidegger says, about the meaning of Being. Well, for Heidegger, the point is that Being has no meaning. From the point of view of the critical theorists, enlightenment would bring about the meaninglessness of Being. It would get rid of religion, metaphysics, myth, anything else that purports to possess meaning itself.

---

1 See, for example, Martin Heidegger, *Introduction to Metaphysics*, trans. Gregory Fried and Richard Polt (New Haven, CT: Yale University Press, 2000), p. 7.

I mentioned picture-thinking. What do you substitute for picture-thinking? There could be not-thinking. When we get to Horkheimer and Adorno's reading of the *Odyssey*, that is one of the options. The point about the lotus-eaters is that they forget that there even was such a thing as thought. That is a great consolation to them, because thought is negativity, action, and so on. But abstraction claims to touch some realm which is not picture-thinking anymore. One of the motifs, then, that runs through this work is, of course, Judaic, the ban on graven images, the nullity of images. The lesson Adorno takes from Odysseus's visit to the underworld—I attribute the *Odyssey* chapter to him, even though that's probably not fair, since the three of them discussed this together—is the nullity of images, the idea that the dead are really just that: images. They are nothing for us. This is a very interesting idea to pursue, because the problem of images, the problem of visuality, is another form of the problem of metaphysics. You remember that Achilles says he would rather be a live slave, breaking stones on a farm, than a dead hero. The nullity is inside death as well as outside of it. It's not just for Odysseus that the dead images are nothing, but also for the dead themselves. He also reminds us that the first image is the mother, that Odysseus must keep the mother away. Tiresias must get the first blood, otherwise the prophecy will be no good. The mother is the temptation of matriarchy. We are in the realm of patriarchy, of the Olympiads and of men. So, regression to the kingdom of women, of matriarchy, would be seen as a historical temptation. Anyway, that is partly what's going on here.

So, what can possibly replace picture-thinking? Mathematics. We are talking about the colonization of the outside world by number. Galileo is the first immense symbol of this process, the result of which is that, in the nineteenth century, if a science can't express itself in numbers, it is not a science. The requirement of demythologization, of true scientific knowledge, is that it achieve numerical expression. Now why should that be? I think this still has to be worked out. There are still people who believe in number. Plato got his idea of number from an essentially religious sect, the Pythagoreans, and the idea was to ask: Where is number, shape, the Pythagorean theorem? Isn't mathematics all in the mind? Maybe, but it is beyond the mind as well. The moment in which one of us thinks that theorem and sees the blinding evidence of its truth doesn't exhaust the theorem. The theorem can become an event, but not entirely. It persists outside of us, but it is not entirely manifested in the real world either.

Nobody has seen it—neither a real triangle nor this theorem—and, indeed, after the world itself ends and perishes, it will still be true. That is what Plato means by "eternal."

Husserl's "Origin of Geometry" is interesting to consider in this regard. It is just a fragment, but it is famous because Derrida translated it. In the mid-thirties—Husserl has already been kicked out of the university because he is a Jew—Husserl writes a book that tries to show that it is the deformation of science and knowledge which has caused fascism and the downfall of Europe. Well, that's a bit idealistic, but what he means is that we have forgotten the truth of abstraction—that abstraction has to come from practice—and that the truths of geometry are to be found in practice, and more specifically, land surveying. This already sounds semi-Marxist enough—Husserl had no knowledge of or interest in Marx at all—but it would need an extra fillip to bring it into full Marxism, and that would be the question: Why do you survey land? Private property. Long before capitalism, number would originate in private property—the first one to say "this is mine," as Rousseau puts it—and, therefore, perhaps, in patriarchy. If I am going to pass down property to my children, that is, to my eldest son—the father, as Joyce says, is an imaginary being—how am I sure of this lineage? In matriarchy, you know who your son is. In patriarchy, how do you know? That is one of the primary functions of marriage under patriarchy: to protect private property, to ensure that what I have, which is measured by geometry and land surveying, is going to persist through the male heir.

So, the question is: What's the matter with the critique of rationalization? The problem is that this critique destroys itself. Marcuse used to say during the student revolts, which were largely against the university, because it is really all the students saw in terms of power: "Don't saw off the limb you're sitting on." The Frankfurt School threatens to saw off the limb it's sitting on. Is the critique of enlightenment not itself a form of enlightenment? Is this not an exercise in enlightenment? If not, why not? How does it escape itself? This is the problem, really. Is it a contradiction? I suppose. It is a very powerful indictment of enlightenment, but on the other hand, what opposite does it put forward?

Up until the Stalin–Hitler pact, Horkheimer was a Marxist, or at least a Marxist sympathizer. You don't really talk about Stalinism until the show trials, I think, since that is the moment at which Stalinism differentiates itself most clearly from Leninist practice, let's say. Horkheimer persisted in this, and I've said that his sympathies were not just with the workers but with the oppressed, and there could be a moment in which those two things separate themselves out, particularly in a country whose working class votes to bring fascism to power. It was partly the Communist Party's fault—there are a lot of reasons for it—but Hitler was elected. He was popular. And, of course, when we get to the students in the US, you hear of the so-called hard hats, the union workers who hated the students—a bunch of pampered upper-class elite—and voted for Nixon. So, there is a point at which the working class maybe isn't enough of a reference, and Horkheimer will then undergo other changes, which we don't have to look at right now.

But, nonetheless, there is a core of this which is certainly Marxist, except that here we are not dealing so much with the psychology of workers. In other words, we're not dealing with the structures of power and domination; we're dealing with forms in the mind. And, little by little, as we proceed through this book, the power of the mind is going to take over from the power of the social or the political. When we get to Hollywood and the culture industry, we are in the power of the mind. At this point, the question would be: Is this not some form of idealism, this idea that Hollywood and thinking and so on could completely control a society, rather than sheer power? Clearly, Horkheimer wants to hold on to the connection between the two forms of domination. For him, this process of attacking religion is a process of domination as well. This is the perfection of domination. Adorno once said that history is not going anywhere in a positive sense, but there is a straight line "leading from the slingshot to the megaton bomb."[2] There is a straight line in science. So, for a moment, science might suffice to make this connection between bad enlightenment, which is a transformation and control of the mind, and physical power. And we mustn't sell that short. A transformation of the mind means the construction of the subject.

I wanted to illustrate some of this by Kant. What unites Kant and Sade? I don't know if you've ever read any Sade—it's incredibly boring—but something important to note are the two sisters of the separate novels: Justine is the one to whom everything is done; Juliette is the one who does everything. "Maso-sadism," if you like. One of the sublime moments of

2 Theodor Adorno, *Negative Dialectics*, trans. E. B. Ashton (New York: Continuum, 1983), p. 320.

Juliette is when none other than the pope gives a long speech about the force of nature being that of destruction. There is a kind of instrumental rationality to the idea that the complete fulfillment of nature would be my own destruction. That is not what interests Horkheimer (or Lacan) about Sade or Kant. The point for Horkheimer is duty. What is duty? Is there a duty in Kant's ethics? Kant is not a puritan. Kant was a very convivial man. He loved society, socializing, meeting the upper class, having his dinners, his wine, and so on. He had some peculiarities, to be sure, but we must not think of Kant as a puritan. In ethics, this is somehow quite scary. You have the good, the categorical imperative: Act as though the principle of one's action were a universal moral law. Your actions should be as though they were universals and not exceptions. If you steal from somebody, well, that would propose a system in which there wouldn't be any order, because theft cannot be universal. How about rape? With this question we are already in Marquis de Sade, who wrote the one extraordinary constitution in *Philosophy in the Boudoir.* Horkheimer doesn't mention it; of course, Lacan does. "Frenchmen, one more effort if you really want to be Republicans." It is an incredible utopia in which anyone can do anything to anyone else, including murder and rape and all the rest of it. That's true freedom in Sade.

So, Sade's is the most rational of all constitutions, right? You can have no logical objection to this thoroughgoing application of the doctrine of freedom. Alright, but here is the problem in both of them, Kant and Sade. Kant would obviously be horrified by this constitution of Sade, so why put these two opposite figures together? Because they're the same in one respect. Kant says, if you do the good because it gets you somewhere, or because you enjoy it, it doesn't count. It has to be done out of duty. There cannot be pleasure in it. That doesn't mean that you must suffer doing it, but pleasure is instrumental, an aim. You give the beggar some money, but you enjoy it, or your friends see you do it, so it doesn't count. So, what must reign in Kant is duty. There is a terrible moment in which Kant says, if a given society decided to abolish its contracts, to abolish itself as a society and let individuals go where they would, before doing so they would have to execute all the prisoners in the prison for the glory of the human race: They made a promise to execute these people, and they cannot stop being a society without first fulfilling their promises. Promises are universal, even if the world perishes. So, Kant is incredibly rigorous in the sense of duty, but so is Sade, because the point of Sade is not sex or pleasure. It's the *duty* to have pleasure. And the duty to have pleasure, as in Kant, is not much fun. These sadists and masochists and all the rest of them—are they really enjoying themselves? No, they are fulfilling an abominable duty, which is to have these orgies, to pursue pleasure, and there are all kinds of rules laid down—just like in Kant! So where is pleasure in all of this? Pleasure is part of instrumentality. Instrumental reason thinks it wants pleasure.

What about Kant's aesthetics? Kant believed that if art had a purpose, there was something wrong with it. Purposeful purposelessness is the definition of art in Kant. The work of art must look like it has a purpose, but it must not have a purpose. In other words, if you write a work to make money, or if you read a work in order to give yourself the distinction of having read this obscure thing, of the appearance of culture, that is not aesthetics, not in Kant's purview. So, to have a purpose is to exist within instrumentality. The work of art is the one thing that escapes instrumentality, and, in a way, Adorno carries over this understanding of art. Art is the one place in which you can get out of this nightmare in which everything has a purpose. But this is a secret you maybe don't want people to share, so you have your workmen stick wax in their ears so that they can't hear the sirens' songs, and then, just to make sure you don't go the way of the lotus-eaters, you have yourself tied up. Then, for a moment, as a member of the ruling elite, you can enjoy purposeful purposelessness. Schopenhauer was saying something of the same thing: This horrible world of suffering—only art redeems it.

Now we're coming back to Adorno and Horkheimer and, finally, the *Odyssey* chapter. The central allegory is that of the sirens. Odysseus can listen to the sirens because he is tied to the mast, whereas his oarsmen have wax placed in their ears so that they can't hear the sirens' songs. But they are working, while Odysseus is appreciating the singing. Odysseus is at a concert; the companions are in the process of labor. An aesthetic climax, if you like, comes with a reference to what Nietzsche would have called *ressentiment*, and it describes how order and subordination, through the subjugation of the world, direct an accumulated hatred "at the image of the vanquished primeval world and its imaginary happiness."[3]

Saint-Just, as a very young man, maybe in his early twenties, who became Robespierre's chief lieutenant, gave the great speech at the trial of Louis XVI, in which he said, "That man must either reign as king or

3 Horkheimer and Adorno, *Dialectic of Enlightenment*, p. 10.

die." But he also made a magnificent statement we attribute more often to Jefferson: "There is a new idea arising in this Europe of the present, the idea of happiness." Not happiness, but the *idea* of happiness is the crucial term here. It's this idea which is either made possible by your awareness of the limits of reason or is suppressed by reason altogether, and it is the source, in a sense, of politics, or at least of a certain politics. It is certainly at the basis of their aesthetic, which we'll deal with much more when we come to Adorno. That is their aesthetic, if you like: the idea of happiness, *bonheur* having a much stronger sense in French, I think, than in English or German, where *Glück* can mean "good luck" as much as "happiness."

Saint-Just did say "the idea of happiness," but Adorno's aesthetics turns on a different quote, from Stendhal's travels to Italy: not *l'idée du bonheur* but *la promesse du bonheur*, the promise of happiness.[4] This is very important. I want to say that this promise of happiness is like *jouissance* in the Lacanian system. *Jouissance* is not pleasure any more than happiness is pleasure in Adorno. In a way, for Adorno, you can't have *bonheur*, only the promise of it. Another related term you come across every so often, which Adorno of course never explains, is "reconciliation," *Versöhnung* in German. That means, somehow, the reconciliation of the subject and the object, of consciousness and nature. That would be somehow *bonheur*, I suppose. Reconciliation is not possible, but the idea and promise of reconciliation is possible. In Lacan, pleasure is not much, but you could say that the idea of *jouissance*, of this superform of the dissolution of the self, is real. That is to say, it's just real. Nobody can have it, or rather, it doesn't matter who has it. It simply exists. If you know that *jouissance* exists, you don't particularly need pleasure.

So, you have this idea that somehow there is a fulfillment of human life, that it is important to hang on to this notion of fulfillment, even though it can't happen. Why? We are not immortal, for one thing. We are not the gods. We are not angels. But, if we lose what we are, do we become animals? No, that would be an offense to animals. Animals are living in the present. Odysseus's companions, turned into animals, are still living a life of gratification. They don't attack the human sailors who come in; they fawn on them. It is a regression, but it is a regression to some state of pleasure. Throughout the nineteenth century there persists a fantasy

4 Theodor Adorno, *Aesthetic Theory*, trans. Robert Hullot-Kentor (Minneapolis: University of Minnesota Press, 1998), p. 311.

of the return to animal life—in Whitman, Wordsworth, and so on—a state in which we would be at one with nature. We are not talking about whether animals are happy, although that is what they are supposed to be. *Bonheur* is a transcendental idea whose domain is restricted by negativity. The minute you say *bonheur* is mere superstition, it begins to fade away until you have nothing.

There is still a question: Will self-sameness lead to domination? Here's the point, and it brings us to Nietzsche. Nietzsche is everywhere in here, of course. They evoke Nietzsche when they write: "Humanity had to inflict terrible injuries on itself before the self—the identical, purpose-directed, masculine character of human beings—was created, and something of this process is repeated at every childhood."[5] Toilet training, language. Nietzsche talks about the torture in learning to forget. In everything that makes us human, we have to leave our animal existence. This is, in a sense, the lesson that they want to take from the *Odyssey.* These monsters are to be overcome in reality. We must make a world safe for the bourgeois merchant. We must cleanse the Mediterranean of these monsters—and even, if you like, of the gods themselves—to create, if not capitalism, then at least commerce, a world in which we are protected in our exchanges. But that is something we have to do to the self, too, since this is also an allegory of the creation of the self.

I mentioned Freud last time. Civilization is built on miseries, on renunciations, an old German theme that goes back to Goethe. But it is not just the nineteenth century. Henry James and the literature of renunciation, which I think one can also be a little fatigued with, is built on the idea that true spirituality, true knowledge, is the product of this torture, in which the instincts are to be renounced. And, in that sense, what Horkheimer calls the dark side of the Enlightenment—Sade, Bataille—makes us see this process of renunciation at work in civilization. Are these people fascists? You know Sade was imprisoned in the Bastille. I won't go into the details of his very interesting life. One of the great enlightened achievements of the French Revolution was the restructuring of land, so that Paris was now redivided into the *arrondissements*, just as the revolutionaries adopted and standardized the use of the metric system all over France. So, each of these *arrondissements* has a mayor. Sade was elected mayor of his *arrondissement.* Clearly, this aristocrat and monster had social virtues,

5 Horkheimer and Adorno, *Dialectic of Enlightenment*, p. 26.

and it turns out, more than that, Sade was against the death penalty. How can you imagine it? Nothing is so bloody as Sade, these tortures, murders, and so on, but, in real life, Sade is a good liberal and humanist. He's against the death penalty! For that very reason, the Jacobins condemned him to death, and he was only saved by the Thermidor. Then, of course, Napoleon arrived and, being a little more, should I say, intelligent than the revolutionaries, stuck Sade in an insane asylum. Then they started to put on plays, and one of the great masterpieces of the German '60s is Peter Weiss's great play *The Persecution and Assassination of Jean-Paul Marat as Performed by the Inmates of the Asylum of Charenton Under the Direction of the Marquis de Sade*. It's one of the great spectacles of modern theater. There is a wonderful film adaptation by Peter Brook. Weiss's play is clearly about Marx and Freud—that is, sexual liberation versus the discipline that a revolutionary has to bring to the task at hand. At any rate, this is to say that enlightenment also has its virtues.

Two things very quickly. We've seen the way in which enlightenment is repressing and training instincts. The animal has to be trained. It is very interesting how Adorno reads the sense of smell as the earliest and most animal-like form of the body, the one that really has to be repressed. You have to have deodorant or something. People lose their sense of smell or domesticate it with perfumes. Repression is what you do to this primal nature in order to make it civilized. But they have another idea of repression—I don't know how much this is in Freud, but it certainly goes along with him, the truly revolutionary aspects of Freud, which Freud himself didn't draw out—and you're going to find it in Wilhelm Reich's sexual politics as well. It is the notion that subalternity is also a result of sexual repression, that the aggressivity necessary for revolution has to be repressed. Well, Fromm, who was one of the original members of the Frankfurt School, has a relationship to Reich and those people. There are already Marxist Freudians in the psychoanalytic circle, and some of their work is inherited by the Frankfurt School.

Almost more important here, in a lot of respects, is the notion of regression. The lotus-eaters are regressing back to an earlier form, to precivilization. The same happens with Circes's transformation of men into animals. Regression, here, proceeds alongside progress. The Frankfurt School's intent is to denounce the idea of progress, a denunciation which is very striking in Benjamin. Social democracy's promises of progress are the basis of his big attacks on it. Does communism offer progress? It offers radical difference, while progress means staying in this society but making it a little better, adding some inventions or slight modifications. So, there is a connection between the fear of regression and this internal drive of enlightenment to progress. Progress takes the place of what used to be substantive reason. What is the end of these proliferating means? I don't know what the end is. Progress. It has no content. The content is just that it will be better. You like what you have? Well, we can do that but better. Progress has an empty telos. It is not a real end in itself.

The other thing I wanted to discuss is whether there is a way out of this problem of enlightenment, and some of you asked that question, a very good question. Horkheimer outlived Adorno, but Adorno outlived the progressive Horkheimer, and he thought that the greatest danger was the expulsion of negativity from thought and from our culture, that our culture was getting increasingly nominalist, positivist, attached to the facts. There was less and less room for negation, because negation means precisely imagining another society, imagining otherness, something different from this ever-sameness. So, the other feature of the ever-sameness that they diagnose is this absence of the possibility of negating it. The labor and suffering of the negative, as Hegel says, is critique. But is critique another aspect of enlightenment?

In a way, the idea of the negative is really all they have left when they get back to Europe. Nazism is gone, but they will certainly look for traces of Nazism. What is Nazism to them? A regression to what they call the "authoritarian personality," and one of its features is anti-Semitism, which is of course still around.[6] Its principal features are regressive. Like Habermas, Adorno was very argumentative. He picked his quarrels and denounced the inheritors of the Nazi regime who were still professors, and he would use the word "fascist." Heidegger, for example. The smallest cell of Heidegger's thought is fascist, Adorno said once.[7] Communism in the East is a regime that you can't endorse—the Communist Party is outlawed—but the hunt for fascism is okay as a cleaning-up solution. The communist solution is closed. For many communist intellectuals—for Brecht, for Althusser—what was important in the immediate postwar years was China. They understood what Stalinism was, and they thought that

6 See Theodor W. Adorno et al., *The Authoritarian Personality* (New York: W. W. Norton, 1980 [1950]).

7 Theodor W. Adorno, *Musikalische Schriften VI. Gesammelte Schriften*, Volume 19, ed. Rolf Tiedemann (Frankfurt am Main: Suhrkamp, 1984), p. 635.

the promise of communism was to be found in the Chinese Revolution, though Brecht didn't live to see the Cultural Revolution. I don't think Adorno or Horkheimer were interested in the Global South.

Of idealism there remains simply this notion of holding on to negative thought, critical theory, which is a way of keeping your own intellectual positions. If Adorno was the daddy or the granddaddy of the students, it wasn't because he had a positive position. It was his notion of the critical and the negative that appealed to them. Marcuse had a far more developed idea, which was simply: Okay, you don't see classes doing much, but now the students are active—because it is the underclasses who are the source of revolt, the students, Black people, minorities—and, at that moment, offer a far more powerful and energizing politics. But, if you want to indulge in this matter of trying to figure out how Marxist their work is, I think you have to acknowledge that there could be many versions of it. Yes, it is Marxist in this way, more Nietzschean in another, and so on.

The other position is simply to say that these are just intellectuals. That was Brecht's position. Brecht called the members of the Frankfurt School *Tui Intellectuelle*. He planned to write a play on it, set in China, in Brecht's classical way of using exotic surroundings. Of course he admired China. A wealthy mandarin is on his deathbed, so he summons around him all the mandarins—that is to say, the *taliban*, the students—and he offers to leave them an immense fortune if they can find the source of evil, not being aware, Brecht says, that the source was he himself, the rich man, riches personified. So, their whole quest ought to lead back to him, just as the whole point of the institute is that it will dissolve itself in the process of its critiques. He never wrote the play. But to understand the significance of this hypothetical play, you must remember not only Adorno's attack on political literature but also that the Adornos and the Brechts both lived in Santa Monica and that the families had dinner together once a week. All of this must be balanced against your intellectual notions of the opposition between the Frankfurt School, the Brechtians, the communists, and so forth.

There is one more thing I want to draw your attention to. You have here a very peculiar sentence: "Wishful thinking is banned. The reason however is that all power in class society is beset by the gnawing consciousness of its powerlessness in face of physical nature and its social successor, the many."[8]

8 Horkheimer and Adorno, *Dialectic of Enlightenment*, p. 44.

This is very interesting, I think, because it makes a missing link. We saw that primitive humans live in this constant fear of the loss of their own life, the fear generated by self-preservation in the face of nature. But now Adorno is fascinated by a phrase that might not seem to us very interesting, in a book that was decisive for all these people: Lukács's *History and Class Consciousness*, 1923. That book plus the so-called early writings of Marx, first revealed in 1932, are the two dominant sources of Western Marxism, let's say. It's not very central, but Horkheimer and Adorno do use the phrase "second nature," a phrase that Lukács uses. I think that is what Adorno is talking about: Society becomes second nature.

So the unsystematized presuppositions of *Dialectic of Enlightenment*, some of which we would have to invent, have their correlate critiques, but then there is the matter of how relevant these presuppositions are today. When we talk about the culture industry, does it make a difference that we are now in the world of computers or of social media? It is possible, of course, that the earlier notion of the culture industry becomes suddenly suggestive in completely new and unforeseen ways. At any rate, they didn't know what would come. And what about the class situation and the world situation? To what degree is this kind of theory out of date and no longer of use to us? Well, those are some questions to keep in mind as we go on to read these final chapters before going on to Heidegger.

August 31, 2021

4

Horkheimer and Adorno (III)

We're going to come across a translation problem in Adorno's *Negative Dialectics*. This is in some ways a very clever translation, but it is very annoying, because the translator does some strange things with Adorno's language; for example, *Vermittlung*, "mediation," a good Hegelian-Marxist word that Adorno uses in that spirit, he translates as "transmission." What can that possibly mean to anyone? This translation wipes out all the political and historical references that have accumulated in this word *Vermittlung*. Why is he doing that? I don't know, and I don't care. It is, however, the only published translation. The other word I wanted to warn you about is *Tausch*, *Tauschgesellschaft*, and so on. *Tausch* means "exchange," and it is an absolutely crucial word for the Frankfurt School, because exchange is related to identity, equality, the commodity form. But he translates *Tausch* as "barter." Do you barter your five-dollar bill for some tomatoes or an ice cream cone or something? I don't think so. If you use the word "barter," you are removing the dimension of commodity exchange, and with it, the whole Marxist problem of exchange and identity. I wanted to warn you about those two words.

Let me reposition all of this quickly, because I do want to get to these two last chapters today. *Dialectic of Enlightenment* is one of the high points of what is sometimes called Western Marxism, a term that was invented or at least developed by Perry Anderson, and what he was trying to show—he cheats a little bit because he doesn't include Communist Party members like Gramsci or Althusser—is a shift from a problematics of economics, capitalism, and classes to a consideration of what are called "superstructures," that is, not just the ideas but the very structure, the mentalities, involved in certain social forms and modes of production.[1] Traditional Marxism, for Engels as for Lenin, is the systematic thinking—I would even call it the ideology—of a working-class movement. In the passage from the '20s to the '30s, the working-class movement in Western Europe fails. The revolts are put down in Germany. Hungary has a revolution, actually, in which Lukács is involved as a commissar. It fails. Obviously, these repressions are bloody ones, and people are murdered, like Rosa Luxemburg, who is killed by the social democratic government. And, finally, when we get to the '30s, Hitler is elected. There is a portion of the working class that is fascist or Nazi. So, to understand this moment would require a different kind of approach than a purely economic one, or at least an additional approach to mentalities, ideologies, culture, which was not seemingly necessary for earlier working-class movements. What Anderson calls Western Marxism comes into view for people who are then no longer members of the communist movement, socialist parties, independent or anarchist, people for whom the problematic of orthodox Marxism has somewhat modified itself to include problems of the superstructure. The great books for these people, whether they have read *Capital* or not, are Lukács's *History and Class Consciousness* from 1923 and Marx's early manuscripts, unpublished until 1932. For people like Marcuse, these manuscripts are mind-blowing. By the time of *Capital*, Marx had abandoned the seemingly psychological overtones of the concept of alienation. Does this abandonment signal a basic change in Marx, as Althusser suggested? That is of no great significance for us right now, but, at any rate, you have to reread *Capital* carefully to see that the structure of alienation—that is, the externalization-internalization structure of the Hegelian dialectic—is there, but it is not foregrounded. The other thing you have to know is that all these people are busy, necessarily, inventing new economic theories, which appeal to Marx's analysis of *Capital*, but they have to go beyond it in ways that are revealing of the phenomenon of fascism. You can certainly call fascism a moment of capitalism. Hitler was able to come to power after the great industrialists met with him, though they didn't like him much and he didn't like them; they decided that the warfare state was the right one, as it has been in the United States since

1 Perry Anderson, *Considerations on Western Marxism* (London: Verso, 1987).

World War II, when it provided the solution to the depression of 1929. Maybe that is not so surprising anymore.

At any rate, Horkheimer's closest collaborator and lifelong friend, Friedrich Pollock, is responsible for the term "state capitalism," which names a fundamental development in capitalism. It is happening obviously in Germany, but it's also happening in the Soviet Union: The market is being suppressed in the name of planning, and the plan involves the orienting of economic production around great organizations. Lenin himself says we have nothing against these monopolies; when we come to power, we just get rid of the private owners of them, and we already then have nationalized industries. As we'll see in a minute, there are reasons for bringing this up. But it is very funny when you read this latest American edition of *Dialectic of Enlightenment* and you see what Horkheimer and Adorno removed from their first version in order that it could pass less scandalously in front of the Western public, including the word "monopoly," because monopoly, for them, seems to have been the sign of what they still considered their Marxism. Now, since neoliberalism, we have grown accustomed to thinking that we have returned to market competition. I don't know if that's true. Was Hayek really a theorist of free competition?

At any rate, they thought we had reached state capitalism, a phase in what they considered a certain historical path, a path which is traced in these chapters and which includes the four periods I've already discussed. These are not modes of production in the Marxist sense. The other missing manuscript at the time, an enormous one—whereas the Paris manuscripts are very short—is called the *Grundrisse*, published in Moscow in 1939. Well, that's not a place and a publication date that would suggest that many people in the West were aware of it. It must have been published first in the West in the original German in the '50s, because I saw copies in East Berlin in the late '50s. It was translated into English in the '60s, and, apparently, for a lot of people, it provides a new kind of Marxism, in particular, in its long section on pre-capitalist formations (Marx was very interested in the anthropologists in his later years). Writing in America in the '40s, Horkheimer and Adorno did not have access to the late Marx's picture of pre-capitalist societies; obviously, they had no connection with Moscow.

So their historical argument is casting a very wide net. As far as anti-Semitism is concerned, remember also that Judaism will be involved in one of the levels of enlightenment, because monotheism gets rid of these images of the other gods. There are all kinds of scenes of the death of gods. (There is a very funny one in Flaubert.) Getting rid of the gods is certainly a part of the process of enlightenment. By the way, it is interesting that they don't seem to like laughter very much. Adorno seems to think that it is aggressive; Baudelaire thought the same. In Wyndham Lewis, laughing is like baring your teeth. You're laughing *at* somebody. Yeah, but laughter can also be, if you like, a good destruction, as was the case with ancient Greek comedy. Hegel says that Aristophanes was the final coup de grâce to the Olympians. Once you start laughing at it, then it's all over. So, monotheism is a form of enlightenment, as is the ban on graven images both in Judaism and in Islam. The graven image invites idolatry, of course, but above all, it arrests the process of abstraction involved in all demythologization. That is, enlightenment generally identifies myth as an image or a narrative that must be left behind.

As you read this, you're tempted to think: Is the object of their critique what we call modernity, and in that sense are they antimodern? Is that what's going on here? Certainly, what is called modernity, whatever you mean by it, has been the object of antimodern movements, I would say, on all political sides. The whole *Dialectic of Enlightenment* could be taken as a book against modernity, in a certain sense. The role of technology is less visible than it is in Heidegger, but I think we could say there is an antitechnological bias that goes along with the critique of science, and of course its salience is then proven in August 1945 by the atomic bomb.

If you read Bakhtin, which I highly recommend to you, you'll find that he was concerned with the novel as a sign of modernity—a sign, and not proof that there is some kind of complete modernity. But what does that mean? For us, modernity is capitalism. So, when somebody comes along and tells us that Odysseus is the first bourgeois, we could say: Alright, Odysseus was the first proponent of modernity. Would that work? Horkheimer and Adorno argue along these lines, but you couldn't really argue that Odysseus is the first representative of capitalism. Of course, it seems more respectable to talk about modernity than to talk about capitalism. It's safer to have modernity as your target than capitalism. In fact, one of the most dramatic moments in the history of the Frankfurt School is the moment in which Horkheimer reads a little published text of Habermas, who was a graduate student at the time; it uses the word "capitalism," and Horkheimer tells him to get rid of it. Horkheimer is terrified that using the word "capitalism" is going to draw attention. He depends absolutely on Adenauer and the German authorities, and the authorities depend absolutely on the Americans. And what's happening in America? It is the McCarthy era. The Americans never liked Marxism very much anyway, but this is the Cold War. So this mention of capitalism is very scary for Horkheimer, but he wants to have it both ways. He doesn't want to have a McCarthyite, anti-Marxist repression, even though he himself is in profound sympathy from his earliest years with the working-class movement, but at the same time, he isn't becoming a post-Marxist or a liberal. He wants to keep the essentials of Marxism, so some kind of game with language has to ensue, which you could compare, keeping all proportions of difference, with the way Gramsci had to invent a kind of shadow language for Marxism in his prison notebooks, because the guards and prison authorities would read his writing. He called Marxism "the philosophy of praxis." They didn't give a damn about that, so they let it be.

What's going on in the organization of *Dialectic of Enlightenment* as a whole? After the first chapter lays out the general process of enlightenment, which we are to understand is happening both to the world and to the mind, we have the *Odyssey* chapter on the formation of the subject, and with it, the notion that every stage of society requires a new kind of mentality. The people who can't function in a new society—they might be people who don't know how to use the internet—they're going to die off, but the people who can adapt to the new things will create a new form of subjectivity. You notice that the first thing they focus on in the *Odyssey* is cunning, *List*. Umberto Eco used to say that the first function of language is lying, because we can't really account for language unless we take into account the possibility of telling a lie. Well, here, it is as though they're saying something similar about subjectivity: Okay, you can't describe consciousness. Psychology is the name for what enlightenment tries to do with subjectivity—measuring things, finding characteristics—so it's no good. But the one thing that you could say about the new subjectivity of enlightenment is that you need cunning to establish sameness, to outwit what you're afraid of. To control nature you need cunning, so cunning is going to characterize the subjectivity necessary for enlightenment.

Then, with the chapter on Kant and Sade, we have ethics. What is the good? This chapter is, as I told you, a diagnosis of duty, of ethical maxims. In a way, I think it suggests that desire is somehow limited by the mode of production, by the form of the social. Many ethical theories are based on the universal, and the universal can't be solved, so to speak. We cannot invent a universal law of ethics. That is what Kant tried to do with the categorical imperative, but he presupposes that the categorical imperative has succeeded, that there is such a thing as the universal to which we can match our actions. That is to say, bad actions we can get rid of, because they don't fit under the universal law. You can't universalize thievery. Is that so? You see that this is a form of taboo, and enlightenment will proceed by taboo, by exclusion. We're going to get rid of myths, get rid of the imaginary, ban graven images, ban anthropomorphism, and on top of it, establish the universal. Establishing the universal, as we already have seen in the Odysseus chapter, is repressing the particular. We have to get rid of everything that does not fit under the universal.

Notice how we are passing from the control of nature to the control of the mind. The formation of subjectivity is a form of the control of the mind, and sometimes we call that "culture." Adorno hates the word "culture," which he thinks is itself a form of enlightenment. It is an anti-intellectual word. The apologists of culture are ideologues: The idea that culture is leisure, for example. You can see how work discipline gets established. The greatness of Ford was to have figured out how to apply Taylorism, how to build factories and transform work itself. Taylor is the supreme manifestation of enlightenment in the world of labor and production. You have your stopwatch. You calculate, figure out the shortest distances, and so on. It is a great pity that Taylor is omitted here. Taylor is one of the supreme heroes of the enlightenment organization of factory work. This is no longer handicraft. This is a way of applying enlightenment to handicraft. Now we're going to produce scientifically, in a measurable way.

The factory is the cathedral of enlightenment. But what about the rest of the day? We call it "leisure" for some reason. The most scandalous feature of Horkheimer and Adorno's argument is the idea that Hollywood —because Hollywood is the exhibit here—is the application of Kant's categories in leisure. There are formulae, not just stereotypes, categories which Hollywood applies, and every successful Hollywood picture is the imposition of these categories on the mind, the organization of the mind, the production of a certain kind of subjectivity, which will be the same subjectivity as the one that I take back with me into the factory. In fact, they say, the entertainment furnished us by Hollywood is the same as the organization of labor in the factories. Today, we might rather speak of algorithms. Algorithms are producing the same kind of subjectivity, organizing subjectivity in such a way that it can be measured, the same way production is organized.

Then, finally, the anti-Semitism chapter, the chapter on the destruction wrought by this new society, on the way in which enlightenment harnesses its negative features. In repression, there has to be a remainder, a portion that is not completely subsumed. Those impulses have to go somewhere, and it is the control of those impulses that will be the task of the forces of order, for example, of the police, of other kinds of discipline, of the Hays Office in Hollywood—or maybe they can be harnessed. Hitler, for example, was able to harness some of these forces. The early Nazi movement was a movement of veterans. These are people who had been wiped out by World War I, absolutely ignored by their government, which was, incidentally, a social democratic one. One of the last things the German army did as it surrendered in World War I was to throw the government to the social democrats like a hot potato. Whatever comes out of the peacetime settlements, the social democrats will be responsible for it. There may be aspects of this that sound familiar, and indeed, we have to ask ourselves how much of this is familiar. We would have said, a few years ago, that we don't have all three of the options that were available in the '20s and '30s: communism, the liberal capitalist state, and fascism. I would have said a few years ago that the fascist alternative had been eliminated in the postwar. Today, I'm tempted to revise that opinion.

As we discuss the contemporary relevance of this book, remember that one of the things it will be arguing against is forgetfulness. This is a theme of Nietzsche: History has progressed by the great power of forgetfulness. You can call it repression, if you like. That is one of the forms repression takes: forgetting. For Adorno's part, independently of Heidegger, he says we mustn't destroy or forget metaphysics. Of course, he says, metaphysics is impossible. We all know that it is a stupid, worthless discipline. It is thinking about nothing. There is no god; there is no meaning to life, as we know from Darwin. But, on the other hand, to forget metaphysics is a crucial move in the enlightenment organization of domination, and, therefore, the forgetting of the past and of the archaic is a very important tool.

We will just take a minute to go through the *Odyssey* chapter. The religious testament of ancient Greece—not that they believe in the Olympians exactly—the Homeric poems, are the basis of all Greek education, and they propose two cultural heroes. One is Achilles. Sometimes you're tempted to think Achilles is like a high school athlete; this is a pre-football hero of some sort, with his fits of rage, but this is an important model. Alexander the Great slept with the *Iliad* under his pillow at all times, carried it with him. The other is Odysseus. Is this a positive, likable hero? Odysseus is first of all, in the *Odyssey*, credited with the winning of the Trojan War. We have a scene in which Telemachus visits Menelaus and Helen in Sparta, and Helen says: "Listen, I'm going to tell you something about your father. He snuck into Troy during the war; he proposed the strategy of the Trojan horse, and I helped him"—this is Helen absolving herself of guilt—"by arranging to show him the weak points of the place." We must understand: The first thing he does in his own narrative is to stop—because they're hungry and have to eat—at a seaport, kill all the men and the boys, and take the women. He took their goods and ate. Unfortunately, this tribe was just the outlier of a larger kingdom which had horses; they came down and killed a lot of people. So, he is presented first of all in terms of bloodshed and war, the first form of survival.

Then we go on to the lotus-eaters, and this is one of the most wonderful parts. Lotus-eating is of course a drug culture:

> They fell in, soon enough, with Lotos Eaters,
> who showed no will to do us harm, only
> offering the sweet Lotos to our friends—
> but those who ate this honeyed plant, the Lotos,
> never cared to report, nor to return:
> they longed to stay forever, browsing on
> the native bloom, forgetful of their homeland.
> I drove them, all three wailing, to the ships,
> tied them down under their rowing benches,
> and called the rest: "All hands aboard;
> come, clear the beach and no one taste
> the Lotos, or you lose your hope of home."
> Filing in to their places by the rowlocks
> my oarsmen dipped their long oars in the surf,
> and we moved out again on our sea faring.[2]

2 Homer, *Odyssey*, trans. Robert Fitzgerald (New York: Anchor Books, 1963), pp. 147–8.

This first thing which one must repress is the bodily image of, if not happiness, then absolute giving-in, not even to ecstasy, but to the forgetfulness of drugs. It must be stamped out from the very beginning. People must be made to work. They must not be made to waste their time.

Now, the cyclops:

> giants, louts, without a law to bless them.

They have no law.

> In ignorance leaving the fruitage of the earth in mystery
> to the immortal gods, they neither plow
> nor sow by hand, nor till the ground, though grain—
> wild wheat and barley—grows untended, and
> wine-grapes, in clusters, ripen in heaven's rain.

They have no agriculture.

> [They] have no muster and no meeting,
> no consultation or old tribal ways,
> but each one dwells in his own mountain cave
> dealing out rough justice to wife and child,
> indifferent to what the others do.[3]

The point is that, after the abandonment of the body that the lotus-eaters represent, we now have the utopian society of the cyclops, which must also be destroyed. Enlightenment wants laws agriculture, labor, production. None of that is here. What about the single eye? I don't know. Enlightenment makes them into monsters in an effort to scare us off.

Okay, the visit to the underworld. The first one Odysseus sees is the mother. In a patriarchal society, we must repress matriarchy. The mother must be kept at a distance. He tries to embrace her, but she is nothing but an image, and in the Greek world, we must distrust images. We learn that we must de-imagize our thought, just as we must demythologize it, because these images are unreal. When we go on to Scylla and Charybdis, we are taught the yes and no of decision-making, the way in which you

3 Homer, *Odyssey*, p. 148.

somehow learn to act. You cannot judge that Scylla is better than Charybdis or Charybdis better than Scylla. For all of its knowledge, this is a risk society, and you must risk your luck to get through. And, finally, there are the Cattle of the Sun and the cave. Both of these episodes involve the crew doing things that Odysseus warns them against. In the case of the winds, the crew decides they could get home faster if they unleash the propitious gales from a bag of winds; instead, all the winds come out. Is this a lesson in patience? Patience is part of repression. Remember that the formation of the worker is dependent on the workweek, on delayed gratification. Marx points this out. In effect, the worker is lending the capitalist his work, giving the capitalist a gift of time which is only repaid on Fridays. For the first part of the week, he is working for nothing. So, you could almost say that delayed gratification is the lesson of the Cave of the Winds, while the Cattle of the Sun teaches a respect for the law.

We don't have time, so we'll have to hold the culture industry and the anti-Semitism chapters for next time, and then we'll go on to Heidegger.

September 7, 2021

5

Horkheimer, Adorno (IV)

First, I want to dispel one misconception, which I think is very easy to fall into, about the passage from myth to science. We are looking at this in a global way, and you have to keep in mind the historical context, including the development of anthropology and of classical studies. There was a Cambridge school, around the time of the World War I, whose interest was in connecting myths to rituals. The idea that myths were really rituals and vice versa left its mark, for example, with Frazer's *The Golden Bough* and T. S. Eliot's *Waste Land*, if you look at the footnotes. Then, in the '30s and '40s, under the direction of Franz Boas, who was probably the most important figure in that moment of American anthropology—and he was, of course, a German transplant—you get a culture of personality school, not so much with Boas himself, but with his followers, who try to understand a given form of society with psychiatric concepts. Ruth Benedict's *Patterns of Culture* is probably the most famous attempt. Like many others, Benedict worked for the State Department during the war, which was when, without ever having set foot in Japan, she produced a study of Japanese culture, *The Chrysanthemum and the Sword*. The great fear—and this was the excuse for using the atomic bomb—was that the Japanese, supposedly being a ruthless people, would resist on the mainland in Japan and cause immense numbers of American deaths. Benedict said no: It is enough for the emperor to say the word, and it will be all over. That is exactly what happened. Hirohito made a broadcast, which nobody could understand because he spoke an archaic Japanese that had to be translated for the common people. "Warriors, lay down your arms." And that was it.

Adorno and Horkheimer could not but have been influenced to a certain degree by all of these developments in anthropology and psychiatry. In particular, there is the question of paranoia, which would require a little more in the way of footnotes and background to see exactly whom they are referring to. But these are the signs of their historical situation, which is no longer our own. Their conception of the archaic period, let's say, was certainly modified by Lévi-Strauss, by the whole debate about power in primitive societies, and by the disappearance of those societies. But I want to insist that, no, this is not a division of what, in French anthropology of the period, they called "primitive mentalities." It is not a debate between a primitive irrationality and a scientific rationality, the terms of which are agreed to from the start. On the contrary, the whole point of this discussion of myth is that myths are also a stage in reason, because reason is a matter of understanding the outside world, diminishing our fear, trying to control what is both unintelligible to us and dangerous. So, this is not good versus bad. This is not good science, progressing reason, and bad superstition—or vice versa. This is a dialectic in which each of these moments is both progress and regress at the same time.

Now, if there has been some kind of progression to what we are in now—that is to say, universal quantification, the rule of abstraction, logic, algorithmic rationality—it means that what used to pass for philosophy, namely metaphysics, is now superstition. Soon we will get to Adorno's "Meditation on Metaphysics," in which he says we can't believe in metaphysics anymore, but we can't *not* adopt it either, and that to denounce metaphysics in the name of positivism as something that must be consigned to the dustbin of history would simply be a sign that the noose is tightening. In Adorno's image, what is under threat is negativity, thought itself. So, the distinction between good and evil, in some sense, returns when Adorno makes such judgments. That is to say, on the one hand, if we don't consider that superstition is bad, then we are prey to even worse kinds of regression, irrationality, and mythic behavior than exists now. On the other hand, he proposes that there is an identity between the irrational and the rational. Hegel's formula in the invention of the dialectic was: the identity of identity and nonidentity—and the nonidentity of identity and nonidentity. So, Adorno will keep only nonidentity. I think this is a kind of a vulgarization of his own thought, but we'll get to that later on.

At any rate, the view of reason in *Dialectic of Enlightenment* constitutes a certain kind of dialectic in which time is inserted, in the sense that, at one and the same time, each development is both regressive and progressive. Does that mean: What exists now is bad, but there's something good in it, a moment of truth? The moment of truth, or the index of untruth, has a historical meaning here. I would like to say it is a more existential notion of truth than an epistemological one but that would probably not be an acceptable formulation for them, since a critique of existentialism also guides their thought. Nonetheless, this is a theory of the process of mental formation, a process of the construction of consciousness, in which you can't simply be on the side of the process itself, because its endless generativity would wipe out the entire past, as Adorno argues in his meditation. We don't want to lose metaphysics in what Heidegger called its *Destruktion.* Its moment of truth must be acknowledged, and therefore, in a way, any notion of modernity must be false. With Galileo, Descartes, Luther—at least in Hegel's periodization—there is this break between the past and modernity. What is the past? "Tradition" was the only word they found for it.

I think you have to understand that Adorno and Horkheimer are not antiprogress in any thematic sense. They are not exactly antitechnology either, although that is certainly involved, as it already was in Marx. Marx showed in *Capital* that automation, the machine, which was designed to be a labor-saving device, in fact, with the installation of machinery in production, made workers work longer than they had in the previous era. That is one of the central discoveries, you could say, in *Capital.* Marx was very interested in new advances in science, but on the other hand, he asked: To what degree can these innovations be mastered by the owners and the capitalists and used against the workers? Horkheimer and Adorno, however, are trying to show that the development of science and technology, rationalization, are processes that involve everybody. In other words, as I tried to emphasize last time, these are intellectuals, academics, and they don't know any working-class people, because, in the Europe of the '20s and '30s, there isn't much of that kind of contact. The one place in which upper-class children or youth would have any connection to lower-class youth is in the army, in national service, and there you have a hierarchy—officers, foot soldiers, and so on. So, the usual associations between the classes are not present in Europe. These people's fathers are industrialists or businessmen, and therefore—Marx already showed what happened to the poor and the workers—they have an interest in showing what is happening in a different form to the bourgeoisie.

I want to emphasize that this analysis of the evils of quantification and the universal, the coming into being of abstraction, the mind colonizing the body, so to speak, this kind of analysis is new for the Left. It is not new for the reactionaries, who have long condemned modernity in the name of religion. The Right has plenty of arguments—not quite the same analyses—but it is well equipped to denounce the godlessness of reason and the bourgeois apparatus of demythologization. But the Left? The contribution of the Frankfurt School, beginning with the first issues of the journal in '32, is to have brought this kind of analysis to the Left.

They don't like the word "ideology" very much. There are political reasons for that, but you could make an argument in their spirit that ideologies themselves are an older stage of enlightenment. Ideological analysis begins, at the end of the French Revolution and the Napoleonic period, with a group called the *idéologues*, who studied ideas in the sense of association, that is, the structure of thinking, if you like. Napoleon hated them, but that's another matter. They did not mean what we normally mean today by "ideology." This word is taken over by Marx in *The German Ideology*, fairly early in his career, and completely transformed, made into what it is today. I think you could make an argument that nowadays those kinds of ideologies, left and right and so on, are old-fashioned; ideology and domination take subtler forms, such that it becomes ineffective if you attack somebody for having, for example, bourgeois ideology or idealist ideology, to use one of the crucial watchwords of ideological analysis. I think the premise here is that we have moved on to another stage, in which even those words—"idealism" and "materialism"—are like myths. We relegate them to the past and we analyze something—"micrology," Adorno calls it—even more minute and complex than those old-fashioned ideologies that nobody cares about anymore. Philosophers don't care very much if you call them idealist or materialist. Maybe some of them do. Should this lead us to say that the very idea of classes is mythical and unscientific? It might lead in that direction, and, in that case, you would have to take a closer look at the economic relations to which the category of class is tied, but it would be a similar undertaking to what they are doing here.

However, I think what is interesting here is a certain relationship they want to establish. They have established that the world is being organized according to new categories of exchange, if not capital. This is what's happening to the world, but what about the psyche? The interior and the exterior are not always the same. We see that Odysseus's cunning is a far deadlier instrument than the sheer muscle power of the cyclops or of these other natural forces. Something is happening to the mind as an organ of the body. What is coming into being is maybe what we call individualism. One of the worst things about the common notion of modernity—maybe you could blame Luther for this—is the idea that before modernity there is no notion of individualism. That's like saying, as in nineteenth-century paradigms, that only in the West are there individuals, or only in the West is death really important, while, in this teeming East, they don't have individuality. Stereotypes have shaped the way in which identity and self-reflection—another suspicious concept—have marked the modern. Luther's notion of the evolution of the inwardness of the spirit, of the way in which religion has to be felt as guilt and as anxiety, as stuff you confess and get absolved of, was for Hegel, for example, a fundamental marker—as was Christianity itself, as a religion of guilt—of inwardization, the creation of modern identity. I think that is a very pernicious simplification.

The one thing I want to emphasize here comes later in their notion of economics. You remember their two basic stages: the market, or market competition, until the emergence of the first robber barons, as we call them in American history, and eventually the moment of monopoly, the end of the market—or so Pollock thought—and the beginning, therefore, of state capitalism. They tend to read subjectivity in the same way. There is a moment of subjectivity which is possible in the stage of competition of market capital but which is no longer possible under a monopoly capitalism, which they sometimes say is no longer capitalism but something new. Under monopoly, what happens to this so-called individualism? Well, it shrinks again. You have the mentality of the bureaucracy, of the employee. Siegfried Kracauer, whom we won't talk about much, though he was Adorno's first teacher, in a way, wrote several very important works under Weimar, including a book called *Die Angestellten*, which is about employees. He tries to show that there is a new mentality, which is that of the employee of the great big business, in which the individualism of market competition is lost, tamed, reduced to forms of obedience. This is a very suggestive example, I think, of the relationship of outside and inside, of society or economics and what I consider the construction of the subject, the structure of subjectivity. We have a more diminished individuality, no matter how we think about it, than the heroes and heroines of the nineteenth-century novel, for example. "The most advanced form at a given time becomes the dominant one. Once, the department store expropriated the old-style specialist shop."[1] That could be about Zola's *Au Bonheur des Dames*. These pages are really a meditation on the emergence and transformation of individualism. You'll say: Okay, but we don't have this kind of mentality anymore because we had the '60s! Then you may prefer to think of it in psychoanalytic terms as the Oedipus complex. All these people deplore, first of all, the authoritarian father. The German family is notoriously authoritarian. The aggressiveness of the world, of families under the authority of the father, who can then revolt against the father—that's all gone when you don't have any fathers anymore. These fathers are nothing. When they come back, they're losers. They deserve no respect at all. In East Germany, there is the notion, accurate or not, that a new kind of subjectivity could be evolved under the form of socialism. That doesn't exist in the West, because there isn't any new system. There isn't any chance for a transformed personality of that type. Freud was not a German, and I want to insist on that, because I think that is very important to keep in mind: Austrians are not Germans. You wouldn't put an English writer into the syllabus of American literature. There are differences to be respected. Freud was not only Jewish but Austrian, and the Austro-Hungarian Empire was of a different type. Besides the structure of economics—whether you have a monopoly or small business affecting the structure of your mentality—there is also the nation itself. I think it is important that what happens to the destiny of a nation impacts the nature of individuality, and this holds very much for the period we are talking about.

Adorno gets back to Germany in the early '50s. You all know the propaganda about East Germany: gray, colorless, completely without character, and so on. But that describes West Germany in the '50s! This place is no longer a nation-state. It is under occupation and under rationing. This is a place without qualities, let's say, to use Musil in another way. So, what is to become of the question of individualism? Do we want to reinvent it? To reinvent it is to reconsider nationhood. They are colonized by the American army. That is what so-called West Germany was in the years after the war. It is not until the early '60s that there comes to be a sense of something like West Germany, which is not really a nation. So, this is why

1 Horkheimer and Adorno, *Dialectic of Enlightenment*, p. 168.

the emphasis on pedagogy will be very important. How is the subject of this new nation to be constructed? What is it that individualism should aim at, particularly if we don't have competition anymore? Of course, these questions will be reconstructed on a Europe-wide basis.

What will emerge in the shape of an answer is the idea of autonomy, the idea that there is such an idea as an autonomous personality, which is not the authoritarian personality, the fascist personality, but maybe not the squashed personality of capitalism either. Some of the later disciples of the Frankfurt School will adopt this notion of autonomy as a goal, and it seems to me that it is a natural consequence of the view they are taking of individualism, consciousness, and identity. Where else would it go? Fascism was the final form in which these *Angestellten*, these employees, found their fulfillment. Like in Hegel's analysis of the Roman Empire, there is a group of nonindividuals, and then the one supreme individual, who is the master of the state, so that you have a pathological dialectic, so to speak, of the one and the many. That is not around for them. The usefulness of Adenauer, after the war, is that he is authoritarian, which is good, because you need somebody to tell you what to do; he is dictatorial, but he is not a dictator because he has no authority. So, it is in that situation that the next generation after the Frankfurt School will have to decide what their psychological goal is, what kind of subjectivity they are trying to bring into being. Anyway, I think this is one of the most interesting parts of this notion that there was a space for individuation in competitive capitalism which was then being gradually wiped out.

I don't want to deal with Adorno's aesthetics in detail right now, since we'll have plenty of time to do that later on, but the allegory of the sirens' song will introduce us to his aesthetics. You have work on one hand, command on the other, and the one moment of the sirens' song. What is it about? Oddly, it's the same as that of the seers or the prophets in the *Iliad.* This translation of the song is from the Loeb Library, which is better here than the translation by Fitzgerald, who embroiders it for some reason:

> Come hither, as thou farest, renowned Odysseus, great glory of the Achaeans; stay thy ship that thou mayest listen to the voice of us two. For never yet has any man rowed past this isle in his black ship until he has heard the sweet voice from our lips. Nay, he has joy of it, and goes his way a wiser man. For we know all the toils that in wide Troy the

> Argives and Trojans endured through the will of the gods, and we know all things that come to pass upon the fruitful earth.[2]

We know the past; we know the future. So, something about the knowledge of past and future is what must also be repressed in Odysseus's refusal of the siren song. The repression of the past, the forgetfulness of the past, the suppression of the past, on Horkheimer and Adorno's reading, would also be the repression of the memory of childhood, which we see again in Marcuse, the archaic memory of happiness that has to be suppressed in order for the individual to become an adult and to fit into the working world, this postponement of pleasure which is required by capitalism and by work in general.

There is much to be said for the aesthetic basis of this reading and the acknowledgement of the class distinction at work aboard Odysseus's ship. Odysseus needs a different control than the workers. The workers can be insulated from the sirens' song. Odysseus has to invent something else. Both sides must be, in some way, "mutilated," as they like to say. In his *Minima Moralia*, Adorno talks about "the damaged life." Both classes must be damaged, but in different ways, just as in the dialectic, if you like, of the jailer. The people who are in jail obviously suffer their own kind of limits. But the jailers don't have much of a life either. I think it is partly this symmetrical damaging that the sirens' song wishes to affirm. This is the sense in which their analysis of enlightenment is also aimed towards a bourgeoisie that is to be instructed in the evils of capitalism and enlightenment.

With the culture industry, here too, is a history lesson. They are talking about Hollywood and radio in the '40s. This seems to us a primitive stage in the development of media and the culture industry. That is to say, there has been an immense amount of change in aesthetics, of formal development in film—radio, I don't know—but certainly in television and in advertising, because some of the ads we see today are highly sophisticated products which are formally much more striking than the older kind of advertisements. So, I think we have to resituate this analysis of the culture industry today, and, of course, the one thing that is lacking here is a modern television culture. You likely know something about the already

2 Homer, *The Odyssey*, Volume 1, trans. A. T. Murray (Cambridge, MA: Harvard University Press [Loeb], 1945), pp. 445–7.

rudimentary television culture in America of the early '50s, with Milton Berle and so on. In Europe all of this comes a little later. But, of course, what Horkheimer and Adorno don't know anything about is social media and everything that comes with the internet. So, the question would be: How can one deal with those new developments? Even if we go back to the first personal computers around 1982, one of our questions, which we probably can't answer, will have to be whether there is anything useful in their view of an older culture industry when looking at the contemporary. There is a lot that is still useful. The consumption of value, for example. They make the point that, if you go to a movie, you want to know what its production values are. Does this cost a lot of money? And what about success? Is this the most widely viewed film? So, with this commodity—since this is an analysis of culture as a commodity, and a pioneering one at that—it is necessary to know how we consume value. I don't know if they do this anymore, but restaurants in California used to serve something on a skewer; maybe you would have lobster, filet mignon, and Cornish hen. Is putting those three foods together a new gastronomical combination? Obviously not. It is simply picking the most expensive of all the restaurant has to offer and then consuming them together. That is one feature of the culture industry. You have to take into consideration, when the bosses of the studio decide that something isn't saleable and it has to be changed or that Stroheim's four hours have to be cut back to two or that Welles has to be censored, we take those facts into account when we see the film. We may not like it, but they are made a part of the aesthetic experience. Economic considerations affect both the production and the consumption of cultural products in a way that they didn't before. We didn't have to know how much money Stendhal was making when he wrote *The Red and the Black*. He wrote it on vacations from his diplomatic duties from Italy, but we don't have to know that.

I want to insist that the notion of the collective is not very strongly developed here, but, if you want to say the Frankfurt School were armchair Marxists who didn't have any relationship to praxis, that's alright, but you have to understand that the collective politics of the German '60s came out of their thinking, whether Horkheimer liked it or not—he didn't like it—and whether Adorno liked it or not—he was in fact a bit more sympathetic. A collective movement did emerge from this work, so we can't underestimate its effects.

We are now talking about an industry that caters to leisure and is supposed to entertain, in particular, to entertain tired, working-class people, people who have worked in an alienated way. The real innovation, I think, is to say that in this system work and leisure are the same. There is a fundamental identity of work and leisure. And they make this argument, again, through Kant's categories. Just as Aristotle was in the classical period, so Kant is today the source of our common sense about things. Their use of Kant's categories is not worked out in any exhaustive way, but they work freely with Kant's idea that we don't have immediate contact with the outside world. How do we turn sensation—that is, pure sensory impact—into thoughts or experience? What Kant proposes is that the mind is organized in such a way as to pass these meaningless sensations from the outside through the grid of the categories, so that what we think or perceive is already going to be pre-formed by these categories. You can see that, in this system, there is no direct contact with the material world, that it's always mediated by something in us of which we are not directly aware. For Horkheimer and Adorno, the perception of that world will be furnished to us, then, in the form of pre-formed thoughts. We're already at sameness, identity. We're not feeling any of the otherness of the outside world. The outside world has been domesticated through a version of Kant's categories, and I think that, in one way or another, this is how our common sense thinks about the world. Do we really think we see things? Do we see the images of things?

From there it is but a step to say that what are furnished by the categories are stereotypes. In a way, the enemy of this step in their thinking is the universal. In the coming decades in France, the enemy is the same, though a different kind of universal: totality. The universal is what is absolutely abstract. It is that under which all of the particulars can be subsumed. So, these are the stereotypes produced by a universal system. Everything we see in Hollywood movies has been predigested: their character types, their categories of actions, their types of images. It is Henry Ford's production belt. It produces standard models out of some raw material that is not accessible to us. It is this, more than anything else, I think, that Adorno—since he is the primary writer of this chapter—objects to. Hollywood produces a second nature, to use Lukács's idea. Hollywood films want to show you something as if it were natural, and the avant-garde will then simply be an intervention showing the unnaturalness of what is presented as natural, as in Brecht's so-called alienation effect. (I think it's better to say *Verfremdungseffekt,* since "alienation" is *Entfremdung,* whereas "estrangement" is *Verfremdung.*) The *Verfremdungseffekt* involves showing how what looks natural to us is really historical, that is, produced by human beings and therefore changeable. The attack on naturalness at least preserves that much, and certainly both Brecht and Adorno learned something about it from each other, because they lived in Hollywood and discussed its products together.

There is also a discourse on style in this chapter, though it is hard to know what Adorno means by it. I think style in this case means period style. He wants to go beyond a narrow historicism to say that, for instance, if there is a modern style, Picasso has to modify it. Style is tradition. Style is preprogramming, let's say, and slight differences can make for genuine art, if you like. So, you can get a notion of art history from this system. You innovate, everybody starts to imitate it, the innovation freezes over into a tradition of its own, and then you have to break with it again. I would say that this is now the standard telos of modernism as the story is told in all the arts. We'll see some version of this when we get to Adorno's aesthetics.

What he wants to insist on is twofold. First of all, art must somehow find expression for suffering. This will be a leitmotif of Adorno's, in particular in the famous phrases about how we can't write poetry after Auschwitz, which is to say we can't do art anymore after Auschwitz; it is the end of the dialectic of enlightenment in a certain way, given the fact that Auschwitz is one of the triumphs of scientific organization. He understands that he has made a *boutade* here, and when we get to his "Meditations on Metaphysics," he'll say (because he works with younger artists): Alright, maybe we can write poetry after Auschwitz, but it can't be the same. Anyway, you can understand how he would judge Hollywood on the impossibility not so much of rendering reality—that's not in question here—but of breaking through the sameness of all the levels of modern life, and then somehow, at the same time—will these two aims be the same?—expressing suffering. This will have to do with one of the primary features of their analysis of the culture industry and of Adorno's work on music, namely that sameness, affirmation—or consonance, in music—gets boring and that new forms of dissonance must break through that sameness. Each form of dissonance gets domesticated, becomes routine. Then something new breaks through that dissonance. In such a process there is a dialectic at work within the arts.

Let me just finish by outlining a few positions in the anti-Semitism chapter. There is an enormous literature on anti-Semitism, obviously, and it is for the most part twofold. One side will wish to analyze the psychology and mentality of the anti-Semite and the other that of the Jew himself. That makes for complications, which you don't see entirely here, because this is not a complete theory of anti-Semitism. I will give you several references. First of all, in one of the most complicated things Marx wrote, "On the Jewish Question," he says that, if you wish to be assimilated to a representative system, you have to give up Judaism. These religious differences have to be abolished if you are to have universal citizenship. Marx has been called an anti-Semite because of this very position. It is a position that shows how assimilation has its own punishment, so to speak. If, on the other hand, you wish to affirm yourself as Jewish, as different from the secular, then you run the risk of simply confirming everything the anti-Semite says about you. How to get out of that problem? Well, I don't know that one can, but it seems to me, with the state of Israel, we are in a rather different situation, one in which nationality is merged with some kind of racial-ideological notion. There are two other texts I would recommend on the topic, which are, however, not references for Horkheimer and Adorno. The great book on anti-Semitism is by Sartre. In English it's called *Anti-Semite and Jew*, in which Sartre asks: How does the object of anti-Semitism get to be an object of any kind, when there isn't such a thing as personal identity? That is part of Sartre's existentialism. In the Sartrean system of otherness, he defines it this way: A Jew is someone other people consider a Jew. There is a lot more involved, but it is a very powerful, extraordinary text. Finally, there would be Moishe Postone's discussion of anti-Semitism in terms of commodification and reification.[3] I guess you could say Postone is also in the lineage of the Frankfurt School, but of a rather unique type, rather different from the social democratic following, the Habermasian descendance.

Next time, maybe, we will even arrive at the possibility of dealing with Heidegger.

September 9, 2021

---

3 Moishe Postone, "Anti-Semitism and National Socialism: Notes on the German Reaction to 'Holocaust,'" *New German Critique*, no. 19 (1980), pp. 97–115.

6

Horkheimer and Adorno, Heidegger

More on the theory of anti-Semitism, which obviously brings up historical questions for Horkheimer and Adorno about an entire moment of German philosophy, including Heidegger, who had a Nazi Party card. They are writing at a time when the occupied powers are undertaking a process called "denazification." The Eichmann trial was a bombshell in the aftermath of the Holocaust, but it is not until the '60s that Nazis are really identified. In the Soviet zone, of course, the Nazis are pursued with great vigor, except for scientists. The scientists found by the Soviets are all taken off to Moscow, given a dacha and a laboratory. The ones found by the Americans are also taken off to America, given a dacha and a laboratory, although the fates of these two groups of scientists are quite different. In West Germany, there arises the same problem that Lenin faced after the Russian Revolution and that the Taliban are facing right now. After you take over a state, you have to run it. There have to be bureaucrats. Where are they going to come from? They're not going to come from a bunch of guerrilla fighters. They know about guns and ambushes, and maybe they have read Sun Tzu—maybe they are intellectuals—but they don't know how to run a sewer system or a transportation system. What Lenin found is that he had to leave the tsarist bureaucracy in place, and, of course, the tsarist bureaucracy did its best to undermine the new state. Who knows what the Taliban are finding? But what the Americans found—and the Soviets to a lesser degree, because the Soviets had the Party, and the Party knew something about administration and bureaucracy—is that they had to rely on the Nazi bureaucrats. What do I mean by "Nazi"? In any revolutionary party-state, as soon as the party comes to power there are opportunists who join the party. They don't give a damn what the party stands for, but they want a job, so they get a party card. There were plenty of these people in the Nazi bureaucracy, and the Americans just decided to keep them all. They had to do something about the worst ones—Heidegger himself was forbidden to teach—but the other ones were left in place to such an extent that the West Germans will eventually have a chancellor who was a former Nazi Party member: Kurt Georg Kiesinger.

I don't think that the Frankfurt School's system is altogether useful for understanding anti-Semitism, and I don't think they have a systematic theory of anti-Semitism, but I would venture a few useful elements of this nonsystematic theory before we leave it there. As I've said, the Frankfurt School's relationship to Heidegger is essential to their notion of anti-Semitism. I don't know what Heidegger thought about the Frankfurt School—if he thought about it at all—but, certainly, the Frankfurt School loathed him and thought he was a pernicious influence. So, I think we have to be very cautious in our rapprochement of these two sources of postwar German thought. Today, this goes without saying, although there are plenty of books about how Heidegger and the Frankfurt School agree on certain topics, and, in fact, yes, of course, from a distance, they may look fairly similar. In the most general terms, both are lamenting something terrible happening to civilization—or maybe it's civilization happening to itself. Both are eventually working in the aftermath of Husserl's late *The Crisis of the European Sciences and Transcendental Phenomenology*, a big book that he published in the '30s, in which he says that science has grown away from its origins in concrete practice. Husserl even seems to say that Nazism itself comes from this bad abstraction. The Frankfurt School develops a role for abstraction in their much more global theory—or tries to—while, for Heidegger, abstraction is, among other things, a sign of the deficiencies of the modern. How can a concept like "abstraction" be used to create a historical narrative, and would this narrative not at some level claim that everything has gone from good to bad or from bad to good? Is this not what is involved in asking how modern science emerged? Or how our subjectivities and our relationships to people and things begin to disintegrate with the abstractions of modern science? It's in the transitions that you find, let's say, the explanatory codes by which each narrative of history makes sense of these things and judges them. This is what we're interested in philosophically, these explanatory codes that the Frankfurt School gives us. I have suggested that the domination of nature is one such explanatory code which can be called upon, not to explain everything, but at least to cast a light on unique phenomena which we might not see otherwise.

Out of the critique of the sciences, in particular, comes a notion of stereotypes; the critique of abstraction is a critique of language, of names, of nouns. One part of the dialectic of anti-Semitism that they don't explore enough is this business of the name. You know what philo-Semitism is: a gentile who is excited by and interested in all things Judaic. So, you have two groups, which may or may not be limited, who are in one way or another obsessed by Judaism. It would seem that, while one is reprehensible, the other one ought to be admirable, but it doesn't quite work that way. The point is that it's all very well to talk about Judaism or Jewishness, but when you start to use the noun, "a Jew," it ceases to matter what your feelings about Judaism are: You are putting someone under a type. Now, a member of the group can do it to themselves, perhaps, also a delicate matter. This is why this whole discussion is very embarrassing. When an outsider talks about a Jew, even if the person in question is in fact Jewish, then you think the outsider must be an anti-Semite, because who else would be interested in identifying somebody as a Jew? There is something in language and abstraction that renders all identification a kind of alienation. A category alienates and creates a stereotype, however positively it might be meant in some particular usage.

The other feature we find developed here is the connection between smell and regression, with all its complications. Imagine smell as the sirens' song. Smell takes us back to animal life, some kind of paradisal, archaic situation, in which smells are all modes of distinction. You may react against that archaic situation with disgust. Why? I would suggest—and this is not yet developed here—that this reaction is a form of envy. As a critique of these bourgeois thinkers, I've noted that the collective doesn't get much attention from them. They know about it, and obviously it is implicit in any kind of critical thought, but as an entity, as an object of study, as an object of identification, it doesn't get much attention. It's clear why not: These are victims of the Nazis. If there was any movement which based itself on the notion of a collective, it's the Nazis. A class society is not based on collectivity in the same way as Nazism, although it could contain within itself or deteriorate into fascisms of all kinds. In East Germany, for example, part of the so-called dictatorship of the proletariat that they tried to institute was that only workers' children could go to the university; if you were a child of a bourgeois family, you didn't have the same educational rights as workers. It's clear that someone who was a refugee from Nazi collectivity is not going to be terribly excited about positing collectivity as an urge behind movements and subjective forces. But I would say that collective envy plays its part here, and that, for the anti-Semite and the Nazi, via notions like regression, "the Jews" are imagined to be a collectivity that otherwise modern non-Jews have lost. There is an imagined solidarity there, to which some reaction must manifest itself, and clearly the chosen reaction in this case was hatred. So, the dialectic of collectivity and envy has to be taken into account, even if it isn't in Horkheimer and Adorno.

I want to go on to one further aspect of their critique of anti-Semitism, which has to do with subjectivity in general. Their analysis of the authoritarian personality, of which anti-Semitism is one possible characteristic, is an analysis of political subjectivity. Horkheimer wanted to produce something interdisciplinary, not in our febrile sense, but in the sense that it could allow people from various disciplines to invent—on the basis of Marxism, actually, but don't tell anybody that!—a common language to speak about the phenomena of modern societies. He wanted to make a unified system, in some sense, but one that had a relationship to concrete reality. In Horkheimer's original system, there were to be collective research projects, interviews, studies on the ground. Adorno never interviewed anybody, but he did make up one famous thing, a questionnaire, the famous F-scale, or fascist scale. It is a series of questions that try to probe your tendency to authoritarianism and thus to fascism. In other words, if you get twenty out of thirty of a certain type, then you're much more perilously close to a fascist mentality than those who only score ten. There was an intent to use that kind of practical testing. But in the United States, where they ended up, with the war ending, people weren't interested in fascism anymore. As a matter of fact, the American army would like to have forgotten all about it, because the Cold War was beginning, and they were much more intent on hiring ex-Nazis to compete with the Soviets. So, the Frankfurt School hardly had a chance to be financed for that sort of work, even as there was increasing interest on the part of Jewish foundations for an analysis of anti-Semitism, which ended up becoming a central aspect of their work. Their work was shaped by tensions in the real world that can't be overlooked.

This is all we're going to do here with the Frankfurt School until we return to Adorno and Marcuse later on, so at least we have a little bit of time to make a beginning with Heidegger. It is clear that Heidegger's mode of philosophizing is quite different from theirs, even on the level of the sentence. They wish to make each sentence the locus of a contradiction, whereas Heidegger wants to use very simple language to show you how these simple words have complexity within themselves. This means that his philosophy is profoundly related to the German language, not a bad thing for Heidegger, because he is a German nationalist, as is Hölderlin, with whom he shares a connection. But, for us, it makes it difficult, if not impossible, to work with him. I am not content with the translations of his work. I'm going to be using a work on television by Richard Dienst called *Still Life in Real Time*, in which he has a chapter on Heidegger. Heidegger granted one interview on television. Unfortunately, it is delivered with his back to the camera. Well, that must mean something. But you can see him speaking in another interview, now on YouTube, in which Heidegger is speaking to a Buddhist monk. That is a very interesting one, because, of course, a connection has been made between late Heideggerianism and Buddhism.

First let me tell you about the word *Gestell*. *Gestell* is variously translated as "enframing," "installation," "emplacement," "construct." So, the safer thing to do would be to reprint the German in parentheses at each mention. Otherwise, you can't understand it. *Stellen* is to put or to place something. "Idea" is *Vorstellen*, which is also "representation." To have an idea of something is to put it in front of you. This is important for Heidegger's critique of representation, which begins with the notion that thought has to do with *stellen* in some way. If you put the thing you are thinking about in front of you, and step back to look at it from a distance, you have an idea of it, a *Vorstellen*. To know something, I have to separate it from myself, and then I have to examine it. That is knowledge, or, at least, it is the kind of knowledge that Heidegger will subject to critique. I said that the most interesting modern philosophies are really, in one way or another, critiques of epistemology, that is to say, of the domination of philosophy by problems of knowledge. Heidegger's is maybe the strongest of these critiques, because it isolates the process of preabstraction that has to take place in order for an idea to emerge. *Stellen* is going to be important for this critique, as are the connections that a word like *stellen* can enter into—*vorstellen*, *entstellen*, *Gestell*. By using these simple words, Heidegger is telling you: Don't worry, you can follow this. He may be telling you something, but he's telling you by way of questions. How is it that this is so? Why is that? Just count the question marks in these texts.

At any rate, this discussion of the philosophical positions within words also entails etymology, or perhaps folk etymologies, false etymologies. The French thinker and editor Jean Paulhan wrote a little book called *La preuve par l'étymologie*, *The Proof by Etymology*. He wasn't necessarily defending Heidegger, but he was pointing out that we have various forms of arguments, not all of them syllogistic, and one kind of proof, if you want to use that word, takes the form of etymology. Part of Heidegger's work will operate through etymology as a mode of proof, and when all else fails, we can fall back on spelling. In the later Heidegger, just to make sure you don't get it wrong—because *Sein*, "Being," is a very frequent word—he will spell *Sein* as *Seyn*. It would be nice if there was some archaic German pronunciation that could accompany this spelling, but this spelling will at least give you a little flavor of the otherness of this supposedly more authentic past. The translators have tried to do this with *Seyn*: "Beyng," which seems similar to Heidegger's invention, but it doesn't really work in English. The people who understood this respelling method best turn out to be some of the poststructuralists, including Derrida, who really spent his whole life developing a critique of Heidegger. He is sort of joined at the hip with Heidegger. His notion of *différance*, which, as a normal word, is spelled *différence*, even though it doesn't sound any different, is certainly a kind of Heideggerianism. Unlike the poststructuralists, Heidegger does not, however, use neologisms, I think, except for *Gestell*, which is, of course, incomprehensible. We'll try to comprehend it.

So, Heidegger proceeds on the basis of a supposition about language. Language is a house of Being. Our relationship to Being—that's what Heidegger is after—can't give us an answer to the question of the meaning of Being because it is an unanswerable question. But we could attempt to think what a proper relationship to Being would be. We could attempt somehow to reawaken the question of our relationship to Being. This is what Heidegger does in the final section of his lecture series. We can't recapture Being, since *Gestell* has gone too far for us really to overcome its effects in any practical way, but we could reinvent this utopian or authentic notion of Being, which we have forgotten. For Heidegger, as for Nietzsche, forgetting is a very powerful force, and reviving this archaic, authentic relation to Being out of what is forgotten—that would be something remarkable. That is why Heidegger's last interview with *Der Spiegel*—it was to be posthumous; it was only allowed to be published after his death—is titled "Only a God Can Save Us."[1] What is this "saving," *Rettung*, or "rescue"? *Wo Gefahr ist, wächst Rettung auch.* The final outcome of Heidegger's late philosophy is the notion that somewhere within the danger we inhabit there is the possibility of salvation, but it is a salvation that has to be reawoken and rediscovered. Now, if you want to do what I told you not to do, you will say that this is exactly what the Frankfurt School thought! Negativity is being squeezed out, so we must at least hold on to the idea of negativity. We can't do anything about it practically, but we can hold on to the *idea* of negativity. As far as art is concerned, art isn't happiness or salvation, as Schopenhauer might have thought. It is the *promise* of salvation. It is the broken promise of fulfillment, not the real thing. Art contains in itself the memory of what isn't there anymore, as well as the realization that it isn't there, that its promise is broken. Yes, okay, there are connections, but they are connections in their shared situation, rather than signs of any unity of purpose.

Alright, let me deal with this business of distance in Heidegger. What is distance? I actually want now—even worse than the comparison with Adorno—to cite Benjamin, who loathed Heidegger from the very beginning. Both Adorno and Benjamin could see the dominance of Heideggerian thought in Weimar in the '20s; Benjamin and Brecht had the idea to create an anti-Heideggerian society, which, of course, they never did. So, it is also an offense to the memory of Benjamin to make this juxtaposition, but I do it anyway, because it allows us to see certain aspects of their shared situation. Benjamin was very interested in the notion of aura, that works of art in the past have had a certain aura about them that is somehow being driven out—by what? By the reproducible work of art, by the mechanical, the machine—by the *Gestell*? Adorno was not happy with Benjamin's essay on the reproducibility of the work of art, because Benjamin suggests that a work of art that speaks to the collective, to collectivity, has a uniqueness about it which is not comparable

1 Martin Heidegger, "Nur noch ein Gott kann uns retten," *Der Spiegel* (May 31, 1976), pp. 193–219, translated by W. Richardson as "Only a God Can Save Us," *Heidegger: The Man and the Thinker*, ed. Thomas Sheehan (New York: Routledge, 1981), pp. 45–67.

to older works of art, and, in a revolutionary era, we mustn't necessarily lament nostalgically the loss of this older aura. Benjamin defines aura as the nearness of a thing, no matter how far away it may be. He is talking about the way in which you absorb a work in the mind, and yet it keeps its distance from you. It may be absorbed in other ways later on, but as you contemplate it aesthetically, it holds a certain distance even though it is nearer even than your glasses. It is inside your mind and yet distinct from you. That is a definition of aura. Heidegger will have his own uses of this notion of distance. For Heidegger, our relationship to Being would have to be something like this fusion of distance and nearness.

Let's probe this idea a little more by seeing how it changes—or doesn't—across Heidegger's career. On my reading, which is probably heretical, I don't distinguish between the two periods of Heidegger. That is, I acknowledge the turn, the *Kehre* which Heidegger himself theorized. But what is the *Kehre* a turn *from*? Heidegger wished to explore phenomenologically what Being could possibly be. Being is the emptiest of all ideas, said Hegel. At the beginning of the *Logic*, to get out of that being which is nothing, Hegel had to have recourse finally to *becoming*. Heidegger turns all of this into a question. Let's question what a question *is*. In a question, we have our whole relationship to Being, somehow. It is something which we can only ask about. What we can say is that there is a certain kind of being which stands in a relationship to Being itself and which is different from all the other kinds of being.

You have to distinguish in German between *Sein* and *Seiendes*. *Seiendes* is often translated "entity," and then, of course, the whole connection to Being gets lost. It simply means things which *are*, as opposed to Being in general, which *is*. There is one whole type of thing, an "entity," which is different from all the others, and that he calls *Dasein*. You will notice that he doesn't want to use words like "matter" and "spirit"; he doesn't want to use "consciousness." He wants to have a specific, different way of characterizing what the French would then call "human reality." This is a very weird and special kind of being. He doesn't want to call it "life" either. He doesn't want to evoke humanism. They come to him after the war and tell him that Sartre has given a lecture on existentialism as humanism. "Are you a humanist, Herr Professor?" He says yes, in some sense, but he doesn't want to use the word. The word distorts reality by naming it. I've already spoken today about the way in which naming a thing is an alienation. Everything for him is already alienated.

Dasein is a perfectly ordinary word in German, and to appropriate it for human reality is a step in this process. It will be analyzed as a being which has to confront mortality and whose very essence—because phenomenology works with essences—is *Sorge. Sorge* we often translate as "care." I prefer that you think of it as "worry," because the essence of *Dasein* is temporal. Worry always means: Am I going to finish this lecture on time? What am I going to do next? What have I forgotten? Our consciousness, as a unique thing, is a constant matter of worrying. That is how we relate to the future and the past. "Care" suggests that we could consciously choose to do this or not. It comes out of the last act of *Faust*, when the aged Faust is visited by all kinds of horrible visions of illness, death, and so on. He drives them all out, but the only one he can't get rid of is *Sorge.* But what is nice for Heidegger is that a lot of social words can be associated with *Sorge. Fürsorge* is a word for the institutions of the welfare state. He can slip all kinds of things into a notion of *Sorge.*

But leave that aside. The point of the *Kehre* is that, after a certain moment—and one should ask when that moment is—Heidegger is no longer going to consider himself an existentialist, because one of the great distinctions between Being and existence is that existence is human. There is *Dasein*. So, Heidegger is an existentialist insofar as he is concerned with issues of *Dasein*. But, with the *Kehre*, we forget about *Dasein* and talk about *Sein.* We revert from existentialism to ontology. Why this *Kehre*? There are some explanations. The more you talk about pure Being, the less you talk about individuals, human beings, and the less you are implicated in political questions. This is Bourdieu's (and to a certain degree Habermas's) objection to ontology. In ontology, all of your statements become emptier. Your complicity with the forces of the outside world becomes less visible. That is one way of talking about the *Kehre*, but there are others.

Heidegger's early book *Being and Time* is still an existential work in which the essence of *Dasein* is time, temporality, and in which the essence of temporality for *Dasein* is *Sorge*, care or worry. The project of this work was to move from the individual *Dasein* to collective *Dasein*, to history. He never gets there. You can see the list of topics, and you can see where it breaks off. In one sense, you can say it is actually a tenure book, because he had to finish it to get tenure, or you can say he couldn't finish it because he didn't know what history was. Where does he come out with history? Ah! He comes out with a new word—others had used it, but at any rate it becomes Heideggerian—and that is "historicity." What makes something historical? This is not the same as to ask: "What is history?" He has a notion of history: the collapse of thought and philosophy into metaphysics. That is his history. After the pre-Socratics, philosophy falls into metaphysics; it stays in metaphysics right up to our own time. Even Nietzsche doesn't really get out of it. He is the last of the metaphysicians. Finally, there is Heidegger, the destroyer of metaphysics.

Heidegger fails to get to history at the moment he is becoming part of it. This is the late '20s, the beginning of the Nazi movement. For Heidegger, the Nazi movement is something like an answer to some kind of dream about an archaic relationship to Being, let's say, a geo-social or geo-ontological relationship to the world. I think you have to understand that Heidegger is a provincial. His father works in a Catholic church in Freiburg, a small town. Germany is very much a provincial country with a few small towns. Heidegger brings a small-town mentality to all this. This is the philosophy of a provincial. He is called to Berlin, like Hegel, like Schelling. It should be the climax of his existence, but he is smart: He knows that, if he goes to the Berlin of the Nazis, he is going to be in big trouble, so he decides to stay in Freiburg. To appreciate the significance of this decision, you would have to read some of the things that the other Nazi philosophers wrote about Heidegger. One of them wrote a tract, which they sent on to the authorities, claiming that Heidegger was a schizophrenic. Another one speaks about—I love this expression—the "personal National Socialism" of Professor Heidegger. Is it really National Socialism? Could you ever work your way through the question of Being and find yourself in National Socialism? Well, he thinks so. So, if you want to consider Heidegger's Nazism a personal National Socialism, you can see that there is a movement of his own personal investigation, his philosophy, towards something which he believes the Nazi movement to be.

I think the worst moment in Heidegger's life and career is when he becomes rector of the university. Here is a little mirror image for you: Horkheimer as rector of the University of Frankfurt after the war, and Heidegger as rector of the University of Freiburg in the Nazi period. At Freiburg, he was a real bastard. You can read all this in his inaugural address to the university on the taking of the rectorship. Obviously, he fired all the Jewish professors. He removed his dedication to his teacher, Husserl, who was Jewish, from the second edition of *Sein und Zeit*. This is a very bad period in Heidegger, the early '30s. Nobody should disguise it. And then there is the moment of the *Kehre*. He becomes disillusioned with this bunch of thugs in power. That is the end of his rectorship, the moment when he goes back to philosophy. There is a story that one of his colleagues runs into him at a bus stop outside of Freiburg and says, "Back from Syracuse, professor?" The reference, of course, is to Plato, who was invited by Dionysius to create the utopia of the *Republic* in Sicily. Sicily was the America of ancient Greece, an immensely rich and enormously powerful place at that time. Plato ended up in jail, as a matter of fact. Back from Syracuse, yes, having abandoned his political ambitions.

Hitler has his own turn in this period. He meets with the industrialists, because they have to check him out, and they are comfortable with him. The army is comfortable with him, and that is the most important thing, but the army, which has its own tradition, doesn't like one thing. There is a difference between the SA, or the *Sturmabteilung*, and the SS. Himmler's SS becomes extremely important during the Holocaust, but the SA was an independent organization, and it was Hitler's personal grouping. Its chief was a man named Ernst Röhm. These are revolutionaries, in the sense in which, if I may dare to make a contemporary reference—although one shouldn't necessarily do that—among Trump's followers you can find people who really think that a social revolution is desirable and possible and other people who are followers for any other reason. The SA are people who believe in social revolution. The army does not like this paramilitary organization, just as the army's relationship to Hitler, as you can see from the assassination attempt of 1944, is always fraught. But after the first victories of the blitzkrieg in Poland and France, they can't do anything about him. In 1934, however, Hitler sacrifices the SA, which he does in a bloody purge in the middle of the night, while the SA is having a meeting. Röhm, a close personal friend of his, was assassinated.

For many people, this is the end of Hitler's revolutionary aspirations, and it seems as though Heidegger understood this, though you can't imagine Heidegger in the SA. Heidegger in uniform? Well, let's not pursue that. But, at any rate, when it became clear that this did not involve a fundamental revolution of our relationship to the earth, which he imagined this right-wing movement to be—and a Catholic provincial like Heidegger has no connection to workers or the workers' movement—after that it's really all over, and he withdraws into ontology. The Nietzsche seminar is a veiled critique of the fascist uses of the will to power.[2] Some of you have

2 Martin Heidegger, *Nietzsche*, 2 volumes, trans. David Farell Krell (New York: Harper Collins, 1991).

noted the famous phrase about turning people into soap, which you find in some versions of this technology essay, which is also a pitiful critique of Nazism. Marcuse was one of his students; he wrote to him after the war and asked him why he didn't apologize or convert. Heidegger would not do that, and, frankly, I think it is a way of accepting responsibility. How can you apologize for what they did? That is to say, I think he is not, unlike almost everybody else in Germany, pretending that he can distance himself from his Nazi past. In any case, we have no answer; there was silence on Heidegger's part.

Instead, in these later works, he asks: Is it possible to imagine a relationship of technology to the question of Being? After the war, he says that the Nazi movement tried to invent an original relationship between technology and Being. In this respect, he affirms his relationship to the Party. I think he is thinking of the *Autobahn*, the Nazi uses of technology, electrification. If you have seen this wonderful series, *Heimat*, about a real village in the Rhineland, you remember that when the Nazis come to power—there are a couple Nazis in this village who don't amount to anything—it is marked historically by the arrival of electricity to the village. Lenin placed a similar emphasis on electrification: Communism is Soviet power plus electricity. For Heidegger, the question of technology is the one which suggests some originality of his politics, and after that, silence. So much for the connection with technology.

Let me then leave you with this. In this early philosophy, before the *Kehre*, the existential philosophy of *Being and Time*, there is another very important distinction. Heidegger distinguishes between the ontological and the ontic. The ontic is the world of all these things that we name and talk about. Behind those, or beneath them, is Being. All of those things *are*, but they are underpinned by Being itself. So, phenomenology, from Heidegger's point of view, would take the ontological analysis of particularities and underneath them to dig out their relationship to Being itself. This distinction of the ontological and the ontic is a fundamental hermeneutic distinction in Heidegger. There is an ontology of each thing—a jug, for example—but what is the relationship of each thing to Being? That is exactly the question that will be asked in Heidegger's first lecture, whose discussion we're now going to put off for yet another day.

September 14, 2021

7

Heidegger

Back to Heidegger. What I was trying to do last class was not only to lay out *Being and Time* in five minutes but also to distinguish it from this later book that we'll be discussing today—and then to reconnect the two.[1] To make all of this a bit simpler, let's say the early Heidegger is an existential Heidegger working in a lineage that runs through Saint Augustine, Pascale, Kierkegaard, and later Sartre. This is the Heidegger who analyzes human reality as a temporality which involves *Sorge*, care, concern, even guardianship. Human reality, or *Dasein*, has a relationship to Being through what he calls "world," *in-der-Welt-sein. Dasein* is a being which is in the world, and I encourage you to think about world in terms of ecosystems. World is a mediatory concept between *Dasein* and *Sein*, that is to say, between human reality and Being itself. And we will have occasion to return to the importance of language already for the early Heidegger. Because, as soon as you name something, you alienate it, Heidegger proposes—and the Derrideans will recognize this—that we could use words like "humanism" or "reality" only if we make clear that we are just giving the idea of something for which language isn't proper or adequate. Therefore, we must remember to forget the very language we have used. Derrida takes up this challenge with the idea of writing *sous rature*, "under erasure." In

1 Martin Heidegger, *Bremen and Freiburg Lectures: "Insight into That Which Is" and "Basic Principles of Thinking,"* trans. Andrew J. Mitchell (Bloomington, IN: Indiana University Press, 2012). Although Jameson references and recommends other works by Heidegger, this book was the only required Heidegger reading for the course.

the print of his lectures, Heidegger actually uses a word which has an X printed over it. I would venture that this is an attempt to combat what we call reification, but Heidegger and Derrida are not using that concept.

So, we have an existential Heidegger. Note what is not there. As I say, *Being and Time* is incomplete. He doesn't get to history. What we have is the existential version of history, historicity, my relationship to history, when I *feel* historical, but not history itself. He never gets to history, except, I would say, late in *Sein und Zeit*—just as he is approaching the question of history but has to stop so that he can turn it in and get a job—when he refers to an essay on generations by Wilhelm Dilthey, the thinker of the late nineteenth century.[2] I would say that Heidegger's understanding of history is generational; that is, it is given at a certain moment, in a certain place, for a generation to have a historical mission. Well, I think you can see what that means. You can see how, in the late 1920s, someone who is anxious to get in touch with Being and the collective might feel that his generation suddenly is given a historical mission, in this case, Nazism and National Socialism. Then there are periods when people don't feel their generational mission; they don't have one, or they missed it. The ones who grew up at the same time as Napoleon and then, in their twenties, became generals of an army that conquered the world—they had a generational mission; the rest of us were born a little too late and didn't have that experience, so our generation is an epigone. Habermas is only fifteen or sixteen when the war ends. He is an epigone. What is his generation to do? When we get to an even younger generation, as we enter into the '60s, suddenly young people feel themselves part of a generation again, with a generational mission entirely opposed to that of the earlier generations. We'll see that later.

For some of Heidegger's most important students—Sartre wasn't a student of his, but he certainly learned from Heidegger; Levinas was a student at one point—the theme of otherness, coming out of Hegel's master-slave dialectic, becomes a dominant theme. The other is not really

2 "Dasein's fateful destiny in and with its 'generation' goes to make up the full authentic historizing of Dasein." *Being and Time*, trans. John Macquarrie and Edward Robinson (Oxford: Blackwell, 1962), p. 436. In a footnote to this sentence, Heidegger references Dilthey's essay "On the Study of the History of the Human Sciences, Society, and the State" ("Über das Studium der Geschichte der Wissenschaften vom Menschen, der Gesellschaft und dem Staat" [1875] in *Gesammelte Schriften*, Volume 5 [1924], pp. 36–41 [Section 2, Chapter 5, fn. 8]).

a philosophical theme for Heidegger himself, except in what he calls *das Man*. It is not *der Mann*, "man." It is from the impersonal pronoun, *man*. Yes, you could translate it as "one," as in, "one does this or that." But I would rather, for Americans, translate it as the impersonal "you." "How do I get to such and such a street?" "Well, you drive this way and take a right." This "you" is the impersonal *man*. You can see Heidegger's conservatism most profoundly in the notion of *das Man*. Heidegger is a small-town Catholic; the big city is a matter of some—shall I say "concern"? In the big city there are the masses, labor unions, crowds, prostitutes, all kinds of people. That is *das Man*, for Heidegger: the inauthenticity of the masses. What would authenticity be? All he can find to describe some closer relationship to otherness is *das Mitsein*, "being-with." *Mitsein* could be a generational concept. I may have a *Mitsein* with certain immediate people, but it is pretty weak as a theory of otherness, so I would say that this is a very crucial absence in Heidegger, or a negative presence. The '20s was a period of rising conservatism. In *The Waste Land*, the dead who are passing over London Bridge, which Eliot gets from Dante, are the mass of people out there, all those crowds in the big city who are not really alive, who are the undead, so to speak. The '20s, besides the parties and flappers and jazz and so forth, is a period of conservative thinkers. Eliot and others want to go back to the old Europe of Virgil and Saint Paul. Others want to recapture the European spirit. Heidegger is among these thinkers as an anti-populist conservative figure.

That is the existential Heidegger. We're coming now to the ontological Heidegger. But let's forget about ontology or Being for a minute to ask what seems to be a much simpler question: What is our relationship to objects? We can have a *Vorstellung*, an idea, of an object, which would mean that this object is for me *vorhanden*, present-to-hand. But, when I pass from contemplating the object to using it, then it is *zuhanden*, ready-to-hand. Here, we come to the so-called pragmatism of Heidegger, for whom we are always in the world, *in-der-Welt-sein*, where our deeper, real relationship to objects is not one of contemplation and science and knowledge; it's a relationship of—we won't call it "action." Can we call it "use"? Not in any utilitarian sense. But it is a relationship to objects in which we are always active, in which objects exist for us insofar as they are part of our practices.

So, *vorhanden* would be the essence of science in the sense I have already discussed, in the sense of a mode of knowing which separates the knower from objects so as to see them objectively, so to speak, to analyze them. That is why science cannot facilitate a true relationship to Being for Heidegger. Here, we see an antiscientific, anti-epistemological tendency of pragmatism, of certain contemporary philosophies, which try to free themselves from the dead weight of science. Kant already set philosophy on a pursuit of scientific truth. He tried to figure out how we could say that a certain experience is true, "experience" being a scientific concept which is not unrelated to "experiment." But what do we do with everything that is not science or knowledge? Ethics, the soul, religion, art. We don't know what to do with these things. But what is real is knowledge. Kant's *Critique of Pure Reason* proposes a foundation for knowledge. Pure reason is this delusion of our *in-der-Welt-sein*. Heidegger is an excellent reader of Kant, and the same questions Kant asked will be relevant for Heidegger.

Although science is not a way to Being, *Zuhandenheit* would be a way to Being, because it shows that the world is a part of my *project*, a word that comes from Heidegger. The world includes my project, which means that it is organized for me according to my own existence. If you want to go on to the knowledge of things, you have to go through the object world and come out the other side. Are there any other paths to Being? In "The Origin of the Work of Art" he lists some of them. There are various passages. Theology is one path. This is not to say that any particular theology is true, but that we can invent some kind of a way to Being through theological thinking. This is the period of the great discussions of existential theology with Rudolf Bultmann and others, and some of these people knew Heidegger. The founding of a new state—that is another way to Being. That also makes sense. You reorganize social reality completely and you inaugurate something that has never existed before. The Roman Empire, the French Revolution, if it had produced a state, the Third Reich. What else? Sacrifice, *Opfer*. We saw that for Adorno sacrifice was a method of establishing equivalence, but in general, in German at least, when you talk about *Opfer* without any qualification it means death in battle, the sacrifice of the soldier. So, there is a kind of sacrifice which is a mode of Being. And then, of course, art, because the aim of "The Origin of the Work of Art" is to show how art is a path to Being.

So, science is ontic rather than ontological. Ontic is the world of objects for which we have names, language. Does this mean that *Zuhandenheit* is ontological? Ontological means going beyond the stage of superficial apprehension into the Being of the object. *Zuhandenheit* is certainly not

Being of a utilitarian kind. It is not in the object's usefulness that its Being lies—you see that we're approaching, finally, the essay on *das Ding*. The jug is such an important example in that essay not simply because it is an object which is handy when we need something to hold liquids—although the moment of use (*zuhanden*, ready-to-hand) is certainly a stage that we have to register. The point of the example, rather, is to tear us away from the notion that—even though objects seem to be independent, as if we can have discrete representations of them, and even though it looks as though, if you wanted to know what an object was, you could look at it from a distance and know it through its *Vorhandenheit*—distanced contemplation is an adequate way of figuring out what an object really *is*. To insist on *Zuhandenheit* is to overcome the ontic prejudice that science lays on the world of objects. Once you get into metaphysics, you begin to touch on the realm of transcendental conditions of experience, which seems to have some promise as an ontological path, but that is not what will then separate him from the standard philosophy which can think only in terms of knowledge.

Finally, Heidegger will raise the issue of what this Being actually *is*. Kant said that Being is not a quality of objects. Let's update one of his examples: You can understand what a five-dollar bill is, but as for its being, if you don't have it in your pocket, then it isn't there. Being is a completely different matter from understanding. People debating the ontological proof of God have long raised the point that God must have every perfection, and one of those perfections has to be existence, because if a thing is completely perfect, but it doesn't exist, then it isn't very perfect, is it? Therefore, God must exist. Kant famously unraveled that argument, which is one reason why Kant is important for Heidegger: Kant separates Being from *Verstehen*, "understanding," the understanding of science.

A few other things have to be said about Being. As I mentioned, Hegel says that it is empty. Sartre says the only thing you can say about it is that it is, it is in itself, and it is what it is. But Heidegger thinks you can say one more thing about Being: It appears and withdraws. In German he uses the word *Anwesenheit* for "presence." Being becomes present—it "presences" itself, in what has become the standard English translation—and then it immediately withdraws. How could Being not be present? Obviously, if you wanted to be completely pedestrian about it, you could say we are talking about the idea of Being. Aren't you saying that suddenly you feel Being and then you stop feeling it? The only problem is that this would be a subjective description, to put it simply, and Being isn't subjective for Heidegger. Heidegger prefers a formula which he gives at the very beginning of the text: Being reveals and conceals itself, in the way that everything presences. "What is this clueless anxiety waiting for," he asks, "if the horrible [*das Entsetzliche*] has already occurred? The horrifying is what transposes [*heraussetzt*] all that is out of its previous essence. What is so horrifying? It reveals and conceals itself in the way that everything presences, namely that despite all overcoming of distance, the nearness of that which is remains outstanding."[3] Well, I don't know what that means, but these sentences approximate what Heidegger considers a very important movement of Being.

Heidegger has some images to associate with this movement of Being, most famously the clearing. What is the clearing? One of his books is called *Holzwege. A Way in the Woods* would be a mistranslation, because a *Holzweg*—here is the Germanic forest again, the very center of German identity, let's say, and the place of the great battles with the Romans—is something you might find if you're lost in the forest. People will tell you just to make a straight line and you'll get out of it somehow, but these are sometimes magic forests that you can't get out of. A *Holzweg*, that is, is a path that goes nowhere. With this title, Heidegger is saying: Here are my essays, and they are *Holzwege*, paths that go nowhere. Do you ever get somewhere in these *Holzwege*? Yes, in the forest, sometimes you come to a clearing, and the clearing is the sense of Being, but then you're back in the forest again. That is the clearing.

I have a lot of Heidegger anecdotes I'm eager to tell you. This one comes from an excellent film on Hannah Arendt. Arendt went to see him again after the war. The film mainly turns on the Eichmann trial. In this film, at her first meeting with Heidegger, he says: *Also, Fräulein, sie wollen das Denken lernen*. It doesn't mean, "So you want to think." *Das Denken* means "thought." So, "You want to learn thought." You want to learn what thought is. Thought is, of course, the approach to Being, but it is not thinking about anything in particular, because how can you think about Being? There isn't anything to think. But thought is something, a *Holzweg*, a wandering, and suddenly, every so often, it meets a clearing that opens and then closes. There is a movement. You can't hold on to it. *Dasein* cannot tarry in Being, but it can have an ephemeral opening to it.

3 Heidegger, *Bremen and Freiburg Lectures*, p. 4.

That is why you might want to ask about this business of truth, since truth was to be the adequation of the thing and the idea. No, no, that's not it, says Heidegger. Truth, for him, is to be found in these languages, in German and Greek. Truth is *alētheia.* Lethe, in the underworld, is the river of forgetfulness. *Alētheia* means de-forgetting, unforgetting something. Rather than the more Sartrean idea of authenticity, although that is implied here, this notion of unforgetting might be worthwhile to consider. Inauthenticity is forgetfulness of Being, when Being suddenly withdraws and you find yourself in a purely ontic world of familiar objects that you can only think about scientifically. Finding truth would be somehow a way of unforgetting Being. The appearance and presencing of Being would be that unforgetting, that moment of truth, so to speak. So, he has a very precise notion of truth, which has its relationship to the Platonic *anamnesis*, the memory of the forms, but only as a premonition of his notion of Being.

Now we come to *das Ding*, the thing, and the case of the jug. You may say he's rigged this thing in his favor by choosing the example of the jug. But let's see what he does here. What does he mean by "the thing"? *Das Ding* comes from an ancient German word. Later he quotes one of the great mystics, Meister Eckhart: "The soul is a 'great thing' [*dinc*]."[4] The soul assembles and collects. Just to jump ahead, the thing would be the place in which the fourfold is gathered together and is *gesammelt*. But what he doesn't tell us is enlightening. This is all well and good, but the *Ding* had a specific meaning. *Das Ding* was the primitive assembly, and it still keeps this meaning in the Scandinavian languages in one form or another. In the old Germanic tribal groups, the *Ding* is an assembly of people. It is German democracy, so to speak, and Marx talks about this in the pre-capitalist formations. So yes, the *Ding* is a thing that assembles. But he is forgetting this quintessential meaning of assembling, which is the assembling of people, the coming into being of the collective, and in that sense the *Ding* is a symbol of the collective. That would take our Heideggerianism in a different direction and would give the notion of assembling, collecting, quite a different resonance, I think, while not really canceling Heidegger, simply adding a dimension to his thought that he is unaware of, except, maybe, in his political moment.

4 Sermon 42, *The Complete Mystical Works of Meister Eckhart*, ed. and trans. Maurice O'C. Walshe, rev. Bernard McGinn (New York: Crossroad Publishing, 2009), pp. 233–7, p. 234; qtd. in Heidegger, *Bremen and Freiburg Lectures*, p. 14.

So, what do we do with the jug? It has a purpose: to hold things. Does that define it? It itself is empty, so does emptiness define it? This is a great lesson, I think, about perception and the history of art. What the architect builds is not a thing but an empty space. The architect constructs empty spaces with pieces of matter. What the architect constructs, for the layman, is a thing, but the adept of the architectural know he makes a shape, a form, and that form is a form of emptiness. Well, the same with the jug. The potter does not make a thing. The potter forms emptiness. So, at that point, you ask yourself: Is the jug nothing? If the material that makes up the jug is inessential, then the essence of the jug must be nothing? Well, not quite. Is it really empty? What about the material it is made of? What about the material and all the various Aristotelian causes, the sides, the upright, and so forth? We have seen that those parts do not add up to a whole. The whole is organic. So that doesn't do us any good either.

Finally, we come to the concept of use. The jug's use is to hold something or not hold something. Taking and retaining: It holds in two manners. It takes the liquid and it retains it. Has Heidegger simply given us a utilitarian definition of a jug? To say so would be to ignore how the holding itself "essences," so to speak. What does holding mean? What is the Being of holding, of what the jug does? It is ambiguous:

> In the gift of the pour there essences the holding of the vessel. This holding requires the empty as what holds. The essence of the holding empty is gathered in the giving. Giving, however, is richer than a mere outpouring. The giving, whereby the jug is a jug, gathers in itself the twofold holding and does so in the outpouring.[5]

So finally the jug is the occasion for a pouring. All of a sudden, a very different but widespread dimension of modern thinking comes into play: the gift. Who knows what Heidegger read, because he never mentions anybody, but "Le Don," the essay on the gift by Marcel Mauss, is one of the seminal works of modern thought. For modern society, gift-giving is a crucial problem. In the anthropology of the period, in Malinowski and so on, it was discovered, so to speak, that in certain societies one's relationship to the other through the gift has to be reciprocal: If you receive something, you have to give something back, in one way or another. Malinowski

5 Heidegger, *Bremen and Freiburg Lectures*, p. 10.

explored the Trobriand Islands, a chain of individual islands of New Guinea, where he found that a certain form of gift must be acknowledged by its equivalent being returned. This gift, therefore, involves something like debt. You can trace indebtedness in the chain of gifts all the way around the Trobriand Islands until you come back to the original giver, who has to be somehow recompensed. In German, it's nice because you can have "giftness" without the giver. *Es gibt.* That means, as Derrida will play with, what in French is meant by *il y a*: "there is ..." The "there is" is the way in which *es gibt*, the gift of the thing, is expressed without a giver. Heidegger is, let's say, an atheist existentialist, even though on his deathbed he asked for a Catholic funeral; he was in contact with theologians, but there is such a thing as negative theology, after all. So, it's not a matter of a god giving something. Being itself is the gift. That is to say, we don't know why it's there. We don't know what it is, but we know it's there somehow. *Es gibt*: There is being, and there is the gift of the pouring.

Now, once you get as far as that in a Heideggerian argument, having been prepared by all kinds of questions, suddenly, this language opens up and we get a lyrical passage. In the language of Heidegger, this passage is the clearing.

> In the water of the gift there abides the spring. In the spring abides the stone and all the dark slumber of the earth, which receives the rain and dew of the sky. In the water of the spring there abides the marriage of sky and earth. They abide in the wine that the fruit of the vine provides, in which the nourishment of the earth and the sun of the sky are betrothed to each other. In the gift of water, in the gift of wine, there abides in each case the sky and earth. The gift of the pour however is the jughood of the jug. In the essence of the jug there abides earth and sky.[6]

The secret is that the Being of the jug is not an object; it is an event. The pouring is an event. The jug is an event, when we see it ontologically, rather than ontically. Ontologically, it is the meeting of sky and earth, mortal and immortal. So *Ereignis*, as the name of Heidegger's late philosophy, means "event," "occurrence," the occurrence being the presencing of Being. When we look at objects and go through these steps of removing the definitions of the object by which we are ordinarily tempted, and which consist in

6 Ibid., pp. 10–11.

a forgetting of the object, then the object appears as the fourfold. It is the moment in which something is given—but by what? The question points us to the immortals—this is all from Hölderlin—and we mortals have the guardianship of Being. Again, sacrifice is the essential ritual of giving. In ancient times, you would pour out a bit of wine to the gods. So, the pouring is also this libation of the gods, the acknowledgement of the gods. It is what you give to the unknown, the stranger in hospitality. In the *Odyssey*, Odysseus is telling his story to his host who is receiving him. The whole point of the *Iliad* is the way in which Paris broke the laws of hospitality. The pouring is sacrifice.

I'm reminded of a joke. I first heard it in Turkey, but it may be all over the Islamic world. You find some guys who are drinking, and you ask, "Doesn't the Quran forbid this stuff?" "Well, not on a close reading," they say. "The Quran says: Thou shalt not touch the first drop of wine. So we don't touch the first drop. We throw that on the ground and then we can drink the second drop!" In the notion of the pouring there is always this *rémanence*, so to speak, of the sacred, of the libation. "In the gift of the pour that is a libation, the mortals abide." The notion of abiding is the notion of the essence. *Wesen* means "essence," but it is an odd word in German, because it is a past form of the verb "to be." *Wesen ist was gewesen ist*. What persists is Being.

> In the gift of the pour that is a libation, the mortals abide in their way. In the gift of the pour that is an oblation, the divinities abide in their way, divinities who receive back the gift of the giving as the gift of a donation. In the gift of the pour, the mortals and divinities each abide differently. In the gift of the pour, the earth and sky abide. In the gift of the pour there abides at the same time earth and sky, divinities and mortals. These four, united of themselves, belong together. Obligingly coming before all that presences, they are folded into a single fourfold.[7]

That is the way in which Being manifests itself, presences itself, before it disappears again. We can't be doing this ontological stuff all the time, but it will appear from time to time.

This is the necessary preparation for the *Gestell*, because if, to use Heidegger's words, the relationship to Being is what is authentic, we can't

7 Ibid., p. 11.

understand what is inauthentic until we know what is authentic. What is the Heideggerian positive relationship to Being for beings, entities, such as we are? What is the positive moment from which the *Gestell* is a falling off or of which it is an inauthentic distortion? We have to have something laid out for us first. The most important thing is the eventness, that Being must presence itself. "The jug is a thing insofar as it things."[8] People have made fun of this language. The world, as he says elsewhere, worlds. That is to say, the object must become an event for us. The event is the deconcealment of Being. Remember that the *Gestell* is the great danger, the *Gefahr*. That is what the world has turned into; it is the disorientation of the world, or if you like, the *Entzauberung*, which has its relationship to technology. The essay that this is turned into is "The Question Concerning Technology."

I don't want us to get caught in this Heideggerian morass, but you have to know what is there in the postwar years, a moment in which it is very easy for Habermas to say, if we want to be modern, if we want to catch up with the modernity of the Western powers, so to speak, we have to get rid of attacks on technology such as Heidegger's, these reactionary, nostalgic, antitechnological thoughts. To what do these attacks on technology propose a return? To the Germanic tribe? Some ur-experience of nature and habitation? We saw where that led in the Nazi period. And yet it is a little more complicated than that. We have seen that technology poses a question not only for Heidegger but also for Horkheimer and Adorno in *Dialectic of Enlightenment*. Do Horkheimer and Adorno blame science and technology for everything? Yes and no. You could certainly think so, because science for them is precisely a kind of thinking which crosses everything out, reproduces itself on top of itself, and ultimately leads to a period in which everybody is afraid of the atomic bomb. A variety of horrors and innovations have come out of war. Antibiotics, for example. Scientific progress can certainly be stimulated by warfare in ways it isn't otherwise, but on the other hand, people aren't thinking about that right now; they're thinking about the rubble and the use of airplanes and bombs, the rockets, the V-1 and V-2 rockets that were sailing over and hitting London. You've read your Pynchon, so you know about that. This is a period in which it is tempting to develop an attack on technology into a fully antimodern position. Heidegger's effort was to produce—although he wouldn't say it like this—a concept with which to grasp the modern. That

8 Ibid., p. 15.

concept will be the *Gestell.* He's given this situation a name, but we don't understand the name. All the pieces are there—*stellen* and so on—but we don't quite know what it is.

One of the great moments of modern architecture is also a way of understanding this concept of *Gestell.* There are several famous bays in the Mediterranean, one of the most beautiful of which is the Bay of Algiers, a superb natural formation. Le Corbusier, who was at the very center of the architectural modern, proposed for the Bay of Algiers, which is surrounded by great hills, that, on the top of these hills, there should stretch an immense *unité d'habitation*. For architectural modernism it would be like *Finnegans Wake.* It was one of the great, unrealizable utopian works. This *unité d'habitation* was to be composed of many little sections in which various units are placed. Inside of each one you might get a little house or a smaller version of dwellings. I think of *Gestell* a little bit like Le Corbusier's plan for the Bay of Algiers, an immense ontological bookcase in which all of these objects are placed.

But I think the most tempting way of understanding the *Gestell* is to articulate it—and now we have to use a certain language which we can put under erasure as fast as we like—as a distortion of Being. The *Gestell* stores things. It is not *Zuhandenheit* or *Vorhandenheit*. It is some third abomination, let's say. Heidegger's question will always be: How can one continue to use this bad storage? To add another dimension to this way of understanding of the *Gestell*, we can say that the surplus is the universal. Instead of having a relationship of singularity to things, we turn everything into stereotypes or instances of universals. The object is always reproduced in some way, always a repetition of self-sameness. Ideas, in a way, are what we store. We are storing language as bad, universal names for things. In any case, this kind of thinking is certainly approaching the symptomatology that we found in *Dialectic of Enlightenment*, but it is attributing the symptoms to a certain relationship to Being. The point is that the relationship to Being is already a kind of Being. It is a tendency in Being. *Rettung*: How can salvation come out of danger?

Let me put it to you in terms of authenticity, which are really not appropriate. If you're in inauthenticity, how do you get out of it? How do we get out of the forgetfulness of Being? One of the ways to get out of inauthenticity is to remember that you are inauthentic. So, the idea of the *Gestell* could take us out of the *Gestell.* To know that we are living in a form of inauthenticity, even if we can't translate it at once into some pure authenticity which may not exist, could perhaps offer a way out of that very inauthenticity. It is a bit like Adorno's notion of the negative. We have to keep the negative alive—to be the shepherd of the negative, so to speak—not just in order to resist but to grasp why things are denatured as they are. So, in a sense, to understand the dialectic of enlightenment would be to see how every step forward is also a step backward. For intellectuals, those are the only solutions. That is, you are keeping the status of an intellectual by giving value to the diagnosis, which of course is a diagnosis in thought. It is diagnosing a condition. That in itself, even if you have no pills for it, is some kind of step forward.

At any rate, Heidegger ends up saying that this recognition of the *Gestell* is itself somehow a presencing of Being. It is a presencing of the Being of the *Gestell*. This is not a Manichaeism. We don't have the forces of the good and the bad that come out of nowhere. This bad thing is part of Being itself, so, in a sense, we have a big problem. Being has produced its own problems. This is the very nature of *Dasein*, to want to pursue power over things. Can we simply try to stop dominating nature? Going back to Adorno's self-preservation would not be a bad way of doing it. But, for Heidegger, to put the question of domination in terms of Being is to say that it is Being itself which is the problem. That is what he comes up with in the *Kehre*.

Anyway, we'll take a last look at Heidegger and then go back to Adorno, with a detour into Habermas's retrospective view of these positions as participating in a process of modernity. We don't need this kind of nihilism, he says, this kind of nostalgia; what we need is some way in which we can proceed beyond domination. We can look at that next time.

September 16, 2021

8
Habermas

What Heidegger has generated, it seems to me, is the critique of representation. I would call it the ideology of form. That is to say, the form of the representation is its ideological message, not the content of the idea. It seems to me that an entire tradition of such criticism comes out of Heidegger. The essay on the world picture gives you a sense of the fall out of a relationship of Being into a relationship with representations.[1] We could talk about how they are subjective and inauthentic representations, but I think the fundamental idea is more profound than that, especially if we consider it in the context of the distance established by science. In a sense, Heidegger would say that science is a body of representations. And yet, if you tug this whole operation too far in the direction of a subject-object relationship—in which you can simply say representations are bad because they are subjective—then we get into all kinds of other problems, some of which we'll actually see in a different form today.

Another thing I wanted to alert you to in Heidegger is authenticity. Authenticity is a word that for us is related to the French. In German it is *Eigentlichkeit*, which is related to *eigen*, a crucial term in Heideggerianese meaning "own." Authenticity would, first of all, be, as Heidegger interprets it, being-unto-death, my death being something that is my own and can't be anybody else's. But then we get into *Eigentum*. I taught a course

1 Martin Heidegger, "The Age of the World Picture," in *Off the Beaten Track*, ed. and trans. Julian Young and Kenneth Haynes (Cambridge: Cambridge University Press, 2002), pp. 57–85.

on existentialism a few years ago, and I associated Stirner's anarchism with existentialism, because Stirner interprets ownness, the ego and *sein Eigentum*, as property. So, here, you get a kind of existentialism which says your notion of your own subjective, authentic experience is itself a kind of property. Ernst Fischer was an Austrian Marxist who considered Romanticism as a moment of literature that comes at the crisis and passage of feudalism to capitalism, which, for artists, means a crisis of patronage. Beethoven lived under both systems, I think. He had patrons who would support him and then he would sell his music on the market. In those days, the scores were sold as books, just as before museums and photography people made prints of works that could be sold. As for Romanticism, the moment when the artist has no patrons anymore, but doesn't really have a market yet, he creates a market by selling the self. Byron builds up his self and sells it, in a sense. The Byronic is his commodity. Fischer implies that subjectivity becomes a kind of commodity. That is not necessarily a bad thing. This is our history, Romanticism. It is also a way, if you like, of trying to find an authenticity in *Eigentum*, in subjective property. Anyway, I wanted to alert you to this other play of words around *eigen* and *Eigentum*, which we'll meet again in Negt and Kluge, though I don't know that we have time to say anything more right now.

I do wish to tell you a few more stories, because anecdotes can convey something that analysis can't. After Habermas is fired as Adorno's assistant, he is hired at a neighboring institution by Gadamer, a former student of Heidegger. People ask Gadamer: Why would you hire this person so ideologically distant from you? Gadamer says he wants the antagonism. He likes the antagonism. As would be natural, Gadamer invites the aged Heidegger to come to a seminar, and Habermas is not impressed. Gadamer takes Habermas aside after the seminar and says to him: I wish you had seen Heidegger when he was great. This is another difference between the post-*Kehre* Heidegger and the ferocious Heidegger of the early years.

I also wanted to tell you about Heidegger at the liberation. Clearly, everyone thought that the Red Army was simply going to roll over everything. In the essay on humanism, the assimilation of early Marx to some possible ontology is a very great admission by Heidegger, and I think it is very tactical, because, in a sense, a commitment to National Socialism, even his "personal National Socialism," is more than a commitment to a single ideology. This is Heidegger's sign that, if and when the Soviets do come, he can still ontologize Marx for them; he can find his place in a new society organized around dialectical materialism. As you can imagine, at the end of the war, there is a tremendous panic. Who's going to get there first? Given what the Germans did to the Russians, it's hardly surprising that they were panicky. At the end of the war, Heidegger is at someone's estate, hiding in the woods, terrified, because he thinks the first thing they're going to do is shoot him. This was the general feeling at the time, especially for somebody as eminent as him. Instead, he is captured, so to speak, by two young French soldiers who offer him a cigarette and ask for his autograph. That is the end of Heidegger's war. Carl Schmitt was taken very seriously and imprisoned for months; he was very bitter about it. Heidegger was prohibited from teaching and making public appearances for five or six years.

When the young Habermas tells us he was a Heideggerian—he had never heard of the Frankfurt School because there wasn't any Frankfurt School—I think that means he had read some *Sein und Zeit*, so it was the existential Heidegger that interested him. In the immense biographies of these figures, Habermas is always mentioned at the end by way of all the prizes he gets; every institution in the world is going to offer him the something-something medal or prize. It just goes on and on. Why? You're going to see that this has something to do with his unique position. I don't want to say he represents the status quo exactly, but there is a sense in which he is the spokesperson for a new kind of stability, especially in Germany. The text we will be discussing today, *The Philosophical Discourse of Modernity*, which I think is a masterpiece of its own type, is composed of lectures he gave in 1985. We are looking back on the period of Heidegger, Horkheimer, and Adorno from the high point of the Bundesrepublik, the new, prosperous Germany. This new Germany is on the verge of overcoming the Berlin Wall and assimilating the East. You must understand that Berlin is not West Germany or East Germany but something else entirely. Of course, it is divided between East and West Germany, but Berlin is really a third area. Berlin did not fall under the various practical accords the Allies drew up. For example, the West German draft did not hold for Berlin. The difference between the early period of Germany year zero and 1985 is extraordinary.

Habermas, in the work that I assigned for today, is rewriting this philosophical past to build up to the climax which is his own philosophy.[2] It

2 Jürgen Habermas, *The Philosophical Discourse of Modernity*, trans. Frederick Lawrence (Cambridge, MA: MIT, 2004). Jameson assigned chapters 1–6 (pp. 1–160).

is not a matter of selfishness. It is a matter of his philosophy becoming the ideology of representative democracy. What is constant in Habermas is the absolute refusal of revolutionary change—including the restoration of tradition, of the Nazi conventions—and the defense of the constitution, the *Grundgesetz*, the fundamental law. I remember the debate between him and Gerhard Schröder, when Schröder was running for prime minister. Someone asked Habermas: "What about the antisocial? Suppose people are inclined toward evil. What are you going to do about that?" He was not interested in this question philosophically. He just murmured, "We have our laws." It is law that he defends, the law of the new system.

The version of legality that he will defend is very original, I think, especially in this context of reshaping philosophical history to climax at the notion of communicative reason, which is fundamental to the Habermasian system. In one sense, the practice of communicative reason will be at one with all the ideologies of the period, from structuralism and linguistics to cybernetics and the languages of computers. But, in another sense, it has its philosophical beauty. There is an almost mathematical process by which he asks himself, faced with the various contradictions and philosophical defects that he uncovers across his history of philosophy, what is missing from all previous philosophical solutions to the problem of legitimacy and social form. This is Habermas discovering what the missing stone is in this edifice. He doesn't discover or invent it entirely by himself; he borrows from Karl-Otto Apel, for instance, who had developed his own notion of communication. But he is the one to give it the significance of an ideology or philosophy which would complete or solve the set of problems that he identifies in the philosophical discourses of modernity.

Nobody has to believe Habermas. One can have a certain admiration for a performance like this. Yes, of course, the tendency is to say that Habermas, like Rawls, is a democratic theorist, and we know what that means. We are exposed to it every day on the news, when people talk about "our democracy, our democracy," as though it were something we carried around with us. What they are talking about, by the way, is another written constitution. But it is wrong to criticize Habermas or Rawls on the basis of the ideology they end up representing. One begins in another way. R. G. Collingwood says all philosophical ideas have to be rewritten and understood as answers to questions.[3] Since you have the answer but

3 See R. G. Collingwood, *An Essay on Metaphysics* (Oxford: Oxford University Press, 2002), pp. 23ff.

you don't have the question, understanding a philosophical idea means reconstructing the dilemma to which this idea is a solution. Suddenly, you have turned the reading of philosophical texts into an actual act, in which something is being solved or mastered.

At any rate, I think the way that you criticize this—and if we don't criticize it, we might as well end this course with communicative reason, the answer to everything—is not with the end but with the beginning. Where does Habermas start? Obviously, the choice of Hegel, in a sense the last philosopher, and the choice of reason and modernity as his starting points are the crucial presuppositions on which his whole theory rests. Once you have granted him that the central problem of modernity is reason, everything follows beautifully. It really is a remarkable edifice. But by refusing this starting point, you can ask some different questions.

Let me give you the answer first. The problem is the disappearance of religion. This is what modernity is, as Habermas defines it. Once enlightenment triumphs over religion—that was a chapter in Hegel, who was ambiguous about this process, as Adorno and Horkheimer are in a very different way—then you have to find another absolute. Why? Because we need to know that life has meaning? No, he is talking about the social. He has another word for this process, from an earlier book: "legitimation," the legitimation of society, the legitimation crisis.[4] That's the point of the search for the Absolute. What is it that finally holds a society together, makes it function, makes people have some common kind of behavior with respect to laws and patterns that can be written out? Legitimation has within it a notion of law, but law needs to be legitimated too. In the early books of the Bible, an immense set of laws are given. Scriptural legitimation is not the only kind, but it is one method that allows us to say that this is a norm and this is not a norm. The reason Habermas tends to seem boring to us is that he is seeking the normative. On what could society be built if not religion? We say "tradition," but what kind of tradition? Tradition would be a legitimizing factor, but how many different kinds of traditions are there? Are they not always held in relation to what we call the Absolute?

We have a very weird word here that I think one always has a right to make fun of: "diremption." Diremption means separation. What Habermas is going to affirm is that modernity consists of diremption, in the fact of what he calls the separation of different value spheres. So, there are two

4 Jürgen Habermas, *Legitimation Crisis*, trans. Thomas McCarthy (Boston: Beacon Press, 1975).

problems, one on each end. One is the foundation of society, the Absolute, the religious basis on which legitimation can be founded, and the other is the fact of diremption, of the separation of spheres.

We begin with Hegel and his failure to solve the central philosophical problem of the French Revolution, which gives rise, according to Habermas, to three types of solution. Habermas wants to show us that, although none of these solutions have worked, they are reproduced in modern thought. It's not just nineteenth-century followers of Hegel who try out these three possibilities; everywhere in modern thought these same three roots are being explored. These possibilities are already present in Hegel. His judgment on Hegel is that he does not manage to escape what Habermas calls the philosophy of the subject. This expression has already been used in France to mean phenomenology, existentialism, anything which attempts to draw its legitimation out of the experience of the individual. In a sense, what is Hegel's Absolute Spirit but the attempt to think out of Spirit itself, which is very nicely desubjectivized by the word *Geist*? I translate *Geist* as "the collective," because when Hegel uses *Geist* in *Phänomenologie des Geistes* I think he is talking about collective spirit. A word like *Geist* makes the connection for you. How can you avoid passing through individual spirit in trying to get to collective spirit? For Habermas, this is a weakness in the immense architectonic edifice of Hegel: It all rests on the individual subject, no matter how sublimated into the collectivity it is, no matter how often I say, with Goethe, for example, that I never had an original thought, since we always think the thoughts of others. All of history would be in our thought, our *individual* thought.

After the Enlightenment has destroyed the validity of religion in the eighteenth century, how can you use the individual subject as a source of legitimation, even if you call it "the Absolute"? Individuals can try to do that for themselves, but we're talking about a collective, a society. The ruler, the dictator—Napoleon, for example—is still an individual subject, and we still have the very dialectic Hegel was talking about in the chapter on the Roman Empire: When the empire brings subjectivity to the single individual, the nameless mass of nonsubjects will evolve out of itself the religion of another individual subject, Christ. To bind legitimation to a single *Führer* is to unleash a dialectical process that outstrips its own origins. This is what Hegel's followers and disciples are left with. If we assume that Hegel has refused nostalgia, going back to the Greeks, all kinds of other solutions, then his political thought will organize society around a monarch, but this monarch is an empty space. This is a constitutional monarchy, at the center of which is a black hole, the emperor who is not visible. In a sense, Hegel's monarch is a decorative device. Everything can work if you have a center to organize it around, but the content of the center is irrelevant. For Habermas, this is still unsatisfactory, and, of course, after the experience of Hitler that solution is blocked.

So, what are the three ways, coming out of Hegel, in which people have tried to solve the problem of legitimation? This is a work of history, and he has done his reading on the Young Hegelians, who continue to pursue religion; they continue the project of the Enlightenment, as in *The Life of Jesus Critically Examined* by David Friedrich Strauss, while the others are constantly working to extirpate religion from daily life. These are the last of the Young Hegelians, but they are still caught up in the problematics of religion. Who will do something new with the Young Hegelian efforts? Marx, of course, who will abandon the question of religion and now turn to labor and production. But, in this branch of the followers of Hegel, beginning with Fichte and his absolute "I," there is an attempt to push Kant further and to continue, like Hegel, to find the Absolute in subjectivity. This will be a failure, but he situates Marx in this column for reasons that we'll come back to.

The second solution would be the conservative followers of Hegel, who insist on tradition and who will see these spheres of value as the very structure of society, that is, of the status quo. These spheres will be reflected in the faculties. You remember that Kant had an interesting wordplay on "faculties," because the faculties are for Kant the faculties of the mind, as well as the faculty of law, the theological faculty, and so forth. So, it's a joke, "the faculties." But the traditionalists will insist on the separation of the faculties, of tradition, and they will continue along those lines. A final diremption, if you like, which is more modern, arrives with the split between civil society and the state. The funny thing is that the term "civil society" is a translation of *bürgerliche Gesellschaft*, "bourgeois society." (Of course, even in English, a burgher is a *grand bourgeois*, a great merchant and not just an ordinary member of the third estate.) If civil society involves labor and production, Marx considers the possibility that elements of it will pass over into the state, because labor under capitalism is a socially organized kind of labor, even amid this modern separation of spheres, which is not resolved in the conservative solution.

So, one solution is the power of subjectivity, another the power of institutions—what is the third tradition coming out of Hegel? It has a name: Nietzsche, whatever that may mean. His point is that Nietzsche will not only refuse but undermine the first two solutions. For Nietzsche, subjectivity is always a form of the will to power, and therefore it ignores itself. As for the second solution, you know what to expect from Nietzsche, a rebel with respect to institutions and faculties alike. If the whole problem of modernity comes from the loss of religion, why not invent a new one? Nietzsche's new religion will be the religion of Dionysus. Dionysus, as Habermas points out, is the hidden god. Dionysus is not always present. He appears, as in Euripides. The beginning of the *Bacchae*: I am Dionysus. He must appear in some way to his following. As Nietzsche himself knows, no matter how powerful the vision of classicism is, Dionysus comes after the Olympians, and he is not a god of the religious institutions of the ancients but the leader of a cult. Nietzsche's solution is the instantiation of religion, the inauguration of religion, but it must be a new religion to overcome all the problems he points out having to do with the earlier solutions to the problem of legitimation. Who actually achieves this new religion for Nietzsche? Wagner and the tragedians. Aestheticism is involved in Nietzsche's answer and project for this new religion, but it seems to me that aesthetics is the missing term in Habermas, at least in this third solution to Hegel's problems.

Apparently, this third solution would not exactly posit a nostalgic return to the past, but what does it amount to? It becomes a mode not only of undermining the other two solutions but of undermining any possible solution, a mode of transgression in general. Bataille figures heavily in this third solution, because Bataille is a much more authentic and persuasive follower of Nietzsche than any of the other philosophers he mentions, particularly with his doctrines of sacrifice. Nonetheless, it seems to me that all these solutions, insofar as they end up in ritual, also involve aesthetics. That is what the other two solutions don't have. It seems to me it is worth interrogating. Benjamin left one of his essays, "The Work of Art in the Age of Its Mechanical Reproducibility," with the idea that, against the fascist aestheticization of politics, we must politicize aesthetics. In our consumer society, it would be well to meditate on the role of aestheticization. Habermas will invoke aestheticization in his critique of Marx; he also knows that aestheticization can be a way of criticizing the Nietzschean path, but he doesn't always use it himself.

Therefore, we have to say a word about Habermas and the aesthetic. Adorno says that Kant and Hegel were the last great philosophers to be able to write something worthwhile on aesthetics without knowing anything about it. Kant never left Königsberg. Of course, he had reproductions of paintings. Towards the end of his life, Hegel did manage to get to Holland and see the Dutch paintings, and, eventually, to post-Napoleonic Paris and the magnificent treasure house in the Louvre. Nonetheless, his is a great aesthetics. I think Adorno's remark is unfair; Hegel certainly understood something about aesthetics. But what about Habermas himself? Habermas collects abstract art, paintings, and has a very high opinion of aesthetics as a subject, but does he know anything about it? And, if aesthetics in Habermas takes the place of the negativity of modernity, how can he incorporate modernism into modernity? How can he hang on to aesthetics when aesthetics is defined as the refusal of the very system that he is trying to establish? Habermas is slyly incorporating modernism as the negative, self-critical side of modernity. He never argues this absolutely, but it is one of the fundamental disputes he has with the so-called Frankfurt School and one of the reasons why I think it would be a mistake to think of Habermas as a member of the Frankfurt School, even though he is so deeply associated with it. And that is why we get this remarkable critique of *Dialectic of Enlightenment*, which really is against everything he is doing, a repudiation of modernism and reason—the notion of instrumental reason, for example—which is very damaging to Habermas's whole attempt to reinstate these concepts. At any rate, it seems to me that, in a way, he gives us a clue about Nietzscheanism by ranging it in this way as an aesthetic refusal both of the institutional solution to the problem of legitimation and of the subjective solution.

How does Marx fit into this? Let me just read you the program of this text. "Starting from Marx's critique of Hegel, I want to trace how the transformation of the concept of reflection"—self-consciousness, in other words, part of your theory of the subject—"ends up in the concept of production, how the replacement of self-consciousness by labor ends up in an aporia within Western Marxism."[5] Of course, that is the critique of his own Frankfurt School. "The metacritique of the Right Hegelians insists with good reason that the degree of system differentiation attained by modern societies cannot simply be turned back." Here, the crucial name

5 Habermas, *The Philosophical Discourse of Modernity*, p. 59.

is Niklas Luhmann, who evolved a systems theory of differentiation, in which modernity consists in a progressive differentiation of its faculties and facets. The notion of systems theory, I suppose, we trace back to Talcott Parsons in the United States, who was very influential in Germany. So, here, in this "metacritique of the Right Hegelians," as he puts it, "the degree of system differentiation attained by modern societies cannot simply be turned back."[6] There can be no return to a theocratic society, in other words. In our world, there would be several attempts to do that. Iran, for example. One possible ideal of Islamic society is to form a society in which religion and civil society are at one, producing a religious economics, a religious law, and so on. I think it is generally assumed that such social forms are no longer viable, and much of the critique of socialist societies has been to argue that they also tried to move categories of state and power back into the private world, from a very different perspective.

At any rate, this is still a defense of the reality of diremption, of the separation of institutions, or, as Habermas will say, of spheres. Habermas himself will therefore have to invent a solution which acknowledges somehow the separate spheres, and which also finds a place for individual existence. In the third path, which he is calling "neoconservatism," he will discuss Nietzsche. "From this tradition there proceeds a neoconservatism that, however, gets into difficulties when it is supposed to explain how the costs and instabilities of an automatic process of modernization can be weighed and balanced."[7] I don't know why he calls it neoconservatism, because he is thinking of anarchism, clearly: If everybody does what they want, then the social machine will not work. Despite what the French followers of Nietzsche claim—because there was a new Nietzscheanism coming out of Deleuze and Derrida, and I think he is right to insist on the role of Nietzsche in these developments—he believes that Nietzsche's philosophy always constitutes a reactionary element in thinking and must therefore be refused. I remember hearing him say: "Once upon a time, France was the country of enlightenment and reason, and we Germans were the very source of the irrational; now," he says, and this is in the '70s, "it seems to have crossed the Rhine. It's the other way around: I, Habermas, defend reason, and the Parisians are all wrapped up in their irrational and transgressive stuff." That was certainly the way he looked at it, though he later reconciled with Derrida.

6 Ibid., pp. 59–60.
7 Ibid., p. 60.

Anyway, this is how he will analyze these discourses, though we still need to look at his critique of Marx. His idea is that Marxism is a productivism and that it is therefore fatally drawn into the sphere of aesthetics; the alienation of the worker by production is the same alienation that is attributable to aesthetics, and therefore—if he doesn't speak in terms of machinery, the notion of the abolition of work entirely, which, for Habermas, would not be a desirable thing, I suppose—it means that we would be wrong to think of Marxism as the solution or path out of the subjective solution. Marxism, for Habermas, has all too easily moved over into the camp of the postmodern, a move he identifies through Marcuse. In Marcuse, certainly, there is the idea that work can be redeemed by an aesthetic investment, that is, that work and labor, production itself, can become aesthetic. The thinker in our time who has developed this in a most interesting way is Paolo Virno, a close collaborator of Toni Negri for a while. In his book *A Grammar of the Multitude* he develops a notion of virtuosity in labor, in which labor becomes aesthetic in the sense that it involves a virtuosity not unlike that of the artists. Virtuosity is, I suppose, a kind of modernistic way in which beauty gets into work. It is not the object of beauty. It is not William Morris or Ruskin or the return to classicism; it is, rather, the type of labor which reflects handicraft and a beauty of execution, let's say.

I'm not sure that he is correct about Marx and aesthetics, although I think it is certainly an interesting idea, if you use these theological notions, like fulfillment. Art has certainly been understood as bringing an authenticity or fulfillment to production. But I don't think that that is what's going on in Marx. Capitalism in *Capital: Volume 1* is a matter of machinery, nonwork, dead labor. The point where I think Habermas does have something to say is in a more political register. *Capital* is not a political book, I believe, though Marx was profoundly political in his nonscholarly life, and we have a lot of testimony about his attempts to organize in the International and his very subtle analyses of the political in *Eighteenth Brumaire* and so on.[8] But *Capital* is not political, in the sense either of analyzing the dynamics of the political, the strategy and tactics of it, or its role in these issues. Much of Marx is based on the reports of the bourgeois English inspectors, who are charged by Parliament to inspect the factories in London. We know these reports probably happened

8 See Fredric Jameson, *Representing* Capital*: A Reading of Volume One* (London: Verso, 2011).

because the landowners were trying to undercut the industrialists; they sent these inspectors to report on industrial conditions. So, there is an immediately political element to these documents, but Marx doesn't look at it. Where he does talk about politics is very early in the chapter on cooperation. All of a sudden, a notion of political relations and an ideal of collective practice emerges, not simply the values that they produce. Habermas points to that moment. He says that, just as Hegel, at a certain moment, didn't go far enough in his analysis of the collective—he probably means the end of the chapter on the Enlightenment—so also Marx arrives at what he would call a communicational collectivity in the cooperation chapter and then immediately diverts his attention to how capitalism functions.

So the problem with Habermas is that, whenever the negative and critique is approached, he immediately wants to substitute—you can't say "the positive" but—something else, because the absolutely negative analysis of Nietzsche, or indeed of Horkheimer and Adorno, is not really what he's after. I take again my basic view of that aversion from the role of art in Habermas, that is to say, this nonrole of art, this assignment to modern art of pure negativity. "Nietzsche enthrones taste, 'the Yes and No of the palate,' as the organ of a knowledge beyond true and false, beyond good and evil," because he is looking for a way to get out of the system of traditional judgments.

> But he cannot legitimate the criteria of aesthetic judgment that he holds on to because he transposes aesthetic experience into the archaic, because he does not recognize as a moment of reason the critical capacity for assessing value that was sharpened through dealing with modern art—a moment that is still at least procedurally connected with objectifying knowledge and moral insight in the processes of providing argumentative grounds.[9]

"Argumentative grounds"—this is essential for understanding Habermas on reason. Reason is giving reasons. Because reason is being able to give reasons, legitimation is founded on argument. This is essential for Habermas: You must be able to construct some notion of reason which can be reasoned with. The irrational is what you can't reason with.

9 Habermas, *The Philosophical Discourse of Modernity*, p. 96.

Before we end, I want to tell you how Habermas worked. It will be a model for all of you I'm sure. In the morning, he has his coffee. On one side of his desk, he has ten or fifteen volumes stacked up. As he reads through them, he moves the volumes from one side to the other, and, when his day is finished, all those volumes are on the other side, and he has done his day's work. I recommend this method for those of you who are wondering how to go about your research. And you can see that he is arguing with his texts; he is finding reasons why Nietzsche reaches a limit of aesthetics, why Hegel is caught in the philosophy of the subject, and so on.

An expression he often uses is the "self-understanding of a society." That strikes me as more than an ideology. It is something we all are somehow supposed to share. It is not legitimation, but it may prove the need for legitimation or a foundation. As I've said, West Germany is not a country in the early postwar years. By the time Habermas finishes this work, in the '80s, it has become a country. Unification, in my opinion, is not really reunification; it is the absorption of one society by another. If you translate Bundesrepublik as "West Germany" then you realize what we have today is a Bundesrepublik, a unified West Germany, so to speak. But this is to reckon with another feature of the German drama, so to speak, namely Europe. As West Germany is becoming, let's say, a legitimized state, there is also something called Europe coming into being and of which it will somehow become a part. That, I think, will have its effect on all of these people and on their thinking. The national context and the language of a thinker is a crucial matter, I think, but we'll talk about that again later on.

September 21, 2021

9

Adorno (I)

Before going back to Adorno, I briefly want to emphasize the role of Hegelian recognition in Habermas's thought. Hegel's master-slave dialectic turns on the fact of *Anerkennung*, "recognition." Though it is very philosophically and politically debated, some people think that the whole prize of the struggle between the master and slave—they're not knights, as in a medieval forest, but sentient beings, more like insects—is recognition. The master must recognize the other as human, from which the other one, the slave, will derive a minimal status as some kind of vague subhuman; but you can't even be a subhuman until you have established the human, which requires the slave's recognition of the master. I leave the debates about recognition aside, but I bring them up because what is at stake in Habermas's communication theory is precisely a certain version of recognition. If we could rephrase all of our political questions in terms of achieving the recognition of the people we argue with, then we would have democracy, according to Habermas. This is the social democratic reading of Hegel: Politics is about recognizing the other, even when we argue with the other. I would say that this is the motif of the Habermasians, who are a bunch of social democrats out to eliminate all the Marxism that was left over from the Frankfurt School. At the same time, recognition does play a part in communication; there has to be a common language for communication to happen. Habermas will have a debate with Lyotard about whether we *can* ever have communication. There is a very funny passage of Deleuze in which he says: "All these people are talking about communication—it's meaningless! Nobody communicates with anybody! We're dealing with a bunch of schizophrenics. We don't know what they're saying and they don't know what we're saying." That is not Habermas's position, obviously.

But today we go back to Adorno.[1] Habermas has said he only knew one genius in his life: Adorno. Certainly, this can be one's reaction to reading Adorno, but I have to say that one's relationship with Adorno is going to be variable. You will be stunned by certain things. At times, you will think that this is the most indefensible writing you've ever read. And then, a while later—maybe some of you have not yet had this experience—you simply get annoyed or irritated with him. I would say that the moment of irritation comes for me with what I will call the insufferable theme of suffering. You know that Adorno himself is not suffering all the time, though he is constantly reminding you of suffering. It can be very tiresome. You think: Why is this person so upset? Adorno, of course, was absolutely brilliant, and my sense was that you could set anything in front of him—*vorstellen*—and he would think about it until he produced something brilliant. But pull it away and put something else there, and then he'll think about that instead. In other words, I'm not sure he thought systematically—or rather, someone else had to set the agenda.

Adorno admires Beckett as much as any composer or writer except perhaps Proust. In *Godot*, you have two bums, and then a moment when suddenly two other people come, the master and the slave: Pozzo is pulling Lucky by a string around his neck. This is England and Ireland. There is a moment when the master, England, says to the slave: "Think, pig!"

1 The primary assigned texts for this lecture are several essays from Theodor W. Adorno, *Essays on Music*, trans. Susan H. Gillespie (Berkeley: University of California Press, 2002), including "On the Problem of Musical Analysis [1969]" (pp. 162–80), "The Aging of the New Music [1955]" (pp. 181–202), and "On the Fetish-Character of Music and the Regression of Listening [1938]" (pp. 288–317), as well as "Meditations on Metaphysics" from Theodor Adorno, *Negative Dialectics*; Theodor W. Adorno, "On Lyric Poetry and Society [1951/1957]," *Notes to Literature, Volume 1*, trans. Shierry Weber Nicholsen (New York: Columbia University Press, 1991), pp. 38–54; Theodor Adorno, "Sociology and Psychology (Part I)," *New Left Review* I/46 (Nov./Dec. 1967), pp. 67–80, and "Sociology and Psychology (Part II)," *New Left Review* I/47 (Jan./Feb. 1968), pp. 79–97. For the following lecture, Jameson assigned Theodor Adorno, *Aesthetic Theory*, chapter 2, and Theodor Adorno, *Kierkegaard: Construction of the Aesthetic*, trans. Robert Hullot-Kentor (Minneapolis: University of Minnesota Press, 1989), chapters 2 and 3. At this point, Jameson's lectures begin to veer further from the syllabus; all assigned and recommended readings will be cited when Jameson discusses them.

And with that, Lucky comes awake, and all of Western philosophy begins to come out of his mouth in an unintelligible way. The name of every medieval philosopher comes out in this long rigamarole, until finally Pozzo pulls the leash and Lucky stops.[2] Ireland is the inheritor of all of European philosophy, and England is a nation of shopkeepers who like to see the demonstration of thought once in a while, but don't really do it themselves. I would even say that, sometimes, Adorno is a little like Lucky, in that he would drive people crazy with his demonstrations. There are many interesting stories about the Mann family, who detested him (though maybe not Thomas Mann himself) and not only because he talked too much. That is the picture one gets of Adorno. On the other hand, he did speak to the students during the student movement. He was, in fact, very sympathetic to their cause. He did call the police at one point during the demonstrations, but I would say that he was much more accommodating than Horkheimer would have been, had he been teaching.

All of this is to say that you will not find a system in Adorno or Horkheimer. Remember that Horkheimer was against philosophy as a system. In any case, Hegel finished off philosophy; only an idiot would try to make a philosophical system after Hegel. Of course, many people did try. In any case, if others think there is still the possibility of a philosophical system, their systems must apparently be undermined. One of the problems of the later Adorno is that he thinks, on some level, that he ought to have a system, so he produces two immense *Hauptwerke*, great projects, which are *Aesthetic Theory* and *Negative Dialectics*. He died in the middle of *Aesthetic Theory*, so it is not surprising that it doesn't add up to a system, though it couldn't have anyway, and so much the better. It is the same with Pascale's *Pensées*: If Pascale made it into a handbook to convert the heathen, agnostic, or atheist, everything magnificent about it would have been lost.

If you don't have a system, but you have a mission to think, then your agenda is going to be set by other people, like Lucky on a leash. It is interesting to look at Adorno's life in that respect. His first agenda is set by a somewhat older comrade, Siegfried Kracauer. You will know him from his film books. He never had a scholarly career because he stuttered and wouldn't have made it in the classroom. The Weimar work of Kracauer is very important, especially "The Mass Ornament," the centerpiece of the

2 Samuel Beckett, *Waiting for Godot* (London: Faber, 2006), pp. 42–5.

kind of cultural criticism he pioneered in those days. Adorno first read Kant with Kracauer, and this first agenda was one of German philosophy from Kant to Hegel. The later "Meditations on Metaphysics" returns to this agenda, particularly Kant's fundamental problem: How do I secure the possibility of knowledge or experience and deal with everything which is neither knowledge nor superstition? Adorno revives this problem by way of a kind of block or separation: You are allowed to think this metaphysical realm but not to philosophize about it in any systematic way, because no one is ever going to get anywhere with that project. You can believe in it. In fact, you have to believe in it. But, philosophically, you end up with Fichte's transcendental ego, which will become the philosophy of the subject, as Habermas calls it.

Fichte is followed by a group of three roommates: Hegel, Schelling, and Hölderlin. It is thought that Hölderlin wrote the primal document, "The Oldest Systematic Program of German Idealism," which lays out the need for a new Absolute. Hölderlin then goes off into this pre-Heideggerian relationship to the being of Germany and nature, which is lost to philosophy, though not to poetry. Schelling is the youngest of them and the first published, the first to become famous, but, in his later years, he reverts to the idea that we have to reinvent myths. So we have, for Habermas, a proto-Nietzschean who reinvents a religion, who wants to find a myth for this modernity, which otherwise has no legitimation. Finally, there is Hegel himself, who takes the whole notion of subjectivity and makes it objective. I would say he makes it part of another constellation, which is that of life itself. That is, the object is life itself in nature, and the subject is logic, thinking, freedom, and so on, and those two things, in the Hegelian absolute, become the same. How can they become the same? Does anyone believe this? In Habermas, we have three variations. With the addition of Nietzsche, these are the immediate constituents of what Adorno is going to take from this moment of philosophy, that is, a constant—almost an eternal—contradiction. Adorno finds these contradictions not only in Kant but in all of German Idealism, which is a bad name for the group of people thinking with and against each other from the publication of *The Critique of Pure Reason* in 1781 to Hegel's death in 1831.

Adorno is a musician. Like any young composer of his period, he heads for Vienna, where he studies not with Schoenberg but with Alban Berg, Schoenberg's disciple and the composer of one of what Adorno considers the two great musical events of the period: *Wozzeck*, the opera, and the other, of course, is *The Threepenny Opera* of Brecht and Weil. That is Weimar's music, and Berg will be the tutelary deity of Adorno's musical side. Then Adorno meets Horkheimer. You understand that he adopts Horkheimer's project, which we call the Frankfurt School, but he is not admitted to this group officially until they return to Frankfurt. Finally, Adorno, the dilettante, the musician, inherits this institution. How is that possible, viewed from this early vantage point, when he is not even a member of the Frankfurt School? He and Horkheimer initially forge a relationship in which he doesn't receive recognition, so to speak. We think of Horkheimer as an organizer, an impresario, and all the rest of it; Oskar Negt has said that when he was studying in Frankfurt, he wasn't interested in Adorno's lectures very much, but Horkheimer—what a magnificent teacher! The fact that Horkheimer couldn't write much should not lead us to underestimate his importance. But Adorno will find a certain space for himself in the critical theory project, and he will receive his assignments from Horkheimer. Adorno's first major contribution is "On the Social Situation of Music," a long article in their journal. Virtually at the same time, his other mentor will be the man whose thesis Horkheimer sabotaged in the Frankfurt faculty, namely Walter Benjamin. The three of them will have meetings, because Horkheimer knew that Benjamin was a force of nature, but Benjamin, with these weird theological ideas of his, was never admitted to the organizational circle of the Frankfurt School, though he was supported monetarily. Of course, he was in Paris when the rest of them were in America. Somehow, nonetheless, he was an influence.

Another important figure for understanding Adorno would be Thomas Mann. I don't know what you people have read of Thomas Mann, and I don't know what people generally read of him nowadays. Everybody knows *Death in Venice*. But the major book for us—and for Adorno—is *Doctor Faustus*. Mann wrote it in the United States, and Adorno was his so-called musical advisor. It is the story of a Faustian composer, Adrian, who invents the twelve-tone system—which we'll look at in a moment—and who falls into a Nietzschean stupor at the end of his life, finally going insane, from this period between 1933 to 1945, when he eventually dies. The book is written by the composer's Catholic, traditional friend, who follows this allegorical fable of Germany itself. It is a wonderful book, whether or not we accept that diabolical reading of National Socialism—I don't know what it does for us—but it is a tremendous read. Adorno had a hand in the musical parts of it. One of the lectures given by one of

Adrian's teachers teaches you to recognize themes in your musical study by giving them names. So, a given Beethoven theme would be identified by a word. In some composition, maybe a Beethoven sonata, one of these themes is called *Wiesengrund*. Well, that's Adorno's name. Adorno was born to a Herr Wiesengrund and only later, in the United States, took his mother's name. He did it because he thought—probably quite rightly—that the Americans were both anti-Semitic and anti-German enough that the name Wiesengrund wouldn't go over very well, whereas the name Adorno would be easy enough for them. I mention this also because, inevitably, it is involved in Adorno's thinking about the problem of mimesis. I don't think anyone has really tracked down where he got all of the background for this concept; certainly, he got a lot of it from Benjamin, but where did Benjamin take it from? One source is certain: some essays by Roger Caillois, a then-well-known essayist and collector of curious topics, who, during the war, took refuge in Argentina and was very much a part of the literary scene there. Caillois wrote several essays on *mimetisme*, the self-preservation of camouflage. In the very beginning of *Doctor Faustus*, Adrian's father is fascinated by mimetic camouflage, and there is a fabulous section about *mimetisme* which certainly came from the Adornian-Benjaminian side of things. Normally, when we think of Adorno's mimetic impulse, we think of it as a creative principle—of course we want to imitate—but it is also a way of staying alive: You take on the coloration of your background in order to live.

So, whatever kind of hostility would emerge between them, Mann was a significant figure in Adorno's life. Of course, Mann is also Lukács's ideal of the left-leaning bourgeois writer, the fellow-traveling modernist, you might also say, and indeed Mann's great project in the '30s, the *Joseph* tetralogy, which nobody reads anymore, is in fact a kind of a praise song to the New Deal. (Joseph is FDR, and the administration of Egypt is the New Deal, and so on.) So, you can see more or less where Mann fits into this notion of the new Europe.

When Adorno goes back to Europe, finally, he is on his own. Horkheimer retires, having drifted into Schopenhauerian thoughts on disillusionment and meditations on the sources of anti-Semitism and the Jewish communities who are set up around the new state of Israel. Horkheimer did outlive Adorno, but he didn't have to face the student movement, though we can imagine what he thought of it. He wasn't there to deal with it the way Adorno was. Now, for the first time, Adorno is actually teaching and involved in pedagogy and is having a whole series of disputes and arguments with the traditionalists, the survivors of the Nazi academy, the conservatives who are still in the institutions. Adorno is busy writing venomous attacks on Heidegger, *Jargon of Authenticity* being the most famous, but I think not the most philosophically interesting. From his point of view, although he didn't believe in Sartrean *engagement* or committed art—in fact he wrote against it—did he believe in Marxism, historical materialism? That was his Benjaminian inheritance. He still kept faith with it, but not in any active way. He is busy tracking down the representatives of conservatism. He is politically involved on the academic level in the denazification of the new Germany, in the creation of a new kind of German culture, which is, in a way, his legacy as a task. Habermas will finally disagree with everything Adorno stands for, but this task of intervening in intellectual life and creating a new nation, which is a republic—this is something that he shares with Adorno.

What I wanted to do today, to begin with, is to tell you the narrative, as it were, of a book. I first heard the name Adorno when I was reading *Doctor Faustus* in San Diego. There was a provost at the university who was a musician and who had worked in Hollywood. He said that Mann had borrowed the musical concepts from a manuscript by Theodor Adorno called *Philosophie der neuen Musik*, translated sometimes as *Philosophy of Modern Music*, which is better than *New Music*, because it is meant in the sense in which Germans say *die Neuzeit*, meaning "modern times." I wondered how one could have a look at this interesting document; sure enough, it was around in German and later would be translated. For a lot of people in our language field, it is Adorno the musician and music theorist who came first.

As I mentioned earlier, Max Weber wrote a little book that affirms something we all knew, namely that Western tonal music, as differentiated from the music of other cultural traditions, is an artificial creation, and it has to do with the way in which our Western musical scales are produced out of an artificial treatment of sound waves, the resonances, overtones and undertones of the human sound system. So, when Bach writes *The Well-Tempered Clavier*, it means Bach is constructing Western tonality in its radical difference from the sounds of other traditions. And with that, in a sense, I suppose you have the coming into being of folk music as something different from the music of the aristocrats and their little courts, patterned on the court of the monarchy. (The old feudal nobility doesn't have this, but the little principalities and the wealthy landowners bring musicians to their courts, who later produce a culture based on this tonal system.) A new history begins at this point. Later, there will be a separation between—Adorno hates this expression, and I do too—classical music and popular music. You all know Adorno's scandalous positions on what we call "popular music," but he will make a place for *leichte Musik*, diversion music, dance music.

Anyway, the tonality system is a new kind of raw material that can be innovated in certain ways. For Adorno, the great climax of the production of these innovations, not only in the number of productions but in their quality and the kinds of things they end up meaning, comes with Beethoven. Adorno was to do a book on Beethoven, because Beethoven—like Shakespeare or Racine in other traditions—is something that cannot be surpassed. After him, there aren't any more discoveries to make by means of his particular way of handling the material, just as systematic philosophy is exhausted by Hegel. This is always the comparison that Adorno makes: Beethoven and Hegel present two immense systems that take what was already there—concepts on the one hand and sounds on the other—and do everything that is available in them, exhaust their possibilities. In music, after Beethoven's death, there will not really be another symphony written in Germany until the 1860s. There are lesser compositions, but the symphony was not a dominant form in the years after Beethoven. It wasn't until Brahms's first, and then suddenly everybody wanted to write symphonies again. You have this notion that there can't be any followers, because they'll all just be epigones and imitators. This is a very important lesson of the logic of the material, the raw material. This is a view that art, whatever form it takes, is going to be an exploration of raw material which is fundamentally social, because remember the tonal system is an invention. It is not natural; it is a second nature.

The second foundational idea here is that one of the fundamental tasks of music, as of all art, is to express suffering. Weber thought that the priests had the socially necessary task of consolation. There isn't anything you can do about suffering and injustice and mortality, but you can assign some religious bureaucrat to deal with them. This bureaucrat will, like a tranquilizer, supply the necessary ingredients, which can at least seem legitimately to address this ailment, which is unspeakable and impossible to express. So, too, is music called on to express suffering. Adorno's critics have pointed out that there is a composer he never mentions:

Haydn. A joyous music, the idea that music is there for an expression of joy and release—this is not in Adorno's aesthetics. Joy will be present, but only as an overcoming of suffering or as a delight in suffering, somehow. The problem here is that the language through which music expresses suffering—dissonance—is going to wear out historically. This is the narrative of Adorno's *Philosophy of Modern Music*. What ages in music is its play of consonance and dissonance. After what we would think of as a first, very rudimentary dissonance, then you have to somehow outbid those techniques for creating dissonance; you have to have a diminished seventh, and then a diminished ninth, and so on, if you want to continue expressing different kinds of suffering. When you get to Wagner, you get expressions of infinite yearning and suffering and misery.

So, music keeps expanding this capacity to express suffering until it reaches a certain breaking point, and that point is named, in German musical history, or at least in Adorno's work, Schoenberg. Schoenberg arrives when suffering has simply become a social neurosis. If you know any of the early Schoenberg, *Transfigured Night*, or even *Erwartung*, *Waiting*, you know that these are extremely beautiful but neurotic and obsessed works. It is hard to see how modern art could go beyond these obsessions. So, by the time of Schoenberg, there doesn't seem to be anything left to do with tonality. Schoenberg was a painter as well as a composer, and quite a wonderful writer, in a way; he ended up in Los Angeles, where there is Schoenberg Hall at UCLA. He was very upset by the publication of *Doctor Faustus*, in which the creation of the twelve-tone system, which belonged to him, was attributed to a syphilitic madman. There is a famous anecdote of him chasing someone down and saying, "I'm not syphilitic! I'm not syphilitic!" He tried to sue Thomas Mann. Mann inserts a little note in a later edition saying that the twelve-tone work is the spiritual property of Mr. Arnold Schoenberg, but I don't think that helped anything.

What is the twelve-tone system? It says you must not repeat any note until every other note has also been sounded. You must not allow any one key to become dominant and form a tonal center. Music is constantly wanting to revert to tonality, and the aim of the twelve-tone system is to stop it from doing so. A sounding of all twelve tones is a tonal row. Each row will be different, and they can take all kinds of forms. The tones can be all on top of each other. The rows are supposed to replace melodies in the older tonal system. There is a moment between the exhaustion of tonality and Schoenberg's invention of his new system which is an atonal period of a kind of musical expressionism. All kinds of weird and interesting things are done in this intervening period. Schoenberg described it as a moment of democratic overcoming. He says that in the tonal system the tonality of one of the keys is like a ruler over all the other keys, who are its servants. When we get rid of this tonal system, we have a democracy of all the keys. They are all equidistant. They all can somehow participate on an equal basis. This one moment of expressionism is either the post-tonal, final fling of tonality itself, or the pre-twelve-tonal approach. Most of what is called modern music in the immediate postwar period is twelve tone; otherwise, it's just traditional. You may know that Schoenberg's students at UCLA did most of their production for movies—for example, horror movies, movies demanding a certain dissonance. His disciples were very well trained to produce the appropriate sounds for those productions.

This is Adorno's demonstration of the telos of the modern. There is a destiny—does one want to call it progress?—in the material itself. The material will, after the seventeenth century, develop to a point, at which it ends up—or so Schoenberg thought—in the twelve-tone system, and a new system will have to be invented at the point where it exhausts itself. So, it will seem that Adorno is celebrating twelve-tone music as a kind of apotheosis of musical history, but it turns out that Adorno has another evaluation of this, and that the twelve-tone scheme becomes an analogy of total socialization, of fascism, a planned system; remember that, for Adorno and Horkheimer, this new society is one of total planning, the disappearance of the market, total control. Okay, but here Schoenberg is symptomatic of this process. His music is also one of total control. So, in a sense, Schoenberg's authenticity is in reflecting the absolute inauthenticity of society in his day and age. The proof is that he doesn't know what to do with the atonal row, so he's reduced to reinventing classical forms inside of his new music. We have symphonies and so on which are then reinvented inside the twelve-tone system. But, if the symphony was based on tonality, why reproduce it? It is what the Frankfurt School calls regression, the appearance of older forms in what was to be a brand-new form. It is the dilemma of art. If it is going to be an authentic reflection of its period—and its period is a nightmare—then the art itself is a nightmare. So, you can see where Thomas Mann got some of his ideas for *Doctor Faustus*.

But we're not finished yet, because this is a double portrait, as in Plutarch, and alongside the trajectory of Schoenberg is the trajectory of the other great modern musician, Stravinsky. Schoenberg will, for Adorno, be somehow authentic in the way in which he pursues his musical logic. Stravinsky is absolutely regressive and, indeed, is allied with fascism in a sense. It's not just that the ballet is an impure form. What characterizes Stravinsky's *The Rite of Spring* is percussion and rhythm; it is all about ritual and sacrifice, all of what seemed to Adorno to be regressive. So, here, instead of finding something that exercises these archaic survivals, Stravinsky is reinventing them in the same way in which fascism regresses to the archaic. You have a double picture here of an impossible musical situation: one reflecting an impossible society, the other regressing from that society into an even worse one. In a sense, at that point, musical history would seem to stop, the end of history in some kind of Hegelian way. Well, it doesn't stop, of course, and there were younger composers who were all supported by important subsidies for the arts that existed in postwar Germany, and in Darmstadt, in particular, there were festivals and subsidies for music. A whole set of younger composers gathered there, Pierre Boulez and Stockhausen, for example. They evolved whole new experiments beyond the twelve-tone system. Adorno would join them and listen. He was very encouraging. He finally wrote a piece in which he says, "Okay, forget I said all that. They are finding a new kind of musical freedom; let them pursue it." With them, Schoenberg becomes academic music. All of these Americans and Germans and French who were composing in the twelve-tone system are thrown out the window (and a whole new moment begins on the basis, by the way, of a French tradition, not a German one).

Anyway, that is the story of Adorno's relationship to music, which is a major part of his relationship to art in general. He never did anything so detailed for the other arts, but he did probe into them. I would say that narrative was never really a primary focus for him, although he wrote about some novels. Beckett and drama certainly was a primary focus. Beckett would then be the step after the well-formed play, expressing suffering in a way the older playwrights were unable to. As for Brecht, he didn't like the politics. Like the many anti-Marxist appreciators of Brecht, he allowed that Brecht was a great poet.

Then we have lyric poetry, on which he has quite a wonderful essay.[3] You may have already begun to understand Adorno's method in these

3 Theodor W. Adorno, "On Lyric Poetry and Society [1951/1957]," *Notes to Literature: Volume 1*, trans. Shierry Weber Nicholsen (New York: Columbia University Press, 1991), pp. 38–54.

essays. It is certainly a kind of *Ideologiekritik*, what Americans call "ideology critique," but he won't use the word "ideology," because even that word is ideological. But his version of ideology critique might not be exactly what you expect, because the minute Adorno shows the ideology of a given position or work, he turns around and shows you that his own critique is ideological as well. It will be very instructive to compare Adorno's essay with Heidegger's "Origins of the Work of Art." Heidegger's essay is a little more historical, perhaps. There is always the choice, in any kind of Marxist or left analysis, between the sociological emphasis and the historical emphasis. It's very hard to get the two together, I think. But Adorno's opening move is very simple: Lyric is supposed to be the solitary expression of a single individual, at best addressed to another individual, but its solitude and subjectivity and its feeling are social. Solitude is a social experience, and therefore everything which is individual in lyric, which seems to be posed against society, is itself a moment of society, so you do get history here in that the very possibility of the protest against the social is itself both social and a historical possibility. He will admit, in a sense, that if this is what lyric is, then it is modern. The ancients had lyric, but they did not have the same kind of society and therefore did not have the same kind of protest against it—the feudal era, as well, in China and in India. So, I think you have to understand that Adorno is confessing that his aesthetics begins with the modern. I'm sure you could go back to the Renaissance and say that someone like Petrarch is the beginning of the modern, but this is a very considerable restriction, and consistent with Hegel. I read Hegel's "end of art" as saying that what we call art, associated with Christianity, with the cult and classical genres, can no longer express the Absolute; now it is up to philosophy. You remember the great beginning of *Negative Dialectics*: "Philosophy, which once seemed obsolete, lives on because the moment to realize it was missed. The summary judgement that it merely interpreted the world, that resignation in the face of reality had crippled it in itself, becomes a defeatism of reason after the attempt to change the world miscarried."[4] That says a number of things. It says you can only complete Hegel—philosophy becoming the Absolute—with Marx, with changing the world. Since philosophy didn't do that, it failed. Its task is over and, on my reading, that means that the Absolute is given back to art, and that modern art from Romanticism onward reinvents the task of expressing the Absolute, expressing society.

4 Adorno, *Negative Dialectics*, p. 3.

At any rate, what Adorno wants to argue here is that the lyric expresses a modern phenomenon of individuation. Again, it is caught in the same confusion of modernism, modernity, and modernization that we find in Habermas. Reason, modernity, and capitalism—are these just words for one another? Certainly, in this view of things, in Habermas's history, they are superimposed. But, for Adorno, individuality arrives with modernity at the same moment in which it is expressed in lyric, even as the critique of lyric "must discover how the entirety of a society, conceived as an internally contradictory unity, is manifested in the work of art, in what way the work of art remains subject to society and in what way it transcends it."[5] In a sense, instead of reflecting the contradictions of society, this modernism, of which lyric can be thought of as a central exhibit, will express society by its absence; that is to say, it is because this society does not allow for the development of the individual subject that the individual must assert itself by way of this lyrical solitude. Adorno's account of lyric implies a series of historical stages, which we can see in a very interesting moment in which he talks about Rilke and *things*. We don't appreciate it in English, but Rilke is really the greatest of modern poets. You can't read Rilke without realizing what an incredible natural phenomenon he was.

> Rilke's cult of the thing [as in his *Dinggedichte*, or "thing poems"] is part of this idiosyncratic opposition; it attempts to assimilate even alien objects to pure objective expression and to dissolve them, to give them metaphysical credit for their alienness. The aesthetic weakness of this cult of the thing, its obscurantist demeanor and its blending of religion with arts and crafts, reveals the real power of reification, which can no longer be gilded with a lyrical halo and brought back within the sphere of meaning.[6]

The path by which the individual lyric tries to oppose the social machine is subject to all kinds of regressions, the regressions that Habermas finds in Schelling and in Nietzsche, the idea that we have to reinvent a new religion, a new Dionysus. This kind of poetry, which tries to free itself from the alienation of society by inventing a new religion, must itself be canceled by a new kind of poetry. If you want to call that new poetry the

5 Adorno, "On Lyric Poetry and Society," pp. 38–9.

6 Ibid., p. 40.

expression of suffering, it would connect these two versions of Adorno. The individual solitude of the work is the suffering which condemns the society around it even as the latter remains absent from the work, just as the very autonomy of the work is itself a condemnation of society. It should not be necessary to flee society into this apparently self-enclosed enclave, and this is itself a condemnation of the inhuman force of the social totality. We'll come back to some of this next time.

September 23, 2021

10
Adorno (II)

We're still on Adorno, or I am, anyway. This is difficult stuff. My aim is to show you how to read his writing, because it seems to me better than trying to make a system out of his ideas. Obviously, we're going to talk about his ideas, but I think they come up as sentences. I think that his writing is a kind of free association of sentences and of concepts, rather than the exposition of one concept after another. That is one reason why it would be very misleading to consider *Aesthetic Theory*, for example, as a series of chapters laying out an argument. It is a continuous thing. The German editor does not have it divided into sections but has given it, as they say in publishing, "running heads," titles for the content of each page. Where did Rolf Tiedemann, the great editor of Adorno's work, get his titles? I'm sure Adorno didn't write them, because he wouldn't put running heads on his manuscripts. I suppose Tiedemann made them up, and the translator has translated them into chapters, separating out the sections that seem to correspond to these different running heads, so that it looks like we have a book in chapters. These running heads are helpful in the sense that they give us a very thorough table of contents, but we must not rely on them, and we mustn't assume that this is a finished book.

I've mentioned to you the most famous thing he ever said: "To write poetry after Auschwitz is barbaric."[1] The one answer would be from Paul Celan, whose poetry is a breakdown of language into small bits. It was

1 Adorno, *Prisms*, p. 34.

partly George Steiner's idea that German was irrevocably ruined and tainted by Nazism, a rather silly observation inasmuch as the very next year, 1959, was the inaugural year of a new German literature. I mention the major works to compensate for the fact that we're going to be reading hardly any literary writing, though obviously culture and literature are part of this picture: Heinrich Böll, *Billiards at Half-Past Nine*—a great but more traditional book—Günter Grass's *The Tin Drum*—an exploding novel on the order of Pynchon—and, finally, from East Germany, Uwe Johnson's *Speculations About Jacob*. When Johnson emigrates to West Germany, then the United States, he produces an enormous novel, *Jahrestage*, which I fear I can't recommend very much. It's a cut-up novel. He writes it in a linear way and then chops it up and mixes it up, a little like Llosa. William Burroughs was the first to invent this notion of the cut-up novel. It is extremely experimental. It is one of the first novels about the Stasi, a profoundly East German work. Grass, being from Danzig, also has a relationship to the East. So, these three kick-off texts of a new moment of modern German literature suggest that Steiner was a bit premature in declaring the German language dead.

Poetry after Auschwitz. The work of Paul Celan, who committed suicide in 1970, is the literature of the Holocaust in some sense. Oddly enough, or maybe not at all oddly, he went to see Heidegger and asked him the usual question, receiving the usual nonanswer. They got along very well. Heidegger was very fond of him. In the days before Celan's suicide, Heidegger wrote to friends saying, in effect, "Someone look after that young man; he's very disturbed." These are the human sides of Heidegger that are nice to mention because nobody believes they exist. Celan's work would signal the possibility of poetry after Auschwitz, but, for Adorno, it is more than the fact that Auschwitz itself can't go into literature anymore. And yet, when he comes to Beckett, he assumes that Auschwitz is present. If you know *Endgame*, you know that way up behind the characters—one paralyzed in a chair, the other his servant—there is a small window with light coming in. Clov gets up on the window and looks out. Adorno believes that what he sees is this desert of Auschwitz, of the dead. This is an example of the way in which Adorno's insights can be reified into themes, as with his standard line about suffering.

Adorno's *Aesthetic Theory* is a great monument to the impossibility of an aesthetics in the traditional philosophical sense. What is beauty? It is a meaningless question. Already in the German Romantics, beauty was superseded by a different kind of category, namely the interesting. Instead of the beauty of the work, it is the interesting nature of a work which is now important. There is a moment in Thomas Mann's *Doctor Faustus* in which the rather conservative Catholic humanist narrator asks his friend whether he knows any feeling stronger than love. Adrian, the hero, the Faust composer, says yes: interest. Here you have an opposition between humanism and the impersonality of the hyperintellectual, with which Schoenberg's music is accused. After all, in Stravinsky, isn't it feeling, the great thumping of the *Rite of Spring*, that you get carried away by? Schoenberg by comparison would seem purely intellectual.

As for aesthetics as a discipline, I still remember Collingwood's *The Principles of Art*, in which he proposes two principles which I've always thought are very sensible. The first is that all aesthetics turns on the way in which two incompatible things come together in an artwork. The work of art must be an expression and it must be a construction. But expression is a matter of spontaneity and feeling, whereas construction is a matter of the raw material. How do those two dimensions come together? I think it is a very interesting opposition, and, while Adorno insists very much on construction, it seems to me that the leitmotif of suffering, if he had an aesthetic, would be the expressive side of his aesthetic. He says in his book on Mahler: The joyousness of the fifth symphony is like Nietzsche's; his voice cracks.[2] Its joy is not real, because how could such joyousness exist in a world of suffering? Construction, which we'll go into in much greater detail, is more consistently present in Adorno. But, really, these two dimensions are always coming together, while, in a funny kind of way, they remain incommensurable. That is why the work of art, when it succeeds, is a remarkable thing. How can a construction express? How can expression construct? How could something impersonal and architectonic respond to a feeling? In Heidegger's "Origin of the Work of Art," the work of art is the contact between world and earth. That could simply be spirit and matter, if you like. But the matter of the work—he is thinking

2 "Mahler was a poor yea-sayer. His voice cracks, like Nietzsche's, when he proclaims values, speaks from mere conviction, when he himself puts into practice the abhorrent notion of overcoming on which the thematic analyses capitalize, and makes music as if joy were already in the world. His vainly jubilant movements unmask jubilation, his subjective incapacity for the happy end denounces itself." Theodor W. Adorno, *Mahler: A Musical Physiognomy*, trans. Edmund Jephcott (Chicago: The University of Chicago Press, 1996), p. 137.

of Greek art, polished stone, and so forth—also includes the resistance of matter. World, in Heidegger, is history, the human project. The work has to include all of these dimensions.

I am beginning with sentences. The sentence is Adorno's method. It is a great pleasure to read these sentences. Here, for example, is one of my favorites. He is talking about the claims of positivism. Isn't positivism better, more truthful than Hegelian idealism? "Even if it were a fact, it could not be the truth that Carnap and Mises are truer than Kant and Hegel."[3] This is the great Adorno sentence. How can a fact not be true? If you can understand that paradox, then the business about truth content begins to fall into place. The facts are the positive, the affirmative, the proposition, the statement. Truth is something else. That, I think, is a good initial sentence, but let me read you a few more from *Prisms*.

This one is about Veblen's notion of conspicuous consumption. Veblen was responding to Adolph Loos, an architect and a commentator who wrote a famous book called *Ornament and Crime*. It is criminal to cover a building in squiggles, says Loos. This is the dawning notion of the simplicity of modernism. In a sense, Veblen, by denouncing conspicuous consumption, is throwing out the baby with the bathwater (which, incidentally, is a section title in *Minima Moralia*, and you notice that, for all his scorn for American culture, Adorno doesn't hesitate to use these American slogans as titles for his little meditations). Veblen knows that it isn't ornament that is wanted, and, yet, if you denounce ornament, you're really denouncing the work itself. So, you can detect a historical movement, internal to art itself, in which art pursues authenticity by getting rid of its inauthentic parts, but the danger is that it will end up killing itself off, as in *Dialectic of Enlightenment*. We should always be looking for this fatal dialectic in the work of Adorno, because it is the movement of Adorno's view of modern history, namely that internal tendencies, which make a work, a thing, or an event, are also what destroy it, so that enlightenment, by canceling the past as superstition or crude thinking, is truer, even as its cancelation of the past is going to catch up with it when it has canceled itself; little by little, we end up in a completely positivistic society in which nothing will be true because nothing would be thought any longer except for mere facts. Thinking would be demythologizing, getting rid of the inauthentic, but as soon as this kind of thinking takes root

3 Adorno, *Negative Dialectics*, p. 385.

it ends up getting rid of everything that motivated it in the first place. Art, too, proceeds by criticizing itself. Finally, it criticizes itself out of existence, because what is art? It's just a leisure pastime. It is a luxury. We still have to feed the planet. We have to do the real things. Art doesn't answer to need, and therefore who needs it? It disappears. Finally, then, the description of Veblen: "It is as if, in claiming to be something special and unique—and this claim must be constantly exaggerated in the interest of sales—each object were mocking a condition in which all men are subjugated to an order whose principle is more of the same."[4] The commodity comes into being in a world of self-sameness, but it does so by claiming to be something new and unique—a new kind of toothpaste—and at the same time it contributes to the logic of "more of the same," creating more sameness.

A couple more. This one is on Huxley and *Brave New World*: "He believes that by demonstrating the worthlessness of subjective happiness according to the criteria of traditional culture, he has shown that happiness as such is worthless."[5] Huxley is criticizing commercial happiness, but, since he is a puritan, he uses that critique to criticize happiness in general. As modern as he was, Huxley was also a follower of perennial philosophy, the idea that there are ancient wisdoms that are always true. That is what makes for the strangeness of *Brave New World*, its attack on modernity and commercialism, which is, however, itself regressive.

In general—and I'm still going fast here—each of these positions is worked over as we move to the beginning of *Aesthetic Theory*, which opens with another of these paradoxical sentences: "It is self-evident that nothing concerning art is self-evident anymore, not its inner life, not its relation to the world, not even its right to exist. The forfeiture of what could be done spontaneously or unproblematically has not been compensated for by the open infinitude of new possibilities that reflection confronts."[6] In other words, traditional art—think of music again—developed a series of listenable, attractive melodies, which, however, we can't use anymore because art taboos those traditional sounds of the past in the name of the pursuit of limitless possibilities. But now we have explored many of those possibilities and they don't amount to anything much. Art's critique of itself ends up in a cul-de-sac where its infinite freedom closes off everything that was promising about it and turns it into something which is no longer

4 Adorno, *Prisms*, p. 78.

5 Ibid., p. 111.

6 Adorno, *Aesthetic Theory*, p. 1.

freedom. There is a truth in a traditionalist critique of modern art, and there is a truth in the critique modern art has of traditionalism, but these two truths kill each other off.

As I've mentioned, Adorno doesn't like the word ideology; I'm using it because I think it's useful: Each of these positions is an ideology, but the critique of an ideological position turns out also to be an ideology. Adorno leads us to a place where critique itself, pure negativity, is being exercised at a level on which one can't be situated, where there are no affirmative statements to be made. Again, I come back to the notion of the affirmative. This is the place to mention again Marcuse's great essay, "The Affirmative Character of Culture," which is about the way in which the cultural, artistic representation of the world, supposedly something distinct from its object, can only show the suffering and misery of the world as an element of itself, an element which allows us to perceive the world as a whole and which is therefore truer than the whole itself.[7] But that very truth of culture cuts it off from the world and makes it useless, powerless and impotent, and therefore it falls back into the world and is simply a worldly product whose negation is impossible. So, in a way, with these more generalized negations, you negate a given affirmative proposition. Logic and philosophy itself are dependent on the idea of a proposition or judgment which says something true about the state of things, *alles was der Fall ist*, or everything that is the case, in Wittgenstein. But the point is that pursuit of propositional truths would end up in an impossible empiricism, because it involves all kinds of presuppositions that undermine the very proposition itself and make the form of the proposition ideological. To affirm the truth of a proposition is to affirm the truth of the form of the proposition, which lends itself to an empiricist worldview. We could go back to Kant, who says, yes, let's try to figure out what could be the realm of affirmative propositions. That will be the world of the categories. We can determine what kinds of things may be true, and we draw a line beyond which we cannot confirm or deny anything, beyond which nothing is accessible to the human mind. The next step would be to commit ourselves to sticking to what we know is true on the basis of that deduction. But that, too, is an ideology, a worldview, let's say. Negating that affirmation—would that entail affirming that the transcendental exists as negation? If so, we

7 Herbert Marcuse, "The Affirmative Character of Culture," *Negations: Essays in Critical Theory*, trans. Jeremy J. Shapiro (Boston: Beacon Press, 1968), pp. 88–133.

would be left in some kind of idealism, in which there would be plenty of other problems for Adorno; it would leave us stranded in the dynamics we worked through with Habermas. Adorno is saying that there is a path of absolute negation which is not simply nihilism. It requires from us that we think an absolute determinate negation. In a worldly situation such as ours, we can say that both alternatives are false. But where does the position of absolute determinate negation come from?

So, this pursuit of the negative—it will become clearer with Marcuse—makes it very hard to talk about their positive views. The idea that we have to preserve some aspiration to the transcendental in a society that is given over to the purely empirical is not a sustainable position, it seems to me. The defense of metaphysics in a world which cannot have metaphysics, which has destroyed metaphysics through a dialectic of enlightenment, makes sense in its diagnostic dimension, but it doesn't make sense as a philosophical position, because it doesn't exactly solve anything. You could say that negative critique is precisely what makes such a position possible. For example, regression: If it isn't clear what the advanced is, what the new is, you can at least tell what is regressive or aims to return to the past. In aesthetics, you may not be able to see what the work of art of the future should be, but you can identify its enemies. For example, what Adorno calls "philistines." These are the people who look at Jackson Pollock and feel obliged to say, "Well, anybody could have done that. My children could do that." The point is that they don't. Regression appears in other guises, the regression of Stalinism, for instance. For Adorno, the East is absolutely closed. In each of these cases, Adorno is so vigilant in his critique of regression that it can only produce more vigilance.

We come now to the theme I have been promising to address: the construction of the subject. Remember the Frankfurt School's theory that both state capitalism and communism are moving towards absolute monopoly, the end of the market, and a totalitarian system in which the individual doesn't have a place. There is an individuality possible in the earlier stages of capitalism, in the competitive capitalism of the market. One can see that the social constraints and structure of society exercise a shaping power on the construction of the subject and that the more it becomes itself and excludes all negation from itself, the less space it leaves for any kind of freedom of the subject. But that gives us our question: If that's so, then, in our system, which is so completely closed and without negation, how do we find the position that allows us to criticize that system except by imagining something which was also an abomination to the Frankfurt School, namely Mannheim's notion of the free-floating intellectual who was supposed to be beyond classes? Everyone must sell themselves in this society, as Brecht says, and while no one can ever situate themselves above their class or above class itself, there can be a provisional position outside of an identification with the system that could permit a certain insight. Horkheimer, more than Adorno, was very interested in rebels, criminals, marginals, and so on, because he understood that the people who were not assimilable to this society could experience it and understand it in ways that the people who have shaped themselves to adapt to it could not. Nonetheless, this strand of thinking still orients us towards the position of intellectuals. Certainly, the very ambition of the Frankfurt School was to shape intellectuals, and in a way that would have made the student movement (which Horkheimer at least deplored) understandable as a movement of intellectuals, the intellectuals who, by virtue of the institution, haven't gotten jobs. The institution is not big enough for them; the students themselves have been pushed out of an institutional society in such a way that they are a force to change the institutions themselves, if not to incite revolution. That is, of course, Marcuse's position, but Horkheimer would not go that far.

Now what was congenial to the French '60s in Benjamin, but also in all of modernism, is the idea that identifying advance means concentrating not on the meaning of the work but on the form of the work. What does it mean to be advanced? Certainly, at the time of the student movements, it means getting rid of metaphysics, which is a matter of meanings. What does existence mean? What are we here for? Where are we going? The Kantian questions. So, an advance in the philosophy of the object means getting rid of meanings and describing processes, or in the case of art, asking not what a novel means but how it is constructed. Not exactly. I would say that getting rid of meaning means discarding both content and form. The question about meaning generally has to do with content. What does this story mean? This is identified as a humanist question. It would seem to be a retreat from content to form. No, I think the question about form is also not the right one. Form is historical. Remember that Adorno is essentially dealing with modern art. He has very little to say about other modes of production. The art that interests him is the art that exists, I would say, in capitalism, since autonomous art is a matter of capitalism, or at least a matter of the dialectic of enlightenment. Having gotten rid of the church, and to an extent, religion, we are left with an autonomous art that exists for itself after what Benjamin liked to call its cultic value. Byzantine art, medieval art, those have their own meanings in the institutions, and they are therefore not yet autonomous in Adorno's sense of the word; autonomous art begins with secularization. Art begins to live for itself. There is a telos in that art. It is going somewhere. Each stage produces the next, all the way until abstract expressionism, and then suddenly it stops. What is to be done now? What can be new now? Hasn't everything been done? That is the end of the telos of modernism. Adorno would not put it this way, but it can be a useful way of putting it. People will ask: Why should I think that Schoenberg is better than Tchaikovsky? Stravinsky famously said in his old age: I would give all of Wagner for one melody of Tchaikovsky. Well, there is a moment of truth in that statement. Tchaikovsky is something, but you're sick of it. You've heard it, loved it, and so on, and now you can't hear it anymore. Now you need something that goes beyond Tchaikovsky. That is the aging of music. In the visual arts, from Manet on, you get a movement which takes you all the way up to Jackson Pollock, and suddenly it, too, stops. I heard a very great art critic say: "Look, this stuff that people are doing now, random objects and so on—my interest has always been easel painting; when easel painting stops, sure, you can do other things—these assemblages in a big museum gallery—but I'm just not interested anymore. Why not? I don't know."

So, the new has to be unpredictable. It is a blind spot. That is why Adorno falls back on the idea that it is intentionless. You can't ask what the artist was trying to do. That is as bad as asking, "What did he mean?" The true artist doesn't have an intention. Nothing comes of that kind of ambition. What comes are certain kinds of language, characters, and feelings which have never been expressed before and are demanding their formulation in language. The artist has nothing to say about what comes out of them. Sartre showed how, with great successes like *Madame Bovary*, there was always some misunderstanding, because the artist was working with private fantasies, but the public experiences the work differently. It is an objective misunderstanding.

I'll try to figure out a way of wrapping this up next time.

September 28, 2021

11

Marcuse

Today we're going to see how the '60s and '70s in both Germanies brings about a reflection on pedagogy as much as anything else.[1] In other words, theory in the German '60s and '70s raises the question of tradition. With tradition having been destroyed, it becomes a question of picking up where Weimar left off, continuing whatever conservative academic traditions remained after National Socialism, inventing new ones, and so on. This is a moment in which there is a great importance attached to pedagogy and cultural revolution, the formation of the subject.

The Cold War could be said to have started at different times in different places, but, in Germany, something decisive happens on June 20th, 1948. This is the moment of what is called the *Währungsreform*, when suddenly you're told overnight that your currency is worthless, and you have to carry it to the post office and have it turned into a new currency. The three Western occupying powers, the Allied powers, so to speak, wanted to reunify Germany under their terms as a demilitarized zone,

1 Jameson recommended the following readings as historical background for this section of the course: Timothy Scott Brown, *West Germany and the Global Sixties: The Anti-Authoritarian Revolt, 1962–1978* (Cambridge: Cambridge University Press, 2013), particularly pp. 119–67; Bruni de la Motte and John Green, *Stasi State or Socialist Paradise?: The German Democratic Republic and What Became of It* (London: Artery Publications, 2015), particularly pp. 330–71; and the timeline provided in Julian Preece, *Baader-Meinhof and the Novel: Narratives of the Nation / Fantasies of the Revolution, 1970–2010* (New York: Palgrave Macmillan, 2012), pp. xix–xxvi.

but there were problems with the currency. Finally, the Americans gave up and allowed the occupied zones to issue a new currency, the deutsche mark. With that, West Germany reemerges, and the East is left with its inherited currency. The *Währungsreform* is a fundamental break, and it is followed immediately by the Berlin blockade and its airlift operations. I don't think West Germany becomes a nation in its own right again until 1966, when the Grand Coalition is formed between Adenauer's party, the CDU, and the socialists. The socialists are really social democrats. Already in 1959, they declare that they are no longer a Marxist party or even a socialist party but are more like a reform party, like the Democrats here from time to time. I would say that it is at the moment of this *Große Koalition* between the two parties in 1966 that West Germany becomes once again a nation. When does it happen in the East? In a sense, with the Wall in 1961. The Wall is very important for the East, because suddenly it cuts off its brain drain problem. You have to hear the Eastern defense of the Wall. It is very persuasive. The East spends their very scarce capital to make their youth into doctors, engineers, and lawyers, but, the minute those doctors, engineers, and lawyers get their degrees, they beat it to the West. There is a constant movement out of the eastern zone and into the West. With the Wall, all of a sudden, that movement stops.

This is also the context in which the student movement is happening, an international movement developing in the shadow of the Vietnam War. Even before the Vietnam War, there are all kinds of American State Department initiatives abroad. Figures appear, like Patrice Lumumba in the Congo. Lumumba is then killed with the approval of the United States by Moïse Tshombe, who becomes one of the leaders of the Congo. Tshombe's visit to West Berlin is a kickoff event for the student movement, the demonstrations against this simultaneous development in the Congo. The next visit which sets off the student movement is the visit of the shah of Iran in 1967. The shah hasn't been expelled by the Iranian Revolution yet, which will take place years later, but there is already a very vigorous student protest against him, in which a student is killed. Of course, that is another solidifying event for the student movement.

There are of course many other tangents of the international student movement, including a more orthodox Marxist element, the Black Power movement in America, and the feminist revolt against the students who are running the student movement, which you get a sense of in the essay

I gave to you by Frigga Haug.[2] For all of them, 1968 is both a climax and a failure, not only after May '68 in Paris but also after the Soviet invasion of Czechoslovakia. After that, the student movement will take a number of different directions, including the Baader-Meinhof direction, which we'll also look at more closely soon.

This would be the time to go on to Marcuse's work. Marcuse is a professional philosopher, but I would say the kind of texts you're going to find here are different from some of the other kinds of philosophical arguments we've seen. In Marcuse's work, it seems to me that there are essentially three moments: *Eros and Civilization* of 1955, what we would call "the Eisenhower era"; then in 1964, *One-Dimensional Man*, an enormously influential argument for the '60s; and finally, in the '70s, *An Essay on Liberation* and *Counter-Revolution and Revolt*, which are, let's say, pamphlets for these new movements, as well as aesthetic works in their own right. What these last texts reinforce is the notion, already to be found in Adorno, that aesthetics is a zone distinct both from epistemology and from commerce, business, utilitarianism—in short, capitalism. As in Kant, you have an attempt to use aesthetics as the alternative. I suppose you would say that art remains the place for Adorno from which negation can be most effectively practiced.

In another sense, what is presupposed in Marcuse's work is the university. The attack on the university—sawing off the branch we are sitting on—is a crucial move for both the American and the German student movement. The University of California is a state institution, as are essentially all the universities in Germany; they are the places where a new generation can have its confrontation with the state. I think that we don't find a reflection on the place of the intellectual or on the university in Adorno, and I suppose Marcuse acknowledges that students can be the agency of—should we call it revolution? I think there is a problem with that word here. He will call it—and this is one of his conceptual inventions—"liberation" rather than "revolution." You can always identify the followers of Marcuse and, to a certain degree, Habermas, because they talk about emancipatory acts and not revolutionary or even political acts. They tie those acts up with Adorno's notion of autonomy, not the autonomy of the work of art but the autonomy of the self. So, there is a

2 Frigga Haug, "The Women's Movement in West Germany," *New Left Review* I/155 (Jan./Feb., 1986), pp. 50–74.

place in the heritage and transition of Marcuse, Adorno, and Habermas in which you find a social democratic moderation reappearing in notions of emancipation.

The aesthetic solution. Another important part of Marcuse's work, already in *Eros and Civilization*, is devoted to Schiller.[3] Schiller, both a poet and a man of the theater, went to live in Jena, near Goethe, with whom he had a long collaboration. In those days, before email, people living next door would still write each other letters, which are a way of getting your thoughts out for further discussion. The Goethe-Schiller correspondence is one of the great moments of German theory, I would say. It is about genres, epic, tragedy, and so on, so it may not seem so interesting for us. But Schiller wished to move beyond Kant, of whom he was initially a follower, and tried to figure out how to use Kant's notions of beauty in a political way. Remember that, at this point, Germany is still divided into principalities, a period in which Fichte will invent a German nationalism of sorts—the student movement then being a unified, anti-Napoleonic, nationalist one. Schiller wished, in that sense, to push Kant towards the political in the largest sense, which he achieved in *On the Aesthetic Education of Man* by underscoring art as a way of overcoming political limitations. Those limitations are ideological, but they are educational as well. Schiller understood that one of the features of this movement had to be a revolution of consciousness, that is, a pedagogy of sensibility. It had to find a way in which sensibility could itself be trained to come out of this state of what we might call dependency or subalternity. That is what he means by aesthetic education. So, art in Schiller is posed as a way of unifying opposites, subject and object. It is a very rich set of propositions, and it is the first source for aestheticization of politics, of work, and so on. This was important to Marx, although I'm not sure whether Marx ever talked about it. Its central motif is the possibility of converting art into a political instrument for creating, let's say, a revolutionary sensibility, for liquidating the subjectivity of the older regime and creating a new revolutionary one that overcomes the oppositions of the old regime. In a sense, it is also a counterrevolutionary proposition, because it finally leads Schiller to the idea that if you could transform people in this way, then you wouldn't need a revolution. A revolution in subjectivity would preempt the very need for a violent revolution on the French model and would take the place of

3 On Marcuse and Schiller, see Jameson, *Marxism and Form*, pp. 83–116.

revolution itself. Revolution is seen as the production of the Soviet new person. The aesthetic revolution is going to take the place of the violence of the Terror as a means for total change.

Marcuse's mode of philosophy is undoubtedly speculative, and he refers to the testimony of Freud's *Civilization and Its Discontents* as a guide. Freud and Lacan are both anti-utopians. Lacan says so himself: The Freudian psyche is necessarily an instrument of repression. The psyche has to take this animalistic infant, with all of its raging instincts, and train it, repress all its instincts, endow it with a superego, a sense of guilt, a sense of duty, in order to prepare it for some kind of social life. Marcuse is going to say that what Freud describes here is a first repression; but there is a surplus repression. Yes, of course, you have to make this *infans*, this animal creature, into something human by an initial repression, but society has other things in mind for it. It must be further repressed in order to work, in order to discipline itself, to accept the delayed gratification of labor and the wage. We can't get rid of repression, Marcuse argues, but we can get rid of surplus repression. That is one of the novelties of Marcuse's argument. You see that it interrogates Freud from the perspective of a search for a kind of psychic formation other than that of surplus repression. Given the Freudian system of the ego, the superego, and the id—or, later on, eros and thanatos, which includes the role of aggressivity in the psyche—what reconstruction of the Freudian system would have to be necessary in order for us to have not even a utopian society but merely a better society, a society in which the aggressivity of war, racism, or sexism do not hold, and in which a different kind of life can come into being? This is a Kantian move. Kant tries to move from scientific truths to the preconditions of those truths. What had to be true in order for us to be able to say that those scientific results are true? And, on the basis of that inquiry, Kant constructs his whole system of epistemology. Marcuse is doing the same with this set of—not empirical—but seemingly convincing and persuasive accounts of psychic forces. He accepts all of what Freud has shown us in his practice, but he doesn't accept that those findings are a permanent anti-utopian weight on the psyche. Can we imagine those reconstructed in such a way as to make something else possible? That is essentially what this so-called Freudo-Marxist book is about.

I want to mention the role of psychoanalysis because it would seem to be once again, for various people, relevant in a Germany where fascism is reemerging as a political movement. This is from a new book by Oliver

Nachtwey, *Germany's Hidden Crisis: Social Decline in the Heart of Europe*, about the economy of Germany since the war. He is discussing the more recent right-wing phenomenon known as "Pegida," or "Patriotic Europeans Against the Islamization of the West," but he describes this phenomenon by going back to Adorno:

> The most important study of authoritarianism remains that conducted by Theodor Adorno. On the basis of surveys indicating the prevalence of anti-Semitic attitudes in society, Adorno and his colleagues sought to discover what psychological foundations underlay such personality dispositions. For them, an authoritarian personality was the key that led to people become anti-democratic, filled with resentment and potentially fascist. The authoritarian personality, in their view, was characterized by a series of connected symptoms that combined into a syndrome: these included conventionality, obsequiousness combined with aggression, ideas of power, lack of empathy, stereotyping, cynicism, obsessive concern with sexuality, and finally, projectivity (understood as the inclination to believe dangerous things were going on in the world).[4]

I recommend this to you because it is one of the best handbooks for what is going on not only in Germany but in all the advanced societies since, let's say, Nixon's abolition of the gold standard in 1973 and the beginnings of financialization and neoliberalism. But what I wanted to show was that one of the strands of this reflection on the changes of sensibility is precisely to do with the nature of fascism or its personality structure, which is inaugurated by the Frankfurt School way back in California with the famous F-scale. Marcuse pursues another direction: What would be the structure of the revolutionary personality? How should sensibility in this period of repression be educated towards revolt and revolution, which was Reich's initial but maybe too simple impulse?

I've already mentioned that Marcuse's answer involves getting rid not of repression but of surplus repression, but it also involves a philosophical discussion of memory. Freud tried to recapture the past in the so-called talking cure. Marcuse emphasizes that memory is not only the memory of trauma but also of happiness, the memory of childhood, of the satisfaction

4 Oliver Nachtwey, *Germany's Hidden Crisis: Social Decline in the Heart of Europe*, trans. David Fernbach and Loren Balhorn (London: Verso, 2018), p. 199.

of the mother. Of course, this reflection on the mother, though he doesn't mention her, comes out of Melanie Klein's revision of Freud. It is the reality principle, eventually the performance principle, that locks us into the abandonment of memory. The reality principle restrains the cognitive function of memory. It is a "commitment to the past experience of pleasure which spurns the desire for its conscious recreation."[5] People are made to forget what happiness once was. "As cognition gives way to re-cognition, the forbidden images and impulses of childhood begin to tell the truth that reason denies." This is a repression operated by conscious adult reason on these more fulfilling memories of what childhood was: "Regression assumes a progressive function. The rediscovered past yields critical standards which are tabooed by the present. Moreover, the restoration of memory is accompanied by the restoration of the cognitive content of phantasy"—and of course fantasy will lead us into art and what frees us in art. "Psychoanalytic theory removes these mental faculties from the noncommittal sphere of daydreaming and fiction and recaptures their strict truths."[6]

This is a very basic beginning of an answer to the question: What would have to be the precondition for a liberation of the psyche from surplus repression? These are the sources of suffering. There is biological suffering, and we are condemned to it, though there are things we can do about it. There are historical sources of suffering, and there we can certainly do something about it. Brecht's estrangement effect is evoked because the making-strange of things in Brecht is meant to be practical, to destroy the idea of the natural and replace it with the historical. The experiences we think of as natural—including feelings, human relations, not just political relations—which are central to our lives, become perceived suddenly, in this distance of the estrangement effect, as historical, that is to say, made by people and therefore capable of being unmade by people. It restores a certain praxis, if you like, to art.

I think that what you have here is the notion, which was an abomination for all orthodox Marxists, that it is not necessarily the working class but rather other excluded members of society who will make revolution. But remember that one of the functions of capital is to reduce work, to create employment, to extend the empire of commodification, and thereby

5 Herbert Marcuse, *Eros and Civilization: A Philosophical Inquiry into Freud* (Boston: Beacon Press, 1974), p. 19.

6 Ibid., p. 19.

to create a kind of worker whom we call the service worker. Marcuse is enlarging the area of agency to include these other groups who are in some sense excluded from the official domain of wage labor, let's say. It is also, of course, underscoring the crucial fact in the United States—but not quite in Germany, because the unions are still powerful there—namely, the pact between labor and capital in 1955, which is sealed by the union of the AFL and CIO, in which capital agrees to a pension system and the workers agree not to strike. The fundamental equilibrium which is reached there makes the labor unions themselves antirevolutionary and wedded to the status quo in the American situation.

One has to be aware of the social conditions for these texts. When Adorno talks about degraded aesthetics, for instance, we have to make the connection—when he doesn't make it himself—with the commodity form and thus with consumerism, where the purpose of the commodity form is not only to establish a self-sameness and equality between the value of the various products but also to make labor invisible. A proper commodity does not allow you to think about the labor that the worker puts into making it. It represses and allows a forgetfulness of a whole dimension of its existence. I think the kind of aestheticism that Adorno or even Schiller consider is really an attempt to recapture that centrality of the commodity and to make it undergo a Nietzschean revaluation of values, or in other words, to capture its positive essence in a different way. This is what Adorno talks about in sections like "Baby with the Bathwater": If you want to get rid of culture, because you think quite rightly that culture is simply the culture of consumption and consumer society, then, at that point, you restore the made world to pure labor, demythologize it, and debunk its objects as pure objects of utility, but you also lose the negative dimension of culture, the one that Schiller, Adorno, and Marcuse are insisting on.[7]

I also want to mention the matter of slogans. Marcuse will promote, as a slogan, "the great refusal," which he takes from Dante.[8] In a sense, I think it is ironic and not necessarily accurate, because the great refusal of Dante is not highly esteemed, let's say. But it was a very powerful slogan. Marcuse created a lot of these slogans. Hegel has a chapter in the *Phenomenology* on the Unhappy Consciousness, which names the way in

7 T. W. Adorno, *Minima Moralia: Reflections on a Damaged Life*, trans. E. F. N. Jephcott (London: Verso, 2005), pp. 43–5.

8 See Herbert Marcuse, *One-Dimensional Man* (London: Routledge, 2002), pp. 66–75.

which consciousness separates itself and projects one part of itself into religion and thus lives its remaining part as sinful, abject, and guilty. This is one of Hegel's fundamental analyses of religion. Marcuse considers a happy consciousness. He is talking about America, of course. This is the critique of America's smiles, its happy Hollywood endings, its reduction of pleasure to fun, its culture industry. Happy consciousness would be one in which a society had managed to negate guilt as well as the true happiness of the past. Of course, there is a big philosophical question about this critique—for which Marcuse has always been attacked: Isn't he saying that there are true and false desires? Isn't all of this happy consciousness a false desire, while he, Marcuse, is telling us what true desires are, just like Plato, setting himself up as a philosopher king? What right does he have? I think there is certainly a problem with starting from Marcuse's position: It is the problem of starting from superstructures. I would say that in all Western Marxism, the role of commodification, rather than that of production, takes precedence, and I would say the base in Marcuse's theory will continue to be not so much production but need. There is an insistence on need, scarcity, as the fundamental thing to overcome, and this is of course happening amid decolonization in the '50s, wars of national liberation, and so on, when need is associated with the kinds of unfreedom that are brought to a world of starvation. But this is, in a way, the program of Marcuse's new sensibility, to restore by way of these changes our sense of need, which becomes then a political project. I myself think the aesthetics in *One-Dimensional Man* and in some of the later work are far more fully exposed. In *One-Dimensional Man*, there is a real philosophical argument about language, in which he diagnoses the removal of the negative even from philosophical language, "the closing of the universe of discourse," which recalls Adorno's elimination of the negative, not just in our daily lives.[9] Here, he targets analytic philosophy, Wittgenstein, whose clarity and wish to be free of ambiguity destroys the history of philosophy, and above all represses affective sensibilities which would be the cornerstones of liberation. But you remember the great line in Wittgenstein: "Whereof one cannot speak one must be silent."[10] That is, philosophy has nothing

9 Ibid., ch. 4.

10 A newer English translation renders this famous line differently: "What we cannot speak about we must pass over in silence." Ludwig Wittgenstein, *Tractatus Logico-Philosophicus*, trans. D. F. Pears and B. F. McGuinness (London: Routledge, 2001), p. 89 [§ 7].

to do with that for which we can't find words or language. That is not far from Adorno's argument for preserving the transcendental as a ghostly reminder or even memory, nor from the Marcusean dimension of feeling.

The other problem is sublimation, but I don't think anyone has ever really solved it. In any case, sublimation will be key, because it is not repression; it is the one place in which artistic instincts can be carried over into daily life, and this is the other place in which work is aestheticized. This is the other presupposition of Marcuse, that the alienation of industrial labor could potentially become something which is nonalienated by being sublimated into artistic work. There could be a satisfaction of labor which is of an aesthetic and nonrepressed variety. Sublimation is a path for the aestheticization of the world which is different from consumer society's aestheticization of the world and production. Beauty would then be negation or revolt, the great refusal.

So much for Marcuse. When we come back we'll talk about what Joseph Beuys might represent, both as repression and liberation, and how a path is made to this new world of the '60s and '70s with a different generation of historical actors.

September 30, 2021

12

Beuys, Mitscherlich, Haug, Backhaus

One reason I asked you to watch the film about Joseph Beuys is that Beuys gives you a chance to see what the '60s group dynamics looked like in a certain place and from a certain angle.[1] The other reason that I picked this particular film about this particular artist is that it marks another development of the themes of reason and rationality with which we began the course, when we looked at Horkheimer and Adorno's *Dialectic of Enlightenment*. We are going to remain within their framework of reason and rationality, in some sense, throughout this course, because it becomes a leitmotif of political speculation, and finally, rightly or wrongly—and not because I want to force Habermas on you, but because for many reasons he is the most symptomatic of these thinkers—we will conclude with a Habermasian intersection of rationality and politics in his spokesmanship for the new formation of the Federal Republic. So, although rationality is one of the key leitmotifs of this string of writers, as far as I'm concerned, I think rationality is not an adequate political concept or slogan. If rationality is pitted against the nonrational, the irrational, it condemns us to throw all kinds of phenomena into a category which is fundamentally untheorizable. The obsession with reason in this tradition underrates the way in which our understanding has become enlarged

1 *Beuys*, dir. Andres Veiel (Germany, 2017); Jameson also recommended Peter Bürger, "Everydayness, Allegory and the Avant-Garde: Some Reflections on the Work of Joseph Beuys," *The Decline of Modernism*, trans. Nicholas Walker (University Park: Pennsylvania State University Press, 1992), pp. 147–61.

so as to include phenomena that used to be thought of as irrational. It seems to me that we can understand many of these phenomena, which we wouldn't exactly want to call rational, in ways that were denied to earlier theories that simply opposed reason and madness, let's say. I think Foucault doesn't go far enough in his history of madness in showing the way in which the madman is not only integrated into society by way of psychiatry and other institutions but also theorized and thereby used to fold madness back into rationality in some sense. Therefore, the very notion of reason itself seems to me a poor starting point for understanding these developments. So, we will treat reason as if from the outside, along with its various opposites, as a phenomenon, rather than accepting it as an unchallenged value.

I wanted you to look at Beuys because clearly, if anything was irrational in the way of fashions, fads, and art, this would be it. There are many other forms of art that one could call irrational in this period, but this is, if you like, an organized irrationality of a quasi-religious kind, and it seems to me, it is part of a false dialectic between reason and its opposites, in the sense that the more dried out and conventional your notion of reason gets, the more room there is and the more need there is for some opposite number. It seems to me that Beuys represents that need.

I was curious to see your various reactions to Beuys. Many different points of view were taken. Some said this was a typical '60s artistic phenomenon, related to Warhol or the Fluxus group, of which Beuys was also a part—this general postwar floundering of avant-gardes. After the war in Europe, the formation of avant-gardes, as an attempt to formalize a certain kind of modernism, is a sloppy process but often a calculated one. Abstract Expressionism in the United States is a unique case; all those people knew each other and had a theoretician in Clement Greenberg, but I think it's not quite the same. Fluxus is another strange current in continental Europe with a claim to the term. The Situationists more so. But, it seems to me, the classical avant-garde is Surrealism, in which you have a dictator, exclusions, a manifesto, a following, at least until Breton emigrated during the war. Had he been Jewish—it went without saying. But the population took a dimmer view of somebody leaving who was not Jewish and didn't have to leave. There are exceptions, but someone who emigrated from France, who was non-Jewish and didn't have to leave, who didn't share the experiences of the occupied country or homeland the way the people who stayed did, is no longer really in a position to offer any kind of leadership. Breton came back and there was a surrealism after the war, but he didn't have the kind of following that dominated the intellectual scene in the '30s.

Anyway, what I want to point out is that Beuys is, if you like, a manifestation of his period. There are differences with similar figures like Warhol. You have celebrities, but then you have gurus; I don't think Andy Warhol was exactly a guru for anybody. I don't think the dictators, like Guy Debord, are really gurus either. So, I think there is something distinctive about the way Beuys develops around himself a kind of cult. You don't necessarily think of Warhol or Breton in iconographic terms, but with Beuys, everything is connected to the hat and coat, and it makes you think: Where else do we find this kind of iconography? I think you have to go back to Charlie Chaplin. Humor aside, Chaplin was an image of the downtrodden, the masses, and was in fact a communist sympathizer himself, having been thrown out of the United States in the McCarthy era. Beuys as a figure is a bit like Chaplin in that sense. His own strange personality plays into it.

We're accustomed to equating gurus with evangelists and their scandals, for which, given our mostly secular positions, we are not tempted to have much respect. (If you go back in time, one can certainly have respect for some of the great religious leaders.) While the very notion of the guru is tainted for us in the West, I think it has to be distinguished in some way from the celebrity. Then we have to decide: How do you distinguish between a guru and a charlatan? The Jonestown community, a false messiah. But in the history of messianism, all messiahs have been false. I would be tempted, in a dialectical way, to say that all gurus are, by nature, charlatans in the sense that they don't know that that is what they are until they have been identified as such by someone else: There is always a secondary figure who appears and shows the messiah figures of the past that they are indeed the messiah. In the case of Beuys, I don't know how this comes about, but clearly, in this period of despondency, from which he is awakened in the immediate postwar, people are assuring him that he has some special status. What I'm trying to say is: Is it possible to distinguish between that special status and charlatanism, and if so, then what kind of a phenomenon are we confronted with? I don't think we can solve that problem now, but I find it to be a question with implications for what is stupidly called "populism" today, which involves the renewal of a kind of fascist leadership.

Some of you talked about the works of art themselves, and I must say that they are more interesting now than they were at the time. But where do they come from, and what is this notion of social sculpture? I assume social sculpture means that, when you are experiencing a work, you are not just looking at a contained work but the work plus all the people who are looking at it and who are somehow part of it in a way that is nondramatic. The notion of "happenings" doesn't completely coincide with what Beuys was doing. To account for this I think you have to go back to the sources of mysticism. Some of you talked about Beuys's origins in Nazism. I think it would be rather silly to make much of his past in the Hitler Youth. He had to serve in it and be a part of it. Why did he choose to become a pilot? Was that a choice of Nazism in some sense? I don't think so at all. First of all, if you had those inclinations and capacities, it would certainly be better to be a pilot than to be a foot soldier in this horrible war and in the situation that his age group found itself in.

His plane is shot down, as you know, in Crimea, and his living body is rescued. In the following weeks he's nursed—not back to health, because according to the official story he is unconscious for this whole period before the army finds him and takes him off to a genuine hospital. Nonetheless all of these obsessions—the notion of fat, for example, being the most striking, weird part of Beuys's repertoire (literally fat, like whale blubber)—percolate into his unconscious while he is lying there wounded. In some version of his life story, his self-discovery comes at the moment when he is able to mobilize all this material of the archaic in his work. You have, for example, the piano which is wrapped in fat. Here you have the instrument of nineteenth-century art and the center of nineteenth-century German culture, when every educated person plays the piano, when music is circulated by scores (Nietzsche learns about Wagner when he's fifteen by playing the score of *Tristan* on the piano with his friends), but it's wrapped in fat. What can that mean? It's not exactly like Schoenberg using the piano to create a new system. Is it a refusal of art? It is a coming to grips with art in some sense.

The film also shows the event with the dead rabbit, which some of you objected to—I don't know that we have to assume he killed the rabbit himself; it could be roadkill—in which he explains to the dead rabbit what modern art is. All of these are provocations in some sense. I don't know what Adorno would have thought of Beuys, or whether he ever wrote about him. Certainly, it is a complete cancellation of Adorno's autonomous work.

Adorno, in any case, was opposed to the idea of avant-gardes. Modernism itself, it seems to me, does tend to divide into two strands: the individual artist—Proust, Joyce, Mallarmé—and the manifesto, the production of a new idea of what art is socially.

We're lucky to have films of these various events, in which art is an event rather than an object, an event that taps the trauma of the past and of the archaic and the mythic in a way which seems to me characteristic of the postwar period. Remember that the crisis which Habermas himself diagnoses in Hegel is the disappearance of the Absolute and of a form of religious legitimation. These archaic forms of legitimation will ask for the involvement of other people, whether the hostile involvement of the German bourgeoisie, which is not an advanced bourgeoisie, as in France, but a *Spießbürgerschafte* or petty bourgeoisie of some kind. It isn't even ripe for scandal. At least in France, in the nineteenth century, the bourgeoisie was able to be scandalized by Flaubert. But the academic bourgeoisie in Germany was certainly able to be scandalized, and Beuys stood for scandal to a certain degree.

What is interesting here is that this kind of art organically develops into politics. Via the archaic, it develops a relationship to what we would call nature, a term which I'm not sure the Beuysians would use until the founding of the Green Party. So, this is one case where a guru who seems to have some kind of fascination and drawing power over people is able to mold that collective following into an actual political movement from which he is then dismissed and expelled, because he is too crazy to keep the support of the bourgeois masses. This wild side of Beuys is good enough for his youth following but alienates the respectable parts of the community. The extravagances and provocations of somebody like Beuys could appeal to a respectable bourgeoisie which is otherwise threatened by them.

Let me then at this point go through some related people, who are going to have to remain names, essentially, because we don't have time to go into much detail, but they're names I want you to know. Mitscherlich's book on the father is one very interesting book that I would have liked to have had time to discuss.[2] When the worker is taken away from the family, the family becomes relatively fatherless, and Mitscherlich's

2 Alexander Mitscherlich, *Society without the Father: A Contribution to Social Psychology* (New York: Harper, 1993).

analysis of the crisis of "fatherlessness" begins from there. But there is a kind of second fatherlessness that sets in after the deprivation of the familial father, according to Mitscherlich, and in its place emerge figures like Hitler. Hitler didn't marry until the last days; he was very careful not to be seen in a familial situation in order to make himself available for all kinds of fantasy investments.

Where do we situate this idea of fatherlessness in the intellectual context of postwar Germany? It is to be situated, first of all, alongside Erich Fromm's *Escape from Freedom*, as a kind of existential Freudianism. I would like to call these cultural critiques, in an ugly sense, because they all attempt to find some way of characterizing a society or a nation as a whole. Mitscherlich's book is an attempt to characterize Germany in opposition to the other European countries or the United States. I think it is related to the anthropological attempts of that period, the so-called Culture and Personality School of Franz Boas, Margaret Mead, or Ruth Benedict. Whether anthropological or Freudian, their studies aimed to characterize named communities of a certain kind of cultural distinction or difference. These are attempts to make a self-identification, of which it seems to me one must be very suspicious. Can minor variations between countries give rise to a whole group, a whole people, it being understood that the concept of a "people" is a doubtful one as well? Is this what you want to call a culture? Countries practice this kind of analysis on themselves, empires maybe less. I've seen a whole wall in a major bookstore in Japan dedicated to Japaneseness, and the same in Mexico: What is it to be Japanese or Mexican? There are moments in American history where Americans ask themselves, as Emerson did in the nineteenth century: What is distinctive about us? We don't do that much anymore, maybe because we don't want to know.

Mitscherlich's book is an example of that kind of interrogation, which, it seems to me, is facing a half of Germany that is trying to reconstitute itself after its failed war and its destruction. I'm not sure that this kind of analysis goes anywhere, but we should realize that it is there in the background. It helps us to see that the question at the time was not so much "What have we done?" *Die Schuldfrage*, as Karl Jaspers called it, the question of guilt. Nobody wants to think about the question of guilt or to analyze it. As for the Nazis, they are bureaucrats; they find places to house themselves in the new government. But to turn back and interrogate them as Nazis and ask what Nazism is—that is a later and very belligerent stage. The East Germans make the *Braunbuch*, the brown book, which comprises lists of all the former Nazis in the West German government. But, if you try to take that book into West Germany, it gets confiscated because they don't really like that kind of operation very much. As for the Nazi war crimes, that doesn't really resurface until the '60s. So, there is a kind of void in the self-image, as it were, of this society, which books like Mitscherlich's look into. But this is not a purely German phenomenon, and when Lacan tries to theorize social things, which he's not very good at, this notion of a society without authority is one of his leitmotifs too, so it's not all that unusual.

The next works on our list are Frigga Haug's essay on the German feminist movement and Klaus Theweleit's *Male Fantasies*, a feminist work as well, at least insofar as it wants to connect in classic '60s fashion the sexism and sexist fantasies of the Nazi leaders and of the military with the very mentality of Nazism as a whole.[3] It was published in two volumes, and it was an enormous success. Frigga Haug is one of the leading feminist theorists of Germany and the editor of one of the most important left journals, *Das Argument*, the oldest continuous radical magazine in Germany. Very little of her work is translated. The text that I assigned to you was also published in a book called *Beyond Female Masochism*. With the idea of female masochism, she means to say that, while obviously, in action it is necessary to attack male positions of domination, the most important kind of revolution is the inner revolution of overcoming one's own subalternity as a woman. I don't believe the term "female masochism" is well chosen, but at any rate, you can see the connections with Beauvoir's *The Second Sex*, which centers around the woman's choice of her own position as a woman. Haug's other great theme is what she calls "memory-work," a kind of therapy of recovery of the past, the past of the women's movement, of the great pioneering women, including Rosa Luxemburg herself; but it also means a psychoanalytic drama in which you recover the pieces of your own childhood. So, female masochism would be a loss of that glimmer of freedom, and memory-work is an attempt to rediscover the places where that loss happened. Her feminism has a very distinctive agenda.

3 Haug, "The Women's Movement in West Germany," pp. 50–74; Klaus Theweleit, *Male Fantasies, Volume 1: Women, Floods, Bodies, History*, trans. Stephen Conway (Minneapolis: University of Minnesota Press, 1987) and *Male Fantasies, Volume 2: Male Bodies: Psychoanalyzing the White Terror*, trans. Erica Carter and Chris Turner (Minneapolis: University of Minnesota Press, 1989).

As an attempt vaguely to fill a gap in these readings, I will recommend a movie by one of the great directors after the war, Margarethe von Trotta: *The Years of Lead*. It is a great film both on the '60s and on the new women's movement, which originated as a reaction against the male-dominated SDS. The years of lead, *anni di piombo*, refers primarily to the long '70s in Italy, but they use the expression *les années de plomb* in French too. For me, it is characterized by the sky, a leaden sky, but obviously, the lead is from bullets. We'll be discussing this more when we get to the Red Army Faction and the '70s. But, in English, the translations of this film are either *Marianne and Juliane* or else they simply translate it—because maybe that's too complicated for English speakers—*The German Sisters*. The Hannah Arendt movie is also by Margarethe von Trotta, a somewhat more conventional film.

Going on to Sohn-Rethel. We will be looking at his notion of the division of manual and intellectual labor, and I want to relate that notion to the work of Hans-Georg Backhaus, who was a student of Adorno's and, as you have seen in his essay, a developer of Marx's value-form theory.[4] This is the point at which something specifically Marxist emerges from Adorno's seminars. It is also the moment at which Hegel reappears in Marx studies. A whole school called Neue Marx-Lektüre emerges, a kind of value theory. Backhaus wants to say that, in a sense, Marx's description of capital is itself Hegel's Absolute Spirit and that capital in Marx's description will function as an overarching organizational scheme analogous to what concludes Hegel's *Phenomenology*. Marcuse points out that Hegel was philosophizing in a society that had not yet arrived at modernity and that there was a whole set of concepts that he could not have conceived on that basis. He could not have conceived of Marxism, in other words. This is an attempt to reunite Hegel with Marxism as its almost structural precursor.

The versions of Marxism which come out of the rediscovery of the *Grundrisse* in the West will take a different form in the East. You will see that Rudolf Bahro's notion of actually existing socialism is based on Marx's theory of the Asiatic mode of production, as it's called. Those would be the twin reemergences of Marxism in these student years and the years immediately following 1968. As for the students, it is important to note

4 Hans-Georg Backhaus, "On the Dialectics of the Value-Form," *Thesis Eleven* 1, no. 1 (1980), pp. 99–120.

that the SPD had renounced Marxism already at the end of the 1950s. It is a very complicated, ambiguous matter when they first come to power. First of all, the grand coalition of 1966, which for the first time includes a socialist minister under a chancellor who has served in the German army and was a member of the Nazi Party, is really the beginning of an autonomous Bundesrepublik. A few years later, the SPD will come to power on its own; Willy Brandt is its first leader, an important symbol for this new Germany and the students. There is a very famous moment, the *Kniefall von Warschau*, when, visiting the Warsaw Ghetto Uprising memorial, he falls to his knees. There was still a complicated relationship to Poland at the time. In Germany, one of the open political sores had to do with the changes of boundary in the eastern zones, which pushed all the Germans towards the West. So, the recovery of the old prewar boundaries was a hot political issue. That is one of the reasons why relations with the East were impossible, and why relationships with Poland, which had inherited these new territories, were also very difficult. For Willy Brandt to fall on his knees in front of this monument to the dead was a very remarkable event in modern Germany history. There was, however, also a scandal when it was discovered that one of Willy Brandt's chief advisors was an East German spy, so he fell from power and was followed by two very powerful and bureaucratic leaders, Helmut Schmidt, a Social Democrat, and Helmut Kohl, from the Christian Democratic Union. At that point, the political development of the West is stalled. Even though the coming to power of the SPD marks a new kind of autonomy for the West, it also marks the separation of the student movement from the socialist party. The student movement is essentially organized around the socialist youth movement of the Social Democratic Party, which separates itself and becomes radicalized.

After that, we're going to deal with three or four more things. One will be the exploration of the public sphere, as it's called, which of course Habermas sets off. It will be a new conception of collective pedagogy, or—as some people call it—cultural revolution. Its central question is: How does one change the mentality of people in order to have a new society? Then we'll turn to the hermeneutic movement, which is, in some odd sense, a sequel to Heidegger. Finally, we have a few other people I want to introduce you to. We'll conclude with Habermas, a different, final Habermas who comes down like a lid on all that comes before him, unifying it all so thoroughly that there can be no place for anybody else.

I once asked Habermas about Marxism in the German university. Willy Brandt, having been this marvelous, charismatic figure, also enforced a *Berufsverbot*, which prevented radical students from being hired, and which fired many radical professors. Later on, after unification, Willy Brandt circulates in East Germany the referendum on reunification, so his later career is less inspiring. When I asked Habermas what became of the Marxists around Backhaus and the school that they developed, he implied that they drifted off into drugs and that the whole thing collapsed. But their work has inspired many returns to Marx and is being revived now in the UK and the US, especially in the journal *Historical Materialism* and in others' interest in the value-form.

How does the recent revival of the value-form in Marx connect up with Adorno? You remember that Adorno complains about the self-same, but where does he get this notion of absolute uniformity? It is a version of the theory of commodification; it comes from Marx's description of the commodity. Adorno's study of the commodity form and his lectures on Marx will be the source of the discussions of value in this group, and there will also be an alternative description of value in terms of Sohn-Rethel's analysis of abstraction. The commodity form discards the use-values and the qualities of things, the nature of their production, the labor that went into producing them, so as to see them as equivalents in value. In the case of Sohn-Rethel, it is a question of going back even further, locating the autonomy of the mind, of idealism and so forth, in this initial separation between manual labor and intellectual labor. Intellectual labor is, then, the beginning of a surplus class—priests and the like—as well as the beginning of idealism and of philosophy itself, insofar as the emergence of secular philosophy in ancient Greece is connected for Sohn-Rethel with a certain commercial social form. So, he too is taking up this theme of value and self-sameness, but at a different, deeper level than the Marxist tradition coming out of Adorno. Abstraction, for Sohn-Rethel, is not only a matter of the autonomy of ideas and concepts—a kind of conceptual autonomy, in which the world of ideas begins to be separated from practical life and from physical labor—but it is also signaled by the appearance of the mathematical, of number. It is very interesting, then, that he will spend a great deal of time on various revolutions in the ancient world, whereby geometry is founded and becomes independent, whereby the phenomena of number theory are imported from Babylon and from India and organized into a scheme that is now somehow autonomous and separate from that of labor. The climax of this study will not really come until Galileo, where we find that the book of nature is written in number; the language of the book of nature is mathematics. The Galilean turn, then, opens the door to a complete mathematization of the world. All of this is elaborated in Sohn-Rethel's research, and we will talk about it in more detail next time.

October 12, 2021

13
Sohn-Rethel

Today, I want to go through some features of the Marx revival in the West and among the student groups. We've talked about the historical features of this revival, coming out of Adorno's seminar, going through Backhaus's essay, and eventually reemerging in the recent debates on the theory of value. The question of value disappeared for a long time and has only somewhat recently been found again in the reconnection of Marx with Hegel and the Hegelian dialectic. Many English, American, as well as German scholars have shown how the categories of Hegel's *Logic* are rediscovered in moments of *Capital* and, much more evidently, in the pages of the *Grundrisse*, which of course, was not known here until the '60s. Between the beginning of his work of the '40s and early '50s of the nineteenth century, Marx, for whatever reason, decided to reread Hegel, just as Lenin will go back to Hegel in 1914. It's not unlike when Mahler, in the middle of his career, procures an edition of Bach's work and studies it; I won't say that Mahler's music turns into a Bach-like production, but this moment certainly shows how going back through a specific, unique body of work, which is both method and content, can make other ways of thinking suddenly seem possible. I think that this is what happens with Marx's rereading of Hegel. At any rate, some of these studies are very complicated and can give you the specific pieces of Hegel that have been transformed by Marx.

Sohn-Rethel has an independent existence. As he says himself, everybody thought he was crazy. He would peddle his writings to various

Marxist groups, but nobody would pay any attention. He wasn't Jewish and didn't emigrate. In the Nazi period, he worked in the war office, where he secretly passed information to the British. He had another career as a spy, which was quite substantial. Finally, his work gets printed and he gains his followers, but for many years his major work, *Intellectual and Manual Labour*—recently reprinted in English translation—remained one of the secret books of Marxism.[1]

Sohn-Rethel set himself a very specific task that, in a sense, bypasses Hegel. But let me first situate this work more generally before we get to that task. Let's begin again with Kant's diagram of his categories: quantity, quality, modality, relation. I'll quickly give you an account of the function of Kant's categories, in a popular and absolutely unphilosophical way. Out there is reality, the things-in-themselves, the noumena. But, fortunately for us, inside of our heads, somehow, we have the categories, which translate our impressions of the outside world into what now, for us, looks like human experience. Quantity will sort things out. Quality will distinguish them. Relation will primarily, but not exclusively, deal with causality; I see, for example, that this brown object falling from a tree hits the ground and I develop a relation between the two moments. Finally, modality will tell me that it exists, or that I've simply imagined it, or that it doesn't exist, and so on. So, these categories turn our being in the world—whatever you want to call it—into intelligible experience. After Kant, in nineteenth-century science, some of these topics will be explored in more empirical ways, but these explorations will be grounded in the categories that produce phenomena; the filtration of the senses will produce objects that we can talk about (although this remains a prelinguistic philosophy).

When Kant is talking about experience, he is talking about knowledge, epistemology. How can we know things? When we get to the late nineteenth century—really much earlier, with the Romantics, but, crucially, when we get to Dilthey—it becomes clear to a wide range of thinkers that, when we're dealing with human materials such as cultural history and its documents, the kind of thinking required by these *Geisteswissenschaften*, these humanistic disciplines, must be of a completely different type than that of the natural sciences. In other words, just to pronounce something that will not emerge really until the twentieth century, it involves the other,

1 Alfred Sohn-Rethel, *Intellectual and Manual Labour: A Critique of Epistemology*, trans. Martin Sohn-Rethel (Leiden: Brill, 2020).

that is, other people, whereas science involves things and objects. By this time, Dilthey and others feel that there ought to be a radical distinction between the way we study things in the natural sciences and the way we study people in the humanistic disciplines. We have a way of looking at nature: Kant's categories. But what about our existence as social beings, our "second nature," a technical term that the Frankfurt School gets from Lukács? How can we know anything about the side of our existence which is not explicable by the laws of physics or biology? We can't use Kant's categories for that kind of knowledge. We don't examine history in terms of quantities and qualities. It requires a wholly different kind of thinking. Is there not to be invented a specific mode of thinking for dealing with all of the materials of human societies? We will return to this question with Gadamer.

So, we get this initial split which is already reflected in Marxism as the split between base and superstructure. I've suggested, over and over again, that maybe the centerpiece of the Western Marxist approach to *Geisteswissenschaften*, superstructures, and to the human materials of this other world that can't be dealt with by science is the theory of the commodity, though it clearly cannot be restricted to a theory of the commodity. Will we say that production is something we can analyze materialistically and that all these theories, Western Marxist or not, about culture, history, *Geisteswissenschaft*, and so on are idealistic? In a way, they have to be idealistic, because they are about ideas. At the same time, if ideas can be discussed in appropriately materialist terms, then perhaps the distinction between materialism and idealism is not the most useful here. But how could ideas be discussed in materialist terms? It's a conundrum. In Conrad's novel *Nostromo*, people wander around pronouncing this mysterious expression: "material interests." How can an interest be material? In Conrad's novel, it is a question for imperialism. This is one of the problems. More generally, this third kind of approach will fall under the sign of the social. That will be a way in which ideas can be understood, if not materialistically, then at least in terms of what Marx called the base. There are, of course, various versions of this kind of approach. In *The German Ideology*, Marx seems to say very strongly that history, religion, law, literature—none of those things have any history; they are only the effects of human beings who concretely produce their own situations. Marx goes from the idealistic view—that the disciplines correspond to something real or social—to the point that they have to be turned back into human action and activities. In a similar vein, Adorno will say that the period of the market, the late nineteenth century, perhaps even earlier, allows the mind a certain freedom which is no longer possible in the epoch of the great monopolies. As a matter of contradiction, one may suspect that Adorno will have great difficulty in locating any possibility for negation and critique in the era of monopoly capital, given that Adorno himself understands monopoly as a structure which limits the mind and presumably limits what kinds of negation are possible, what kind of art can be produced, what kind of thought, and so on. So, there is an attempt in Adorno to move from the superstructure back to the economic situation. The economic situation is seen not as determining those phenomena but as giving the condition of possibility, as a determination, as the framework in which they will take place, which later on, as it gradually gets reduced, will make only a more limited number of things possible. Adorno also was opposed to connecting works with moments of history or social history, but he was perfectly happy to connect something to a general mode of production. So, he would connect various phenomena to stages in capitalism, but not so much to history, whereas I think that would have been another possibility. But, in Adorno, there are already a number of remarkable kinds of mediation at work, and clearly, for Adorno to center his cultural evaluations on this enormous moment shared by Beethoven and Hegel certainly implies something about the situation that makes them both possible, even if Adorno does not allow us to say much about what that "something" is. What he does allow us to say is that theirs is a transitional moment in which the French Revolution opens up an immense but potentially illusory freedom.

It would seem to you, looking at the title of Sohn-Rethel's book, *Intellectual and Manual Labour*, that he has a rather different position on the question of mediation, and that he would prefer to take his analyses back to the laboring body. But that is not quite true, because what he means by manual labor is a social relation; he means a society in which the individual human being expends energy in a particular way. Nonetheless, he sees this form of social relations—and this is in *Capital*—as emerging from the moment of cooperation, that is to say, when there develops a general sense that, in order to exchange something—you're making baskets, let's say, and somebody else in the village is making metal—there has to be an agreement that you will furnish certain things and they will furnish certain things but that this agreement cannot immediately be made on a measurable basis.

What is important for Sohn-Rethel, however, is not so much the emergence and breakdown of a cooperative society, but rather that of thought itself, philosophy, if you like—eventually, that is, the question of abstraction. Even if one prefers to say that the Platonic form was the finalization of the emergence of abstraction, the question remains: Where could abstraction come from? That is, at what point does thinking develop a certain autonomy from the material world? At what point can one speak of the *logos*? This question has come back in contemporary philosophy. Again going to France, Deleuze talks about—he doesn't use the word "autonomy"—the realm of the concept. Nobody wants to be caught in this materialist-idealist dilemma, so we have to find some way of forgetting it. It is obviously wrong. It is obvious that the body and the mind are not separate, but since we are talking about them separately, and they seem to have different objects and contents, what do we do with this separation of languages or codes? Deleuze opts to think through the realm of the concept, which is autonomous, in the sense that it derives neither from the body nor the mind. The concept is not something that emerges from the personal mind, from one's own thinking. The idea of an impersonal concept goes all the way back to Plato, which is the final consecration of the realm of the *logos*, let's say, as it comes out of pre-Socratic philosophy—hence the return to pre-Socratic philosophy, as if thinking could take place before the split of body and mind, in the utopia of a thinking which was not caught in those oppositions. For them, as for Sohn-Rethel, Parmenides's theory of being is the beginning of philosophy.

Part I is essential and will require some dedication if you want to work on this legendary book. Part II is a more traditional look at modes of production. Part III looks to refunction historical materialism so that it is not caught up in Stalinist orthodoxies. This book has two polemics. The first is an attack on bourgeois philosophy, that is to say, empiricism, the fact, positivism. The other one is an attack on orthodoxy and Stalinism. As Gadamer might say, one must always keep the nature of the question and the audience in mind. Who is he arguing against now? What are the positions that are under fire, and for what purpose? Going back to our previous discussion, his question will be: Where do Kant's categories come from? This is a question which can be asked in many ways. Kant scholars debate their historical origins and the validity of their deduction. Other kinds of questions are also possible. Could there be other kinds of categories? In our world of quantum physics, are there not other notions that ought to be understood as categories? Probably not, because the categories govern not only science but also daily life in some more ordinary way.

(Here I open a parenthesis. There are three parts to Hegel's *Logic*, an immense work in which Hegel develops what I think we can still call categories, and in which he shows that the progression of each of these categories undoes itself in some way. None of them are satisfactory in themselves and so they lead on to something else, something more complicated. In the *Phenomenology*, as you know, there is a similar kind of progression, which finally reaches the moment when there are no longer any complications, which would be the Absolute. What it is, nobody knows. Is it Hegel's own mind? Probably not. Is it history or God? Or capital? This is the connection that the theorists of value wanted to make. But the progression of the *Logic* is not the same as that of the *Phenomenology*. The first book of the *Logic* has to do with what the Germans call *Verstehen*, "understanding." That is our physical body in the world, and it begins with being. Why, exactly, is a major question—but isn't that the most obvious category? Things are. We are. Out of being, nothing, and becoming—and there are many problems with Hegel's transitions, but to deal with those is to enter into a discipline unto itself—we end up with quantity and measurement. So, instead of simply positing the existence of categories, as does Kant, Hegel wishes to show how they produce themselves. Somewhere in this enormous stream of movement, of figures, of transition and metamorphosis from one to the other, you can find Kant's categories. At a certain moment, understanding reaches its limits, and we pass into what happens in the mind, the categories of reflection. These are now much more intellectual-seeming categories, like identity and difference. When that is exhausted, we reach then what he calls "speculative philosophy"—speculative because it can't be argued in the usual sense—in which he distinguishes the meanings in the mind and the meanings in whatever exists outside the mind. Is it nature? At any rate, he calls it "life." Anyway, so much for Hegel.)

You can see how the problems posed in Hegel might suggest to somebody like Sohn-Rethel that one need somehow to ground this matter of the categories and of abstractions. Where would they come from? Clearly, his first division is this first fall—or was it there all the time? When we are talking about origins, it doesn't make any sense to distinguish between consciousness and what we do with our bodies. So, it will be somehow in the act of doing things, of satisfying needs, of using our hands, all of those things will be involved in the production of the first categories. The category of the object, for example. Where does that come from? Schopenhauer used to say that Kant left out the category of the object. That is a very profound insight, and it will come back here in the form of reification. Somehow our work on things is going to produce a category of the independent object, of separation, of individuality. But that would be another stage.

Sohn-Rethel argues that abstraction comes from the market and the problem of value. At the moment of exchange, the produced objects must somehow be turned into thought. The social in its most elementary form will be the source of these values. How is that possible? The notion of the commodity is going to come from the separation of two kinds of value in the object: use-value and exchange-value. Value has no content in the sense that it can always be split into the form of exchange-value, the only form which is relevant for capital. It doesn't matter what you're going to do with the thing; value is based on something else. This is reflected in Sohn-Rethel's idea that use-value comes *after* exchange-value. It is not until the object has been produced and is now suspended between its buyer and its seller that we see it as a static thing, so to speak. The fact that we give it an exchange-value is accompanied by its independence as an object. Therefore, it is from that moment that we not only have a commodity but we have produced the idea of substance, first of all, of the unitary, because we have to know: Are we exchanging a single thing? Then: Is it larger or smaller? Quantity. And then, finally: What do I do with this? What is it good for, and what are its qualities?

So, out of exchange will come abstraction. If you didn't have a market society, why would you have to talk about use as the special or particular quality of an object? Everybody would simply be using things. There wouldn't be any need for an idea like use. It is the very idea of exchange that produces the idea of use and will produce its further qualifications. This is a single act which differentiates and produces second nature. So far, Sohn-Rethel is following Marx fairly closely. I'm not sure that it contradicts Marx at all, but what Sohn-Rethel has added is that the fact of exchange as a social act, the fact that I have to go find another person in order to do something with my product, even if that search is mediated in certain ways, will produce categories, forms. One of the things we have to realize, something which underlies all of Marx's work, is the idea that labor itself is a commodity. In fact, it is really the other way around in Marx. It is the fact that labor is a commodity that makes things into commodities.

In Sohn-Rethel, it is a little different. You have seen already in Backhaus that Marx had different versions of the theory of commodities. There are at least four versions, as Backhaus says. But, for Sohn-Rethel, the commodification of labor will follow the commodification of things. That is, labor is not abstract to begin with, as you may well know. What we call labor, however, is a complete abstraction. Each thing we do is unique and special, just as each of us, we are told, is unique and special. At what point does labor become generalized enough as a concept for it to be hooked up to the money system of quantities, such that we can speak of it in terms of time and ultimately in terms of value, something which can apply to all the very different kinds of human effort that we now call "labor"? The most original—that is to say, the least orthodox—part of Sohn-Rethel's theory is to say that this moment comes much later. Nothing in Marx, I would say, either corroborates or contradicts it.

Marx directs his understanding of the labor theory of value against Proudhon. In short, Marx says that a wage system requires that a portion of work be surplus, and this surplus labor produces surplus value. In the rival socialist movements in the nineteenth century, most notably that of Proudhon, who was the founder of a certain political anarchism, it is possible to speak about and argue for a just wage, that is to say, being paid adequately for your work. You may recognize this idea because it has been taken up in a form of social democracy that still exists today. But, for Marx, a just wage is a myth. There is no just wage. All value will be connected to surplus value and surplus labor, which is extracted from the worker. Even if it is under some other system, like socialism, wage labor will involve surplus value and social reproduction on the basis of expanded production. So, it is a question of the political nature of this slogan, "a just wage." This is a union's demand. I don't say that the unions are Proudhonistic but that they are frozen in a pre-Marxian notion of what value and wages are. In our society, it's common sense. You have to ask for more money. In France, Proudhon was a very interesting figure. The Paris Commune, which is celebrated by the Marxist tradition, was Proudhonist. These were Proudhonian anarchists. Marx, you could say, appropriated the Commune for his own needs.

As Sohn-Rethel shows, a great deal is present in this moment of the exchange situation, how it transforms its elements, what it leaves out. In showing that it involves a real abstraction, out of which these Kantian categories are produced, he goes back before Kant and tries, in some sense, to tell the story of the emergence of the categories, not as some innate feature of human nature, but rather, as part of a history of the socialization of the human being. What is going on in that process? If you have, on the one hand, the production of abstraction in terms of objects and substances, then we have to have a force which turns them into those things in the first place. That would be reification in its literal sense, the turning of processes into things. The process of production in the early period is gradually being turned into objects but also into static abstractions. The abstraction is this vessel which includes all kinds of concrete but maybe unnamed things. I tend to think that reification in the broader sense of objectification is a universal process and that it is ambiguous, that is, that reification is positive—if you're trying to reify your thoughts in writing a paper or a novel, then you'll be very happy to produce an object out of those misty and unsubstantial things which are thoughts—and on the other hand negative—if somebody makes your labor into an object and pays you money for it, you may not be so happy. So, this notion of reification has no value; it can be positive or negative.

What distinguishes Marx and Hegel is that Hegel has a notion of objectification as intellectual production. All of Hegel is an immense but idealistic production process. What Marx does in the early writings, when he produces a theory of alienation, is to show, against Hegel, that not all objectification is positive. There is a negative dimension of objectification which is called alienation. Alienation means the separation of a worker from his object of production, from his tools, from his own life and time, and ultimately from his fellows, because, of course, in a competitive situation, your fellow worker can just as easily be an enemy, an adversary, who is fighting for a part of capital that, with layoffs and unemployment, you may not get. These are the four senses of alienation in Marx.[2] For all of them, the term is "separation." Then there is the question of what kind of autonomous system is being produced here. We'll save that for later. But the logic of separation and differentiation is crucial here, even though it is not formalized in the work of people like Sohn-Rethel, except in this initial, very dramatic gesture of separating intellectual and manual labor.

We'll move farther east and talk about Bahro next time.

October 14, 2021

2 See Karl Marx, *Economic and Philosophical Manuscripts* (1844), in *Early Writings*, trans. Rodney Livingstone and Gregor Benton (New York: Penguin, 1992), p. 322 ff.

14
Bahro

Among other things, the film that I assigned to you, *Deutschland im Herbst*, *Germany in Autumn*, by Rainer Werner Fassbinder and others, depicts the burial of the businessman who was killed by the Red Army Faction. The whole government is participating in this burial, images of which are superimposed on those of the alleged suicides in prison of the final RAF leaders, in particular, Andreas Baader. The weapons were allegedly smuggled in by their lawyers. They were in high-security prisons, so you can believe what you want to believe about all that. When something like these suicides happens, one is never to be blamed for assuming something else, and in left circles, that is exactly what was done.

The woman with whom Fassbinder argues in the middle of the film is, in fact, his own mother, who is from an earlier generation which experienced the early years of the Bundesrepublik. Kluge was the overall manager of this film, and his contribution is the section about the history teacher who is digging for history. This is literally a dig into history, replete with the teacher's spade. She is trying to find out about everything, about the past of Germany. She is a character in some of Kluge's longer pieces, and maybe we'll say a word about them when we get to Kluge.

This film is a document, and it was certainly very important. Some national events become national traumas; the Japanese had one with the subway poisonings, although they were having a perpetual one with the Sanrizuka airport movement, which was the longest lasting of all left uprisings; ours was, no doubt, the Kennedy assassination. Habermas likes to talk about these communicational events, and it seems to me that the Kennedy assassination in '63 was an unparalleled event, in the sense that, despite or because television had not really reached the proportions that it was to reach, everybody remembers exactly where they were when they heard about it. It was an unusual kind of communicational event that should be reckoned into all these other accounts. Since we're talking about Kennedy, I should also point out that, for Bahro, whom we'll get to in a minute, Willy Brandt would be the German equivalent of Kennedy—young, charismatic—though he wasn't assassinated. The assassination attempt on Rudi Dutschke, the student leader, and above all, the killing of the Iranian student, which is really the beginning of the German political '60s, signaled a change from *cinéma de papa*, "grandpa's cinema"—this being grandpa's government, in a sense, Eisenhower or Adenauer—into something new which promises a change in state policy. Let's leave off what kind of change that would have been for a moment.

So there are interesting parallels, and they give you a better sense of what this moment was like. In '69, Willy Brandt takes over as the first socialist chancellor. He isn't assassinated, but in a sense, he is assassinated by the East, by the discovery of their spy in his government, at which point he has to resign and is followed by managerial figures like Kohl, all of whom have very long terms, because that was what West Germany wanted or needed. But, by the time the Social Democrats come to power, they have already renounced any radical kind of program and have agreed to be the caretakers of the state. Far from a domestic affair, the change is in the relationship to the East. Brandt presides over the repressive laws that are put in place there, which are like those that Bush pushed through after 9/11, but also in intellectual business, with the *Berufsverbot*, the ban on teaching by radicals, which was particularly important because it allowed them to get rid of all kinds of troublemakers. The only reason something similar didn't happen here is because, on the one hand, we have many private universities, and on the other, because our repressions of the Left had already been made popular by victories in wars. The victory in World War I was followed by the Palmer Raids and all kinds of repressions of radicals and communists; World War II was followed by McCarthyism. But we lost the Vietnam War, so it did not lead to an equivalent red-baiting and communist hunting in that period, although plenty of other kinds of repression happened. Nonetheless, some radicals came into positions in the university. Today is another turning point in the politics of the university.

At any rate, this did not happen in West Germany; there weren't any more wars. When the Social Democrats come to power, suddenly the Left, which had lived in a certain condition when the Social Democrats were out of power, now sees that it must take its own initiative. The student movement of the '60s begins. The Red Army Faction emerges in its wake. Soon there is the famous hijacking of the plane that lands in Mogadishu. The suicides take place soon after that. The massacre at the Munich Olympics has already happened. All those things have to be reckoned with in our understanding of the period. I've written an essay called "Periodizing the '60s."[1] I don't remember what my conclusions were, but it should give you an idea of what one has to do to think a period, and specifically to register the internationalist nature of this period, which will become public and conscious with what we call "globalization." It would be interesting to follow the use of this word, which comes into being after Vietnam. It is a sign that suddenly everybody realizes a different situation has emerged on the international level. (I'll come back to globalization when we talk about the East.)

The first radical movement of the '60s culminates in a series of failures. The end of the student movement is simultaneous with a new kind of worldwide economic stabilization or, at least, the hegemony of a new kind of worldwide system, which we recognize as neoliberalism. It is important that in the ideological situation of the Cold War, you could take sides—there is an idea that the collective action of individuals, parties, or groups has an effect, until suddenly there is a new feeling of helplessness and impotence. Individual acts become less plausible somehow, and, in a sense, the end of the Red Army Faction is as symbolic of that feeling, if you like, as is the whole change in the intellectual climate which we are tracing here.

Now those changes don't produce immediate effects, and, of course, none of this is synchronous, but they mark out a pattern, which serves as the background of this film. The discontinuous nature of the film, its mixture of fiction and documentary, is typical of Kluge. Kluge was a young lawyer, a great protégé and favorite of Adorno, but also a filmmaker, among many other things. He wrote the manifesto for the new wave of German filmmakers. We will have more to say about him soon.

1 Fredric Jameson, "Periodizing the 60s," in *The Ideologies of Theory* (London: Verso, 2008).

With that, I would like to go across the border and say a word or two about the DDR. What position are we to take on the East? First of all, you will say that it is gone, so we don't have to think about it anymore. But it was a very important experiment, it seems to me. Do we repeat the Western anti-communist propaganda or repeat the communist propaganda? The people who fled Hitler going to the East rather than the West, the people who went to Moscow, were believing communists. A lot of them had fought in the Spanish Civil War. Brecht, as always, was unique in that respect, because he fled through Moscow and then got out as quickly as he could via the trans-Siberian railway, Shanghai, and then California. Stalin was not very suspicious of him or the others who left in that manner. As Rudolf Bahro says, psychological explanations are not as useful as objective ones. At any rate, Stalin killed many of the war veterans in the purges. They asked one of the theorists of the bourgeoisie, "What did you do during the French Revolution?" He said, "I survived." For somebody like Lukács, who was sitting in Moscow at the time—they remembered him a little too late for the purge trials, not realizing he was with the Hungarians they wanted to get rid of—that was all there was to do.

The people coming back from Moscow to the Russian zone of occupation are, for the most part, believers. These people believe in communism and want to build it. Nobody liked Ulbricht, who was their leader and later the head of the DDR, but he was a faithful reproduction of Stalin in many ways, in the mistakes that he made as much as anything else. When they finally got sick of him in his old age, the East German politburo wrote to Brezhnev and said, in essence, "Free us from this person!" So, Brezhnev got rid of him without a word of thanks.

I propose to take the point of view of the critique of the regime by those believers, of whom Bahro was one, a much younger one at that time. With that, we come to the truly remarkable figure of Bahro. He was ten or eleven at the fall of the Nazi regime. He was a committed communist and did a variety of jobs for the government. He was always a troublemaker, criticizing the bureaucrats and the party, so he would periodically be fired and then be rehired. But it was, for him, the Soviet repression of the Dubček regime in Czechoslovakia in 1968 that was essential. At the same time, the students are driving de Gaulle to a secret rendezvous in Germany with his German occupying troops. There is a whole set of refugees from the party, the first coming with the Stalin–Hitler pact, then in the '50s, and then finally in '68, I would say a more definitive disillusionment with Dubček's idea of "socialism with a human face," a transformation of the regime, but not as with Imre Nagy in Hungary. Nagy's mistake was to propose to abandon the Warsaw Pact. The invasion of Hungary was Khrushchev's biggest mistake.

At this point, Bahro begins to write his book, which is finally published in the West in '77.[2] He is writing in the East, where he benefits from the sympathy of certain people in the regime. The regime of the Stasi is really there from the beginning, although it only later becomes a recognized institution. Once, in South Africa, I visited some teachers at a university, who were mostly white, and who were constantly raided by the apartheid regime. They were all young, clean-cut. I'll do an embedding; here's another story. In the Polish '68, when the students were being chased in a demonstration sparked by a play by Adam Mickievicz, *Dziady*, which was violently anti-Russian and made the authorities very mad, the secret police were chasing them into churches, which seemingly they respected in that period. Somebody asked the priests, who had let the students in but kept the secret police out: How do you know the difference? They're all young and look the same! Well, the priests say. They know who the secret police are because they always cross themselves when entering a church. In the South African situation, the apartheid regime would come into the university and take a look at their books. One time they pick out Althusser, *For Marx*. The secret policeman says, "Yeah, but the Repressive State Apparatus isn't any better." So, you have to understand, as Christa Wolf says later on when she was attacked for being interviewed by the Stasi and giving the names of her neighbors, that these were the only people they could talk to, the only intellectuals of the regime. They understood what we were protesting, the dissidents say; the apparatchiks and bureaucrats didn't.

So there was a lot of sympathy for Bahro's critiques in the East, but it couldn't be published, and, after a little bit of imprisonment and a perfunctory trial, they let him go west, where eventually he, like Beuys, joins the Greens and ends his life in a situation in which the hard left thinks he has become too mystical. You can see why. If you were an orthodox Marxist, you would likely find much of this unpalatable, largely because of the deemphasis of class, but also because of "the alternative." The book

2 Rudolf Bahro, *The Alternative in Eastern Europe*, trans. David Fernbach (London: Verso, 1978). Jameson assigned chapters 10 and 11 (pp. 253–348).

itself is called *Die Alternative*. The editors decided to retitle the translation, *The Alternative in Eastern Europe*. Incidentally, I have always objected to this decision, because it seems to me Bahro is proposing an alternative for the West as well, so I think the retitling is an abusive limitation on the value of this book. It is an extraordinary book, but I believe you have to learn to read it philosophically.

Bahro has his eye set on what the system is and how to transform it. This is, as I say, a protosocialist or communist perspective, and I think it is the great statement from the experience of the East on the political limitations and possibilities of the period. But he's using all of the anti-communist arguments from the West. This is fascinating. All of them get transformed. Yes, he agrees that this is a bureaucratic regime, but for him, bureaucracy was an important stage. I jump ahead to his two solutions, which are really one, because they both make a connection with Sohn-Rethel. The first is to abolish the division of labor. In the DDR, nobody was supposed to get a higher wage than anybody else, or at least not by any astronomical amount. In the East, when the Wall fell, people who were unaware were seemingly distressed to find out about all the luxurious dachas of the politburo. Bahro's solution is rather simple: Make sure that your rulers also collect the garbage one day a week. The second solution is much broader. Maoism being supreme in the '60s and '70s, he calls for a cultural revolution. What is this cultural revolution? Well, it is based on a concept that he has fashioned after Marx himself, as was the fad in a number of Western theorizations: surplus consciousness, the part of your mind that has not been completely organized and programmed by your work or by your bureaucratic position. The Italian intellectuals fastened on that moment in the *Grundrisse* where Marx talks about the general intellect—that is, the spread of scientific knowledge of enlightenment, the way in which the very knowledge of science itself has transformed the consciousness of people—and Bahro is doing something similar with the idea that surplus consciousness involves a surplus of knowledge that needs to be invested. Much of fascism was also understood as the product of, let's say, an excess of libidinal energy that has no place in the system. In Europe, for intellectuals, this has to do with the lack of jobs, as well as the enlargement of the educational system to accommodate thousands of new students, just as happened in the US in the '60s. In Germany, you have classes with thousands of students, but nowhere for them to go. So, they go out in the street.

I think the crucial innovation here is on the level of the mode of production. Bahro takes in an entirely new direction the whole second section of Sohn-Rethel on the modes of production and division of labor. You remember that there is a page or so in the introduction to Marx's *Contribution* in 1857 about his own intellectual progress and what he believes. This is really the summary of Marxism as it stood then, although there is nothing about the theory of value in it; the problem of value had to be elaborated elsewhere. He says there have been five or six modes of production. There is primitive communism, tribal society; slavery of ancient society; the Asiatic mode of production; feudalism; then capitalism. With that, Marx says, the prehistory of humanity ends. All of these modes of production are part of the prehistory of humanity, and history will begin with socialism. This is one of the great scandals in Marxist theory: When Engels writes up a theory of anthropology and the family after Marx's death, following Lewis Henry Morgan, there is one great absence, which is the Asiatic mode of production. What happened to it? In the early Frankfurt School, a man named Karl August Wittfogel, who was a Chinese specialist, wrote a book called *Oriental Despotism*, an anti-communist classic in which he says that Stalin exemplifies Marx's description of the Asiatic mode. Why did Engels leave it out? According to Wittfogel, Engels must have dimly suspected that socialism would result in this despotism, so he had to leave it out because it would have given the game away. In this respect, he replicates Bakunin's critique of Marx, in which he said that communism would be a bureaucratic, dictatorial society. Wittfogel simply anthropologizes this critique by defining the Asiatic mode of production as the oriental despotism which lies in store for any future socialism.

What is interesting here is that Bahro adopts the idea of oriental despotism, which was a very strong part of traditional anti-communism and, in fact, a very subtle part of it in the sense that it is supposed to have caught Marx criticizing himself in advance. But what is the Asiatic mode of production? For many people, a mode of production will be the way in which a certain type of production produces not only a material world but also a culture or superstructure all of its own. People have written against this notion of a base-superstructure distinction, the English especially. The Asiatic mode of production is the most doubted one of all. Perry Anderson has suggested we give the concept of the Asiatic mode a "decent burial."[3] The

3 Perry Anderson, *Lineages of the Absolutist State* (London: Verso, 2013), p. 548.

problem with getting rid of it as a category is that then almost everything else is feudalism, by default. You lose perspective, a shade of historical specificity, whereas, if you can differentiate the Asiatic mode, at least you can see how other forms might provide different analytical possibilities.

What distinguishes these theories is that, allegedly, and according to the record, the only societies in which capitalism imminently develops are those coming out of the feudal mode of production. That is to say, capitalism has only originated in feudal societies, and the interesting way that people have defended this proposition is with the case of Japan. In another part of the world altogether there ensues a similar process to the European one, which furnished Marx with his example. Bahro adopts a similar principle here. Historically, there is a certain line, often identified with a second feudalism in the East, which can be traced in the transition from feudalism to absolute monarchy in the West, typically corresponding to a return to a greater feudalism. For Bahro, it would be called the Asiatic mode, whose exemplary line runs through Germany and Poland. There is a reason, then, why either the Mensheviks were right that tsarist society had to go through a democratic, capitalist period to arrive at socialism; the attempt to catch up to the West and to create a genuine socialism without passing through capitalism has to be dealt with in a different way. Bahro's position is that socialism must absolutely destroy the capitalist state but that the state was nonetheless necessary as a prestage for this process. What Stalin did in his so-called Asiatic mode was to produce this state, to ready it for destruction, which will then generate a kind of structure that can be transformed into socialism.

The point is that you can distinguish feudalism from the Asiatic mode very simply. Feudal societies have aristocracies, because they deal with relationships between the various nobles and their separate demands. The Asiatic mode does not have an aristocracy; it has a bureaucracy, as was developed in an exemplary way in China, where the state and bureaucracy form the conditions from within which capitalism, in some sense, has to survive. It is not often enough asked what the state means in these situations. In the '30s, the great innovation of the state was the notion of planning. The idea of the five-year plan—my God, why didn't we think of it before! State planning was like a thunderbolt in political thinking. In the United States, there was the Tennessee Valley Authority. The TVA was to be the first great state enterprise under the New Deal. For its part, fascism was understood as a regime in which at least the armaments plans, but potentially all production, followed the dictates of the state. This is also what Pollock meant by his notion of monopoly capitalism. Monopoly doesn't just mean big enterprises; it means planning according to certain dictates. It is suddenly recognized that the nature of the state is to plan, not just to be the board meeting of the capitalist class, the way it was in the nineteenth century. No, the state can develop its own autonomy and set its own quotas, agendas, and regulations. During the war, this will be the function of a great many states which may not have much else in common. You don't have to wait for some development in political theory to understand what planning becomes, especially in the United States, where it persists after the war and develops into the military-industrial complex, that is, a state in which the Depression has been solved not by Roosevelt's New Deal domestic measures but by warfare and the army. This is also the case in Nazi Germany; Hitler's great triumph was that Germany never felt the Depression, at least not in the way that other countries did, in part because they were busy rearming, although that is not quite how people understood it at the time. If you isolate this notion of planning, which was the most stunning conviction of political theorists in the '30s and '40s, you understand better what Bahro means by this reformulation of bureaucracy and leadership. As for the USSR, Bahro is quite explicitly not interested in psychological accounts of Stalin as a cult of personality. The philosophical presupposition of this position is that, in the East, a genuine socialism would necessarily emerge in a different way out of a state bureaucracy.

The necessity of the state in Bahro is followed by the work of cultural revolution to destroy the state. We don't have time to discuss everything this implies, but it hinges on a notion of total knowledge. We can discuss total knowledge negatively in terms of Taylorism. The great hero of nineteenth-century putschism, Auguste Blanqui, says that nothing is so disheartening as not to be able to get an overall view of a game on which life depends. This is exactly what Taylor says, but the other way around: Individual workers must not be allowed to understand the totality of the production process the way a manager does. We must produce the place of the manager, of total knowledge, in such a way that the workers cannot assume it. So disheartening! What creates the sense of misery is this lack of knowledge, of access to the totality. I think this would be Bahro's reply to both the aestheticization of labor in Marcuse or in the Italians and to other notions of what is attractive in leisure, what should replace work, and so on. There is a specific satisfaction in this access to total knowledge. This is not knowledge in some intellectual sense. This is about an awareness of one's position in a process which is necessarily larger than any individual. There is a notion of space involved here, a kind of cognitive mapping, supplemented with an emphasis on work-gratification, which is a more interesting notion of labor than can be found in many of Bahro's Western counterparts.

Whereas the old way of dealing with this problem is to make a pluralism out of Marx so as to account for all the different modes of production, Bahro refuses this option; he is aware that surplus consciousness can violently pass into imperialism, into capitalism, but with important differences. The passage from a slave society into capitalism will be different from that of bureaucratic society to capitalism, for example. Older modes of production persist in capitalism itself. The patriarchy, sexism, the position of women, subalternity of various kinds, the dominance of the city over the country—let's say these kinds of oppression are not forms of capitalist oppression. Capitalism may be sexist, for example, but one certainly must be able to deal with the role of sexism in earlier modes of production and its persistence beyond them. Obviously, slavery is a significant survival, and one doesn't have to accept Bahro's notion of survival to account for its modern forms. For Bahro, the liquidation of those vestiges and survivals is central to cultural revolution. Marxism cannot be attacked for not taking them into account, Bahro says, because they are not technically part of the mode of production of which Marxism is a critique. This part of Bahro can help us to see capitalism as an impure system which has managed to incorporate plenty of inheritances. Today, one might appeal to Fanon or other theorists of decolonization for a way of thinking about the particular social inheritances of race.

What happens to the party in Bahro? He proposes a league of communists—a Yugoslav expression—and that it be independent of other parties, that is to say, that it allow the existence of other parties in order to be able to argue against these other parties and to acquire its own rationale, to make its converts through argument. Finally, there is the evocation of the Paris Commune, which then returns as the model for the new state.

Bahro's book is a complete revolution in Marxist and socialist thinking, alighting a revolutionary path which really was not taken. Bahro himself went back to the East. There was a long period in which the possibility of an

Eastern state was proposed, but so much money was spent by the Western parties that it was obviously impossible to reverse course at that point.

Next time, we will talk a little bit about how Bloch fits into this picture. Clearly, he cannot be counted as an example of Eastern thinking. He is a member of an older generation; he was a contemporary and good friend of Lukács. Max Weber would hold unofficial gatherings in Heidelberg, and Lukács and Bloch were both participants. They went two different ways. Bloch was the first great Marxist thinker to utilize the explosive notion of utopia. His first book is a blast of utopian thought which includes all of its predecessors. It is prophetic. When we get to his later masterpiece, *The Principle of Hope*—which he wrote in the East, though he began working on it in the '30s—we get a final testament to thoughts that began elsewhere. It is an encyclopedia of utopian thought. We'll come back to it next time.

October 19, 2021

15

Bloch, Enzensberger, Negt and Kluge

In Germany, the student movement begins in 1964 with the visit of Moïse Tshombe, the ruler of the materially rich part of the Congo and the murderer of Patrice Lumumba. At least in Germany, the '60s begin with the student movement and stop in '77, precisely with what you have seen in *Germany in Autumn*, that is, with the end of the RAF. This German "autumn" doesn't have any equivalent in the DDR, because the ideology of the East, party socialism, has nothing to do with such demonstrations of terror as those of the RAF (although the East did hide and save some of those who fled after '77 for quite a long time, until '89 or '90, when the West was able to get its hands on the relevant Stasi documents).

But, today, I want to talk about Bloch before returning to this moment through the prism of the public sphere. Bloch is obviously a much older figure, coming from the generation of the '20s and '30s. He taught at Leipzig. Bahro was not much interested in Bloch's teachings, but other people were. I think it would be wrong to say he was forced out of the DDR. He was in West Germany giving a talk, and he did not go back, but he never attacked the regime. He kept the faith, so to speak. You could certainly think, as I suppose Ulbricht did, that Bloch was less a Marxist than a prophet, particularly the Bloch of *The Spirit of Utopia*.

I'll give you an overview of his career, and then we'll look briefly at the later writings that I recommended to you.[1] The catchphrase from *The*

1 Ernst Bloch, *The Principle of Hope, Volume 1*, trans. Neville Plaice, Stephen Plaice,

Spirit of Utopia, which covers a lot of ground, is the "darkness of the lived moment," *die Dunkelheit des gelebten Augenblicks*. This idea, the blind spot of the present, is enunciated in a prophetic tone which is even more striking in German than in the translation, which is not a philosophical or theoretical fashioning. I've quoted this phrase often because I think it is very interesting: Kierkegaard said that the present is not a temporal idea. In a sense, Bloch is following Kierkegaard's insight. Normally we think of the present as what we are conscious of. No, he says. The present is precisely what we are *not* conscious of. But there is a part of the present that we can uncover because it appears, so to speak, in our anticipation of the future. The future is somewhere in this darkness of the present. The prophet is the one who can see this union of the present and the future. The reference is always to the great biblical prophets, who are evoked primarily to differentiate the role of the prophet from the intellectual or political leader and thus to reassert the necessity for Marxism of a less programmatic understanding of the future.

In the '30s, he developed this approach to the darkness of the present through an idea that you will perhaps be familiar with: nonsynchronous synchronicity.[2] This emerges from his account of fascism, which presents a variety of levels of historical time as happening at once. The standard Marxist phrase, developed in the Soviet context, for the overlap between different phases of historical development is "uneven development," a phrase which is used to explain the simultaneity of various capitalist and non-capitalist modes of production in a single time and place, typically a single country. Fascism, for him, clearly represents the persistence of the archaic, or the misrecognition of a return to the archaic as a path into the future.

The Paris Commune was a climax of Bahro's history of Marxism, but a different set of references are more common in Germany. There was, for instance, a quickly repressed commune in Mainz which escaped the domination of the imperial forces for a while. But I'll give you a different reference. In the English '60s, what had to be dug up again (à la Kluge) was the English Revolution, Cromwell's dictatorship, the Levellers, the Diggers, and the great figure of Gerrard Winstanley, who would have

and Paul Knight (Cambridge, MA: MIT Press, 1995), introduction (pp. 3–20) and chapter 15 (pp. 114–78).

2 Ernst Bloch, "Nonsynchronism and the Obligation to Its Dialectics," trans. Mark Ritter, *New German Critique* 11 (1977), pp. 22–38.

been the utopian figure of that first national or bourgeois revolution. The English Revolution remains expressed in religious terms, which have to be translated to see its as-yet-unrealized *novum*, to speak like Bloch. In China, something similar had recently happened with the overthrow of the Mings. But Bloch will deal with something else: the peasant rebellion, the crucial moment in German history that he wants to resurrect, if you like. Bloch wrote on the ringleader of this revolution, Thomas Müntzer. Luther set forth forces in the peasantry that he couldn't control, a peasant uprising which attracts some sympathy among the lesser nobility. The peasant revolution nonetheless fails. Luther is as violent in his language as he ever was about the Whore of Babylon or the Catholic Church. He writes denunciations of the peasants and urges that the nobles drown them in blood, which, of course, they do. In the East, there is now an immense monument to Frankenhausen, which was the great battle of the uprising. The East Germans understood that the uprising was a part of their socialist past, so to speak. At any rate, Bloch's book is important to register in this regard because it means that there is a precedent for Bloch's religious language, a precedent which is identified in his own work.

Bloch's ontology of the future also involves a concept he calls the "not-yet," which is hidden away somewhere in this darkness of the present. Our great prophet, the late Donald Rumsfeld, in his theory of historical time, which he formulated while speaking about Iraq, says that we don't just have the known and the unknown. We have the known-known, the knowledge we know we have; the known-unknown, what we don't know but can look up on Google or in books; and the unknown-unknown, what we don't know that we don't know. In a sense, what Bloch calls the not-yet is the unknown-unknown. But there is also the category of the unknown-known, what we don't know that we know, something which is known but hasn't quite been worked out yet. The not-yet or *novum* may also appear there.

I want to say that we ought to think of Bloch's achievement in grammatical terms. I've always loved that Varro, in the first version of his fundamental grammar of the Latin language, forgot to include the future tense. That is the whole message of Bloch: We have forgotten the future tense. What is the future tense? The future tense is very often empty or simply formal; it has no content, because we don't know the future yet. And yet, the futures that we posit contain nothing but what we know already. They don't contain this richness of the future. Not only prophecy but the future tense itself is only possible if the future can be found inside the present.

In the negative moment of Bloch's analysis, he will identify what represses the future: everything that prevents us from seeing this experience of the not-yet, from feeling it, from living it. He attributes much of this repression to a bad objectivity. We would call it positivism, the ideology of the empirical fact. How can the fact have a future? It exists already. How can anything empirically perceived have a future? Bad objectivity of this kind blocks all thoughts of the future. Then there are other kinds of resistance to the future, which he needs to register for his system. If it has become impossible to access this sense of the future, then he needs to be able to say why. He needs a doctrine of futurological repression. A significant aspect of this repression is a certain resistance to the future, a resistance to change, a horror of change. People don't want to change, or they have chosen to remain in their particular unhappiness, if you prefer a Sartrean existential version of this futurological repression.

The first part of *The Principle of Hope* is a detective work in which he finds these traces of the future everywhere in daily life. We could think of aspirin. Aspirin projects, if not a utopia, then at least a future in which you will not have your headache. Everywhere in daily life, there are sediments of these other futures. To uncover how we ourselves produce these potential futures requires an analysis of fantasy and daydream. The daydream has to be radically distinguished from the nighttime dream. As Freud understands it, the nighttime dream taps infantile experience, but the daydream is something in which the ego is more actively involved, in which you are still able to project yourself into the various positions of a fantasy. In Bloch, the daydream is the personal shell of something impersonal. The daydream is what we project our class feelings into, but it must go beyond merely manifesting those feelings. In a comment that would obviously alienate the regime, he says that we must dig into ideology to find what is *utopian* in it. I'll start using that word in the particular sense which Bloch gives it as early as 1919: Utopia is the ultimate projection of the futuristic not-yet.

There is a potent politics—a politics which can also be found in Benjamin —in the idea that, if fascism is an archaic distortion of the principle of hope, then we ought to be able somehow to find the progressive response to the opportunity that it has seized. It is a kind of politics in which you try to recuperate the energies of the Right, of fascism, to appropriate them for the Left, for revolution. It is certain that much of the Nazi movement, for example, mimics a revolutionary movement. Is it possible to capture the energies unleashed by the Right and turn them in a different direction, or do they remain wedded to *ressentiment* and privilege?

Everything I'm saying is quite topical today, but I'm not necessarily going to spell it out. This is obviously a major political issue as we witness the rise of seemingly revolutionary energies in various strata of the Right. The anti-fascist politics of Bloch doesn't presuppose that the magic formula for recapturing those energies has been found, but Bloch implies that such a recapturing is dialectically present in the sense that, if it is possible to identify a resistance to the future, then that resistance cannot simply be understood as a force in its own right but only as a force relating to the horizon of a particular future. If you reconstruct Bloch's politics as an opposition between the utopian instinct and its repression, then one can dialectically identify the two in such a way that some passage from one to the other might be possible. Of course, there is also a passage in the other direction. That is to say, it seems not only possible but probable that fascism itself can appropriate utopian instincts and is itself a form of distorted utopianism. We don't have time to go beyond that, but I hope I've given you a sense of how Bloch is completely unique. He can also be very frustrating. *The Principle of Hope* says the same thing over and over again, but I hope to have shown that there is a use for it beyond its immediate references.

As a way of entering into a discussion of Enzensberger, I quickly want to raise the issue of translation, particularly as it concerns the term *Öffentlichkeit*, sometimes translated as "public sphere." It seems to me that this expression is rarely used unless speaking about East Germany. What is the term we use when they say "public sphere"? I think it is "the media." So, we see there is already an immense gap between the objects in question. It is true that Enzensberger bridges analyses of the public sphere with the topic of media, not only because he uses the term "media," but also because he is quite aware of the problems involved in translating between the two. But there is, of course, a third term here. We have "media" in English, *Öffentlichkeit* in German, and then "civil society," which occasionally rears its head. That is a translation of *bürgerliche Gesellschaft*, "bourgeois society." There is a wordplay here on the meaning of *Bürger*, which could mean "a bourgeois" but also, allegedly, "a citizen." The people who translated Enzensberger wanted to avoid the term "bourgeois" and to translate *bürgerliche Gesellschaft* in some respectable way. The relevant reflection on civil society goes back to the eighteenth century, before it is taken up in Hegel and Marx. "Public sphere" suggests a space, whereas "media" suggests an object, a device, or a transmission. Both are connected to a sense of the public, but *Öffentlichkeit* comes out of a different meaning of "public," one which does not have to do with any strict opposition to the private. In this sense, *Öffentlichkeit* has been subsumed into the tradition of philosophizing civil society in ways that are not visible in English. Enzensberger, however, avoids this discussion completely and really does write about the media.

Enzensberger is a poet and the longtime editor of *Kursbuch*, perhaps the most important leftist periodical in the '60s. It had a staggering circulation. One asks oneself how such an immense circulation was possible. Well, he says, in each of these German villages, there is perhaps one person who is a fledgling leftist or intellectual, and they're completely isolated from the wider political world; so, they get a copy of this journal every so often, and they find out what's happening. In other words, this journal is able to make its way around Germany in numbers which don't match the circulation of leftist journals in other countries because it fulfilled a social and political role that didn't have to be filled in other countries.

Enzensberger is an eloquent, even elegant figure, a kind of dandy of the Left, not associated with Marxism much but not with anarchism either, a gadfly both of the East and of the Left in the West. He spent some time in Cuba and wrote on what he calls "revolutionary tourism." Later, when the '60s ended, his politics ended as well. I've heard him give talks more recently in which he says the best thing for Germany today would be for it to be boring. "We Germans," he says, in effect, "must now be average. When Germany gets interesting the world should shudder." After *Kristallnacht* in '38, Goebbels said in his speeches, "There! Now people can't say we Nazis are boring." Enzensberger's late remark that it is better to be boring has to be taken in that context, but also in the context of the post-Romantic, post-Schlegel shift from beauty to interest.

Enzensberger's "Constituents of a Theory of the Media" was a very powerful essay.[3] It is an attack on left-wing puritanism as much as Stalinism. But his most important observation is that Marxism has no theory of

3 Hans Magnus Enzensberger, "Constituents of a Theory of the Media," *New Left Review* I/64 (Nov./Dec., 1970), pp. 13–36.

the media. One of the tasks of the student movement, of which he is one of the leaders, is to invent a new theory of how the media can be used. I'm not sure he succeeds in doing so here. He begins with the obvious answer to the notion of media as propagandistic, namely the utopia of response, of being able to reply. The radio is nice because the people who listen to it can't reply. You can't reply to television. How would a reply to media be possible, a responsivity in which you can hear the reply of the other side, of the underclasses? When Mitterrand came to power in 1981, he legalized all the outlying broadcasting stations, opening France up to all kinds of oppositional media. Everybody was very excited, and the Trotskyists, as always—like when the Soviet Union was opened up under Gorbachev—thought that, finally, now that they could get Trotsky's message out, everything would change. It turned out that most of these stations fizzled out into nothingness and had no listeners. The only successful ones were a gay broadcasting channel and an Israeli channel, their success having nothing to do with their ostensible ideologies but simply because they had good disc jockeys and played good music. That was the end of the open media.

So, appropriating free speech in the sense of the right to reply is not necessarily the solution if people are less interested in political expression than commodities, as Negt and Kluge will show. But this is a very important document in the German '60s, insofar as it provoked a greater reflection on the question of the media. The other major document, the first to develop the formula of the public sphere, is Habermas's dissertation, published in 1962. It traces a history of the public sphere that begins with the famous coffeehouses in London in the eighteenth century, where a literal space for discussion and argumentation is opened up. We know that, for Habermas, reason is being able to give reasons, to justify one's beliefs and actions, to argue. In a sense, this category of civil society or bourgeois society that he is analyzing is essentially a space for argument, not a space for the multiplicity of opinions or repressed ideologies. Already in *On Liberty*, John Stuart Mill says that even a very small minority position should be allowed its own publication, an idea which forms the basis of liberal repressive tolerance, or at least of an empty evocation of freedom. By laying the foundations for this openness to debate, Habermas is deducing a rationale for representative democracy. That is, in order for there to be representative democracy, there should be a public sphere that facilitates the contest of arguments. But Habermas does not produce a manifesto; it is, rather, a history. One way of beginning a critique of this foundational history is to ask what it leaves out, not empirically but theoretically. In a way, even though it claims to be providing a basis for dissent, it leaves out the negative. He has a confidence that, if *Öffentlichkeit* is allowed its right, if it functions properly, reason will prevail. As we saw in *Dialectic of Enlightenment*, Adorno and Horkheimer did not exactly share this confidence.

Obviously, there are many changes that have happened in the public sphere and the media since Enzensberger's theory and Habermas's history. Negt and Kluge's reply concerning the proletarian public sphere is itself already fifty years old, and it is also in many ways rather out of date.[4] In this regard, I think you may find their introduction enlightening, because it shows why they see no reason to change any of their positions in light of more recent technological and political developments. Like with Mitterrand's opening up of the airwaves, it is not clear that their notion of a counter-public-sphere makes any difference. In the current *Öffentlichkeit*, does an oppositional public sphere exist, or is it somehow appropriated by the prevailing forces? These are questions I think we have every right to ask Negt and Kluge, although they certainly allow us to think of these problems more comprehensively than Habermas or Enzensberger do.

Negt and Kluge approach the matter of *Öffentlichkeit* in terms of the concept of experience. For much of the theoretical left in the West, at the time they are writing, the concept of experience is associated with the taboo of humanism. The most violent theoretical arguments in the French and English left are directed against a humanistic concept of experience which presupposes an individual possessed of a certain wholeness and self-transparency. The sort of humanism that you find defended in a text like Sartre's "Existentialism Is a Humanism" later comes under attack in the revolt against the philosophy of the subject, bourgeois ideology, Cartesian individualism, but which Heidegger's "Letter on Humanism" refused as a reified name or value. The point of the structuralist critique of experience is to find a way to avoid positing the human being as the

4 Alexander Kluge and Oskar Negt, *Public Sphere and Experience: Analysis of the Bourgeois and Proletarian Public Sphere*, trans. Peter Labanyi, Jamie Owen Daniel, Assenka Oksiloff (London: Verso, 2016). Jameson assigned both forewords and the first chapter. Other assigned works by Negt and Kluge are discussed in the following lectures. See also Jameson's overview of their work, "On Negt and Kluge," in *The Ideologies of Theory* (London: Verso, 2008), pp. 194–221.

center of the universe, the measure of all things, but rather, following Freud's Copernican Revolution, as a satellite of the whole system, just as the earth is the satellite of the sun. In short, the attack on humanism sees individual human experience as an effect of many contingent factors.

For Negt and Kluge, this is not the case. Their notion of experience, perhaps a more Hegelian notion, is not exhausted by a phenomenological notion of the subject, although it seems to me this notion of experience is not completely incompatible with phenomenology. Their use of this concept is very clear. Whereas the public sphere is perhaps supposed to be some advanced, enlightened, literate form of communal consciousness, Negt and Kluge remind us that, out in the countryside, this enlightenment has not yet reached the people. If the whole purpose of a public sphere is to include more and more people, like the great literacy campaigns in the Soviet Union and in Cuba, its properties will be shaped by the particular way it expands from one part of society to another. For Negt and Kluge, this expansion derives from a class position. Bourgeois experience is incompatible with proletarian experience, so the question is how one can imagine people with proletarian experience accessing and participating in bourgeois institutions, or rather, why such access would be desirable. It should be possible to create a *proletarian* public sphere, a place in which a different kind of experience can find not only its means for expression and reflection but also its development.

For "proletarian," I think one could read "subaltern." Like Bahro, Negt and Kluge understand that the category of subalternity covers a much wider range of social positions than does the notion of the proletariat. Marx's politics always understood that factory workers—which is not the same as proletarians—are going to be a minority; there is never going to be a majority of the population who are actual factory workers. Meanwhile, those factory workers are also consumers, so there is a way in which they participate in a part of the bourgeois experience, but there are many other social strata which are part of subalternity, not necessarily the proletariat. I think Negt and Kluge take that for granted.

Here we have to introduce another interesting leitmotif in these discussions. The word "emancipatory," which comes out of the late Frankfurt School, has replaced the word "revolutionary." This alternate terminology could accommodate Gramsci's two kinds of politics, wars of attack or trench warfare, a revolutionary politics or a politics of the famous long march through the institutions, leaving aside the matter of how you evaluate those two politics. One is a politics of gradual infiltration and appropriation, the other one of head-on attack and the destruction of the enemy. In that sense, "emancipatory" is a useful word to cover both of those approaches to the political. You don't need to decide in advance which side of those alternatives you wish to endorse. I do, however, think that the later Frankfurt School allows the force of the revolutionary to disappear into a weaker post-Marxist position. In other words, if you don't feel that you're imprisoned by something, then there is no point in trying to be liberated from it. To be emancipated, you have to be emancipated *from* something, and if you don't think you're suffering, then how or why would you want to be emancipated?

Kant defined the Enlightenment as the process by which people free themselves from their status as minors, in the legal sense of the term. In a monarchy, "the people" is a minor who does not yet have the maturity to judge and make decisions for themselves; someone assumes that role and makes decisions for you. For Kant, the French Revolution was a step out of that minority, a moment when it was possible to become *mündig*. "Emancipatory," in many of its modern uses, doesn't have any relation to this Enlightenment-era notion of emancipation as maturation. Nonetheless, it continues to have a meaning with respect to autonomy, because the emancipation of proletarians is in some sense an overcoming of their minority status.

Negt and Kluge do have a notion of development or education, for which they use the expression "learning processes," *Lernprozesse*. I've never heard anyone use this expression in English, except in connection with these translations, but it makes a lot of sense. Here you have a population which has been subjected to a long period of brainwashing under the Nazi dictatorship and which emerges as an occupied country, a country lacking *Mündigkeit*, in the sense that it is being overseen by an occupier, whether American or Soviet. The question comes back to Bahro's cultural revolution: How do you transform this population? Apparently, nobody is a Nazi anymore, so what are they? They are nothing, degree zero. If this is so, how is the population to be trained and educated? Who is going to do the educating? That is why the matter of learning processes is going to come to the fore not only in Negt and Kluge's work but also in the work of contemporaneous thinkers like Gadamer. All these theorists are prompted by their shared historical situation to consider how, and to what end, learning processes can transform the experience of a population.

The notion of learning processes runs throughout Kluge's works, which span an immense range of topics and styles. Kluge's first book of stories is *Lebensläufe*, which has two English translations: *Attendance List for a Funeral* and *Case Histories*. I would say that *Lebensläufe* is the best introduction to Kluge's writing. There is another characteristic one—the title is translated as *Air Raid*—which constructs a nontraditional narrative about the bombing of his birthplace, Halberstadt. Finally, there is a book called *Learning Processes with a Deadly Outcome*, translated by one of our own students, Chris Pavsek, who has written on Kluge's filmmaking.[5] This book is a futurological experiment with Nazi astronauts on the moon at the end of the world.

How, then, is *Öffentlichkeit* to be seen in light of those learning processes which shape our experience? Again, this is more powerful as a negative diagnosis of the problems facing a proletarian public sphere than as a solution to those problems. In a sense, if there had been a "solution" to be tried, it would have been secession, which was tried in the West for a long time. Sartre used to complain that the Communist Party, which, in France, was quite large, had its own newspaper and publishing houses, its own culture, its own festivals; in other words, it could exclude bourgeois writers. A working class was connected to the Communist Party such that it didn't need any other institutions, such that it would seem possible to build a proletarian public sphere as an enclave within bourgeois society. But this was not taken into account as an option in Germany, even though it would be possible to analyze the absence of this option in terms of the *potential* proletarian public sphere. In Germany, opposition was understood in the sense of a society in which a wide range of populations were intermingled, as is the case with us today, but in which the Communist Party in the French style had ceased to exist.

Obviously, any effort at opposition was faced with the problem of commodification (which is not, I think, properly registered in Enzensberger). The power of the bourgeois public sphere is that it can commodify anything that appears within it; it turns facts into finished products; it even gives the human the semblance of a product. The notion of the public sphere can be understood according to the notions not only of

5 Alexander Kluge, *Learning Processes with a Deadly Outcome*, trans. Christopher Pavsek (Durham, NC: Duke University Press, 1996). See Christopher Pavsek, *The Utopia of Film: Cinema and Its Futures in Godard, Kluge, and Tahimik* (New York: Columbia University Press, 2013).

self-sameness in Adorno's sense but also of reification: There is a bourgeois way of consuming finished products, the contents of the public sphere, news, events, anything which can be turned into a commodity for the bourgeois public to consume. The subaltern or working-class public can be trained to consume in the same way, and therefore it needs some way of affirming its own horizon of experience instead of allowing it to be invaded by the products of the bourgeois public sphere. In the bourgeois public sphere, each individual is also endowed with privacy, with the illusion of an unpublicized experience. The bourgeois public sphere functions to create a notion of the private, of the personal, and of the intimate and subjective, if you like, in order to compensate for what is otherwise experienced as the widespread commodification of the public sphere. It, therefore, also produces the possibility of taking over the place of what could be the proletarian private sphere. As you can probably already see, all of the positions we have examined so far, even if they can be translated into each other's terms, remain in some contradictory opposition with each other.

I don't think Negt and Kluge get much further than intimating the possibility of a proletarian public sphere. Negt himself was a leader of the student movement and a student himself of the Frankfurt School. He was not, however, one of the innovative thinkers of the student movement, who tended to arrive with the next generation. He didn't have the kind of Marxist formation that somebody like Rudi Dutschke or some of the other student leaders from the East had. So, he has a different perspective than some of the other '60s people, which is maybe what makes his collaboration with Kluge so interesting. It is his intervention to which Habermas reacted, calling him a left fascist. This was one of Habermas's most deplorable moments, and I think he regretted his attack, since it was against one of Adorno's students. We'll go on with Negt and Kluge next time.

October 21, 2021

16

Negt and Kluge, Gadamer

I've been trying to explain to you how the absent frameworks of collectivity —it could be the nation or some other group—impacts the individual personality. The collective and the individual are not parallels. Although their relationship is a long-standing problem in political philosophy, it is not something that anybody has really worked out. I always think of the languages of small countries, like Hungarian, which apparently has some very great poets, but nobody else is going to know about them. Hungary's connection with Austria under the empire was very important for it; Hungary, in fact, supplied the army, so there was a reason for this combination, the Austro-Hungarian Empire. But, after the war, once it has been reduced to a small country, it must distinguish itself in other ways under the threat of becoming provincial. But what is the other feeling, the bygone feeling of being part of an empire? Hardt and Negri have written about this problem, but I think they have not posed it directly.[1] We have to pose it directly today, insofar as the United States, in my opinion, is not a nation-state of the European type but is rather something else, something that has accompanied the rise of globalization. What I want to say is that one's connection with groups, both noninstitutionalized and institutionalized, is profoundly formative of one's situation, despite being absent from the immediate horizon of experience.

1 See Michael Hardt and Antonio Negri, *Empire* (Cambridge, MA: Harvard University Press, 2000).

In any case, the narrative I've been playing around with is that, in year zero, the divided Germany has no past to affirm. The Hitler period was unsuccessful. Weimar was unsuccessful. The monarchy was unsuccessful. They start from zero. There is nothing from which to construct the new nation-state. Nonetheless, a gradual process of construction ensues in both Germanies. National identity is only reached for West Germany—and probably in the East as well—in the early '60s, with the Wall. The Wall is the determinate episode for the East, because it announces that there is such a thing as the DDR, and it is marked by a boundary. In West Germany, I think the decisive moment arrives when Brandt comes to power, proving that it is possible to transition out of the Adenauer years. Until then, the Americans are in charge and Adenauer is their surrogate. When that period ends, something else begins—meaning the Left itself has an opportunity. That is to say, what also begins (again) is the Left. The youth movement's demonstrations are not quite the same as they are either in France or in the United States. The youth movement in West Germany is more like a political party. It is a political party that manages to express itself and to struggle in all kinds of ways. But it ends with the literal '60s, just as another, extraparliamentary violent movement begins, namely that of the Red Army Faction. Suddenly, all kinds of new problems are raised. Once a state is institutionalized, can it be challenged? Is there a social contract? These questions become unavoidable when, all of a sudden, this finally legitimate state, this national identity, is faced with its own use of violence. Immediately, repressive laws must be passed to put down the young people's expression of dissent.

I have insisted that the philosophies we are surveying have to be understood against the background of the emergence of these two states and the final incorporation of one into the other. As I will show you in a moment, Negt and Kluge have a different point of view on this trajectory than either Enzensberger or Habermas. Habermas's solution is simply to argue that, because the state is set up in a certain way, its citizens must behave in a certain way. The only interesting contact I've had with Habermas—I'll tell this story again—was when I saw him in a debate. Somebody in the audience asked him what he would do about extraparliamentary violence and lawlessness. At that point, nobody was thinking about violence from the Left, which was long gone, but rather that of the skinheads and what is now clearly a Nazi Party, particularly in the former East. I expected him to give us a long, philosophical solution about the nature of violence, this and that. But he simply brushed it off and calmly said, "We have laws."

As you may know, Kant was a great admirer of the French Revolution. He was an "enthusiast," which is a word that did not have a very good connotation in the eighteenth century, because it meant you were driven by an irrational force which caused you to believe that you were the source of truth. At any rate, Kant had an enthusiasm for the French Revolution which never left him. He did not renounce it during the Terror, when everybody else did. I mentioned his idea that never before in history has a people given itself a constitution. The whole idea of the written constitution is that it is the sign of the people's will, and therefore, in a sense, Habermas is inscribing himself in that tradition. It is based on a *Sollen*. Now that we have a written constitution, there is the problem of its application: You have the law, but how does it apply to individual cases? The cases are particular, so there has to be some hermeneutic in which you judge the individual cases on the basis of a necessarily abstract, written law, and there can never really be an end to this dynamic between law and case. That is, these two levels—the level of written generality, of universality, and the level of the individual event, individual people—are irreconcilable. The whole point of what Gadamer calls the juridical hermeneutic is that it must finally come to the moment in which you adjust these two codes so that they address each other; otherwise, there is no capacity for judgment. When Habermas says we have laws, it means that the ones who judge are legitimized by institutions and that the matter of interpretation is no longer open, or rather it is subject to the *Sollen*, the ethical obligation to fit oneself into the demands of the law.

I think Negt and Kluge have no systematic solution to these questions, so I'll have to look at their work in pieces. Their aim is not to figure out who should own the television stations, what kind of news we should get, and so on, but rather how bourgeois experience is modeled by our setup in the public sphere and our position within it. It is not the content of the bourgeois public sphere which bears the greatest importance but rather the fact that it functions to conceal totality. Its function is to make it impossible for you to see the social structure as a whole and to see your position in it, to see how the system gives you a certain position. That is its ideological effect. You can say, then, that the ideological effect of the bourgeois public sphere is formal. Nobody believes that the medicines advertised on TV do all the things they promise; nobody believes what the politicians promise in their speeches. But the form of the address is what makes it impossible for you to judge where your position is.

Then there is the portion of their work about fantasy. On the one hand, one could say fantasy is hope in Bloch's broad sense. On the other hand, one could say it is narrative in some more contemporary or colloquial sense. Again, it is both a form of alienation and an acknowledgement and a critique of alienation, as they say. Many of the stories Kluge tells in his later books exist somewhere in this ambiguity between acknowledgement and critique. These narratives can no longer be affirmative of what they represent. That is, they can no longer be political in the sense that they tell you what to do, but they can undermine the very category of fantasy. What kind of a solution is that? Their solution is cultural revolution. It is not a new system of *Öffentlichkeit*, but, rather, a new system of experience which involves such learning processes as one finds scattered across their works. It is a very rich book, but you mustn't expect anything systematic, like Enzensberger's program or Habermas's injunction to participate in normative communicational acts, with its confidence in the recognition of the other.

We must move on now to Gadamer. *Truth and Method* is a fundamental work by somebody who has a remarkable background in philosophy and a remarkable mind.[2] He will make some distinctive proposals in the area of the hermeneutic. If you want to find a school for him, it would be hermeneutics. And, since he says so, his is a hermeneutics that comes out of Heidegger. When Gadamer was a student, Heidegger said to him that he really is not suited for philosophy at all; it would be better to learn the classical languages and to become a teacher of Greek and Latin. Later, Heidegger may have changed his mind.

Gadamer takes up the second of the two lines we've been pursuing, one coming out of the Frankfurt School, the other out of Heidegger. Both are quintessentially German. None of these people knew much about French theory until the '70s. Much later in Gadamer's life he has a debate with Derrida. But where does Gadamer fit in this sequence? Chronologically, he was certainly of the older generation. He did not fight in the war. He taught his Plato and kept his mouth shut. I think he cannot be associated with Nazism the way Heidegger is, despite being a student of Heidegger. So, Gadamer provides a distinctive voice of the past, and in many respects, he wishes to be a voice from the past.

2 Hans-Georg Gadamer, *Truth and Method*, trans. Joel Weinscheimer and Donald G. Marshall (London: Continuum, 2004). Jameson recommended focusing on pp. 291–306 and 341–71.

The strain coming out of Adorno and Horkheimer is irreducibly paradoxical, because Adorno and Horkheimer marked the perpetual crisis of reason, of negativity as a critical phenomenon. Gadamer agrees with them, by the way, as he attests in a footnote in which he endorses their *Dialectic of Enlightenment*, which would not have made them happy, I think.[3] You've seen how Adorno and Horkheimer go nowhere; that is, they offer pure negativity. When somebody like Habermas tries to turn their project into an affirmative position, he has to abandon them, because what is wanted in this new situation that I've outlined is a productive kind of learning process. Something new has to be invented, a new kind of state, new citizens, but it is not a revolutionary state. These are forward-looking matters. What can be the future of this state? What can be the nature of the new subjectivity it might produce?

Gadamer says we have forgotten another of the three dimensions of time: the past. However pedagogical Gadamer is, he is offering a defense of the past and an affirmation of tradition. But what could be the tradition for German thought after these catastrophes? Well, Gadamer and others will go back, of course, to Kant and Hegel, but, ultimately, beyond them to the Greeks, which is seemingly a perpetual move of German thought. Gadamer is, in fact, a Platonist. You remember Plato's notion that the truth of mathematics is eternal. It is not material or personal; it is just there. It is something which transcends human individuality and maybe even history itself. If you have a notion of truth, presumably mathematical truths are among your eternal, nonhistorical truths. Can we really accept such a return to truth after the end of religion, the Absolute, and so forth? That is at least the proposition on which his notion of tradition is based.

What are Gadamer's politics? Remember that he hired Habermas at a moment when Habermas is thought to be a rabid left-winger, so he couldn't have been all that reactionary. But what Gadamer's hermeneutics gives us is a way of interpreting the past in a broader sense which is not reducible to that of tradition. In year zero, Gadamer found that there wasn't any past, since it was destroyed. Now, along with a construction of the future, there must be a construction of the past. This is the function of Gadamer's hermeneutics in this great book. But it contains more than that, including, every so often, interesting reconstructions of various historical figures. A bit like Habermas, he is a philosopher who wants to argue and discuss.

3 Gadamer, *Truth and Method*, p. 373, n. 14.

There are *Auseinandersetzungen* and arguments with all kinds of people here. He wants to engage with other positions.

As a history book, a book of philosophical history, this book is full of useful insights. What interests us most of all is what we would today (or yesterday) call the "theoretical" aspects of Gadamer—not the philosophical parts, but the *novum*, let's say, the new ways of dealing with the past. What is the history of hermeneutics? "Hermeneutics" of course comes from Hermes, the god of secrecy but also the messenger god. This is what has to be kept within a doctrine of hermeneutics: a way of opening up the past so that we can get at what the Frankfurt School called its "truth content." They were perfectly happy to use this expression. Everything in the past—maybe except Heidegger—had its truth content. The whole thing may be false, but there, at the very center of it, since it is a human experience, is a little seed or grain of truth, which we have to rewrite in order to see what it is, and in a way its discovery is the task of hermeneutics.

But hermeneutics begins by taking two forms. One is the higher criticism of the Bible that gets going in the eighteenth century as a critique of the historical data in the Bible, the inconsistencies of its various parts, and eventually the central question as to whether there was a historical Christ. One of its outcomes is allegory, that is, the idea that the Old Testament prefigures the new one, with the new one prefiguring something else. With 1453 comes the rediscovery of the Byzantine: The scholars fled a Byzantium which had been conquered by the Ottomans and brought these texts to Italy, an event which we are told begins humanism in the specific sense of a relationship to classicism. Remember that Luther himself was a humanist, and his translation of the Bible is one of the great monuments of that humanism. A certain hermeneutic comes into being in the Protestant study of the Bible. Therefore, you also have a double meaning of the word "humanism." Is this the kind of thing that Heidegger is going to attack in his "Letter on Humanism," or does it mean the scholars who are defined by their knowledge of Greek and Hebrew? Or is it both of those things? In that case, what is the connection? Both beget a hermeneutic, which gets going in the eighteenth century, with the emergence of philology, the study more often than not of ancient Greek texts. It is concerned not just with what a word or object means but what its lifeworld is, its historical context. What do these words mean in Homer, these abstractions, which are not exactly the same as what we find in Sophocles? This would be one of its questions.

In the early nineteenth century, something happens which Gadamer is very interested in, namely Romanticism. He is not however interested in the famous poets but, rather, the theologian Friedrich Schleiermacher. Schleiermacher invents his own romantic hermeneutics, and for the first time he will introduce subjectivity into the process of hermeneutics. It turns philology into a relationship with another subject. We can call it "intersubjectivity," but this is not a word Gadamer tends to use. It is always a very suspicious word, because it presumes as solved the problem of the relationship with the other, understanding the other. Schleiermacher turns the practice of philology into a practice of understanding the other. Obviously, this is going to have a great impact on both of these sets of texts but above all the Greek classics. So, it is Schleiermacher who revives this word, "hermeneutics," not that it has a great fortune in the nineteenth century, but it will be taken up by people like Dilthey, who are concerned with the difference between our understanding of historical texts and what the scientists are busy doing. A very big difference is that, for the scientists, the wrongheaded past of science is to be consigned to the ash heap. For the humanists, the followers of the *Geisteswissenschaften*, as Dilthey was, nothing is ever completely wrong. The text always has *something* in it.

So, Gadamer is concerned both to confirm and to deny the tradition of hermeneutics. For him, as for many of the people we've looked at, what must be avoided is a simple psychology. Once you see psychology at work, it must be wrong. That, by the way, was an insight of Durkheim: Once someone is tempted to give a phenomenon a psychological meaning, it is already wrong. We've seen Bahro refuse Khrushchev's characterization of Stalin in terms of a cult of personality; he wants to know what went wrong in the system, not some hypothetical speculation about Stalin's paranoia. But, with Schleiermacher, this mistake is already made. It is a necessary error in the development of a strong hermeneutic that Gadamer will offer, but it is still wrong, in the sense that we are seeing ourselves as a psychological identity trying to make contact with another psychological identity in the past. This person, whether overtly, like Montaigne, or in some mediated form, like Shakespeare or Homer, is another subjectivity who is speaking and expressing some kind of self. But to speak of selves is already too psychological, and therefore we have to figure out some other way of performing an analogous operation.

Not only do we *want* to understand the past, we *do* understand the past. This is precisely the way Kant would put it: We have *a priori* judgements, so how is it possible that we have them? This is the difference between Negt and Kluge and Habermas. Whereas Habermas is imagining the public sphere that he would like, Negt and Kluge are only interested in what is at work in our present experience. So, Gadamer wants to find something which will free us from psychology but maintain understanding. Understanding is a complicated word, as we've seen with *Verstehen*, which can mean a simple, limited understanding of space and matter, as opposed to *Vernunft*. But in the hermeneutic sense, Dilthey's sense, understanding means having some access to the primary text.

Meanwhile, in terms of history, Gadamer wants to avoid not only psychology, on the one side, but also two other things, on the other side: historicism and the philosophy of history. The philosophy of history is easy; we know what that is. All history is the coming into being of Spirit. That's Hegel. All history is class struggle. Or is it the overcoming of class struggle? That would be some kind of Marxian philosophy of history. All history is the development of life. That's a certain version of Dilthey and the vitalists. All history—and this is the common position today—is the development of complexity. This is the current buzzword in the sciences and also in so-called big history. Whenever you see the word "complexity" used as a value word—I don't tell you to draw your revolver, but nonetheless—be suspicious enough to have a closer look at it, because this is a form of *doxa* today. Complexity has replaced the notion of life. Life is just one form of complexity.

So those are a few philosophies of history in which history is going somewhere and has a meaning. But what is historicism? That is a real problem. Everybody attacks historicism, but what do they mean by it? It seems to mean all kinds of different things. Let's simply take Gadamer's work. It certainly has to do with the past. Would you say it has a fascination with the past? A historian specializes in a certain moment in the past. Even literary scholars have their contact with the past. Benjamin talks about how certain moments of the past mean more than others. Is that historicist? In any case, this is what Gadamer says about historicism: Historicism forgets its own historicity. It does not include the historicity of itself, of the historian, in its view of a historical period. What Gadamer wants to do is to restore that historicity in some way.

The other thing that historicism seems to do is to break up the continuity of history. If a philosophy of history sees all history as one process, an immense continuity from the first hominids all the way to the atomic bomb, then historicism sees history in distinct periods. Someone may say, "I'm really interested in the Byzantine period, but I don't care much about Italy at the time, or Ming China, or the empire of the Zulus." Benjamin was fascinated by the Paris of Baudelaire. There is a certain moment of the past that you lift out. Historicism typically involves a fascination with a certain moment of the past which tempts you to leave yourself out of the historicizing procedure. Stanley Cavell talks about film as viewing the world without myself. Something similar happens in historicism. However rich a certain enthusiasm for the past may be, and however much we all wish to be somehow involved in it, it does not fit into a notion of what genuine understanding or hermeneutics is.

That is why we have to be careful what we think of his notion of tradition. I think it is as much a provocation as is this other, more famous idea, which he calls "prejudice." The Enlightenment, he says, has a prejudice against prejudice. Gadamer is working in a leftist environment, among the students, and he wants to convey that to become a Platonist is going to be an act. It is not currently popular to be a traditionalist of this kind. "Prejudice" doesn't quite have the American resonance, which includes racism and so on, but it is not innocent either, because certainly any philosophy will want to start from zero; they don't want to bring any *Vorurteile* into the process. The greatness of Descartes is his attempt to figure out how one can start from zero. What is the standpoint from which I can reinvent or ground all knowledge without the past? Of course, he didn't do that, but Descartes is the very prototype of the Enlightenment attempt to start without prejudice, to make philosophy a blank slate and to see where we are.

So, what *does* Gadamer mean by prejudice? Is prejudice a form of ideology? What is he asking us to do? If we do swap the term "prejudice" with "ideology," it is clear that he is not asking us to get rid of our ideology but to be aware of it, to understand the way in which your ideological baggage is confronting the past. It means thinking about myself historically. In this new version of hermeneutics, there will be two historicities. Remember that historicity is Heidegger's way of getting from *Dasein* to history. *Dasein* is itself historical, and therefore you don't need to find out how *Dasein* plays a part in history. To say "play a part in history" presupposes that you could refuse to play a part or step outside of history. No, you are profoundly historical. You are history.

Gadamer will draw on the Heideggerian notion of *Vorverständnis*, "pre-comprehension." He uses this term to present the hermeneutic circle. The hermeneutic circle is an infernal machine in which you have no beginning; you are always in the middle of it, just as you are thrown into the middle of existence itself. You start a sentence, and if the sentence isn't finished, you don't know where it's going. How can you know what you think until you hear what you have said? How can you possibly say anything completely if you have to begin with the parts, and if you can't understand the parts until you know the whole thing? With his notion of *Vorverständnis*, Heidegger seems to cut through the hermeneutic circle as though it were the Gordian knot. We already know ourselves as *Dasein* and therefore we are already embarked, as Pascal might say, and we understand what we want to understand ahead of time. Remember that Pascal, in his account of his mysticism, has Christ say to him, "You would not be searching for me had you not already found me." That would be a religious hermeneutic circle in which there is no absolute beginning to faith. The very fact of looking for Christ means you have already found Christ. According to Gadamer's autobiographical accounts, it was the Heideggerian motif of *Vorverständnis* that set him going in philosophy and was the source of his own version of hermeneutics.

So *Vorurteil*, "prejudice," means more than the baggage you bring to any interpretation. The relationship of the self to history will produce something called *Wirkungsgeschichte*—*Wirkung* meaning "effect," *Geschichte* meaning "history"—which is going to be exploited by the so-called reception theorists, including Hans Robert Jauss and even Stanley Fish, who provides an American version of these methods. *Wirkungsgeschichte* is history beginning to work on you. Our relationship to the past, our being in the world, has a "horizon," as Gadamer calls it, because our world is finite. A horizon is what completes our world but also limits it. It has an ambiguity similar to that of boundary and limit in Hegel, which is his disproof of the thing-in-itself in Kant. For Hegel, when you touch a limit, you're already over it. You're claiming to name this thing that you don't know, but since you're naming it, you *do* know it, and therefore it isn't a thing-in-itself anymore. I think horizon is not enough understood in terms of this dialectic of the limit. By setting in place the known-knowns of your world, you define the unknown-unknown of what lies beyond the horizon, but in doing so you make them known in some abstract sense. It is this movement of perceived knowing, if you like, that puts Gadamer's hermeneutics in dialogue with the critique of ideology. Our horizon is what limits us in our experience. It is very clear in class terms. What we have never experienced of the other classes is something we don't understand. Lukács's account of ideology in *History and Class Consciousness* presents the matter in another way by taking us, among other places, to the limit beyond which bourgeois consciousness does not know the experience of the other classes, and it does not even know that it doesn't know it; it marks off an unknown-unknown.

So one brings one's own horizon to the text, but understanding the text means figuring out *its* horizon. If you like, you can think of it in terms either of experience or expectation, terms that Koselleck will take up. A text is a horizon of expectation. What else do I think is out there? What is in reality? What don't I know about reality? That is, supposedly, the difference between ourselves, today, who know so much more than the people in the past, and the people in the past themselves. They didn't know that there was something beyond their horizon, which was modern art, or quantum theory, fascism, or whatever else would come after them. What is it that they were not expecting? To think of this in temporal terms as expectation is a good way to understand the difference of horizons, but I don't think this is the only way one can think of it. Another way of talking about it—and this is how Sartre translates it—is in terms of situation. This is a word that both Sartre and Heidegger get from Karl Jaspers. It means that my world, in the phenomenological sense, is a situation. It is not an inert landscape. It is a set of commands, expectations, disappointments, limits, all kinds of things which are set up for me personally and which I have to deal with in some way. Situation is a profoundly existential idea, and I think it is important to associate the notion of situation—which most of the Germans don't do—with that of horizon. The notion of horizon takes on its full resonance if taken in existential terms, which is certainly appropriate enough for a philosopher of Heideggerian origin.

This is where we get into a problem. We have two horizons: me—but I'm not a person or a subjectivity anymore, just a horizon of expectation—and the text. But the text is clearly not a person either. Rather, what we have is a situation confronting another situation. Gadamer's solution to the confrontation of these situations is the fusion of horizons, the moment of hermeneutic understanding, the moment in which the text is opened to me somehow. What does it mean for the text to be open to me, this text of the distant past? How could it be open to me? We'll look at those questions next time.

October 26, 2021

17

Gadamer, Blumenberg, Koselleck

Today I want to go on with Gadamer and then to see how this chimes with Blumenberg and Koselleck. After that, when we get to Jauss and the Constance School, I will suggest that we have returned to literary criticism, just as with Gadamer we have returned to philosophy. These are the disciplines. It seems to me that we entered this whole realm of German thought looking for theory, but we don't talk about German theory; we talk about French theory. I was at a conference once where a Czech scholar stood up and said, "Why do they keep talking about French structuralism? It's *Czech* structuralism, because we preceded them!" Of course, they did, in some way. But I think the return of the disciplines is something we should try to figure out, and these comparisons between the intellectual situations of different nationalities may prove helpful in that endeavor.

Gadamer is really the first traditional philosopher we have read so far. Adorno was certainly a prodigious thinker, but I don't think the study of philosophy suited him, whereas Horkheimer wanted to destroy the disciplines and create a new unity of disciplines. So, there is an initial distinction to make between theory, whatever that may be, and philosophy. Most interesting modern theorists, I think, have wished to destroy philosophy. Marx wanted philosophy to realize itself. His work was not economics but a *critique* of political economy. I think the upshot of Hegel is that philosophy was at an end. For both Heidegger and Derrida, who is in this sense Heidegger's follower, what is called "metaphysics" can be translated into the traditional term "philosophy," in which it held a certain esteem, and, certainly, they felt that it was something to be destroyed or deconstructed and replaced with something else: for Heidegger, a return to the ancients and a kind of mysticism, and, for Derrida, I'm not quite sure, although I think his endgame is what you call "positive deconstruction," ending up oddly enough somewhere in the realm of social democracy where we find Habermas (with whom, despite some bad beginnings, he had a kind of understanding, so to speak). Nietzsche, before them, certainly wished to do away with traditional philosophy. And so on.

This return to the disciplines, I think, is a sign of the consolidation of the past. Does the consolidation of the past entail a return to tradition, in Gadamer's sense? I suppose he would have thought so. But, with Gadamer, it is as though the Greeks already constituted philosophy, and therefore nothing new can ever really be invented, only retrieved from the past. The problem with Gadamer, as I said, is that we have to pick out the nuggets of theory that are present in his work and to look at them separately from the philosophy. What we find in his hermeneutics is that history is primary, and suddenly everything else that has preoccupied the thinkers of the past—and not only the German ones—turns into questions about history, indeed as though they had forgotten the future tense. What one feels is oppressed by the hermeneutic relationship to history is the dialectic, although the dialectic is always a question, even when it isn't asked explicitly. Heidegger had a powerful critique of representation which seems to me very much still with us but which doesn't seem to be visible in Gadamer. He is certainly a very thoroughgoing critic of philosophical positions, but one rarely finds him taking on or criticizing a contemporary theme.

So critique is absent in some sense from this work, because it is providing a way of looking at the past, which is not criticizable by virtue of the fact that it is not there anymore. What else is absent? I think the concept of ideology is absent, although, as I say, it can be reintroduced into Gadamer's thought. Is prejudice ideology? Yes, of course it functions that way, and I think what can be very stimulating about Gadamer only emerges if one substitutes "ideology" for *Vorurteil*. You remember that one of Althusser's fundamental ideas, directed against orthodox Marxism and party orthodoxy, was that ideology is not opposed to truth. That is to say, by criticizing ideology, one does not necessarily arrive at truth. Maybe you arrive at the critique of certain ideologies, which is more a question of praxis or action, but in that sense truth—although I don't think he would say this—is an existential idea. It is part of a family of concepts which includes authenticity. These are not scientific terms for Althusser. Using Lacan's terms, he will say that ideology is necessary in daily life for us to understand our position in what is also an idea, namely the outside world, our situation, our class situation, which would be the Symbolic order. For him, we are always in ideology. Even if we are in utopia, in communism, there will be ideology, and we will still have ideological positions because we will still have selves. All you have to do is look at the various Marxisms, which are all ideologies. It is in this sense that we can understand ideology alongside Gadamer's *Vorurteil*: You never get rid of it. It is your whole past. You can change yourself on the basis of it and come to consciousness of it, and indeed, Gadamer presents the interpreter precisely with an injunction to become conscious of his or her historicity. One is no longer so embedded in *Vorurteil* when becoming aware of the present, one's own time, but it can't simply be escaped. The concept of ideology would have been helpful for Gadamer.

I want to say two other things about hermeneutics and philosophy. First of all, there is a basic problem that was absent from much of traditional philosophy and that has returned in a distorted form in modern philosophy, although very few philosophers have posed it in the right way, namely the problem of the other and of other people. There are many ways of approaching it, but as a proto-Sartrean, I would say that Sartre's idea is the most relevant. Philosophy fastened on to the problem of solipsism. Descartes told us that we exist, so we don't have to worry about that anymore, but what about other people? Descartes himself couldn't figure that out. He thought that maybe you could think of them as automatons. Sartre says nobody has ever really believed in a solipsism of that kind, so we must be looking for the problem in the wrong place. In fact, he says, the problem is that we know in advance that the other exists because we are alienated from the other. The child doesn't know what it is, but it certainly knows what the other is and that it depends on it. So, one would have to redesign this whole inquiry. The answer to the question of the other cannot be Christian charity or understanding. This was the mistake that Schleiermacher made with his idea that we have to somehow feel our way into the other, to understand the other. Well, maybe not. Maybe it is the other way around, although of course the other poses the same problem to us.

When we are dealing with seemingly literary matters, matters of interpretation, we are dealing with the other. These literary texts are mediations between ourselves and the other, even an other from the distant past, from some other country, class, race, and so on. The text is always a mediation with the other. The question is: What to do with this otherness? How to make that mediation productive? How not to turn it into a projection? How not to absorb it into ourselves? For most people, to do so entails a certain kind of reaction: "I know how that feels. I understand." That is to say, we take this alien text, which can be both familiar and strange, and we place ourselves in it, project ourselves into it. This notion of understanding the other is a psychological projection, and therefore it cannot be satisfactory.

The other thing I want to say is about historicism. Historicism often involves positing a cultural moment and describing what constitutes that moment. The baroque is the easiest example that comes to mind. What were their values? What were their institutions? What kind of art did they produce? (That is always the secret key.) What was their religion? These are all questions posed as though they were all asking about a mere part of something larger, complete and stable in itself, which we're looking at from the outside. The idea of a historical period involved here has been transformed in modern thinking and in modern historiography. Now I think what people look for is not the culture but the break, the moment of transition. To what? To something else. The notion of culture, the notion of the historical moment, that kind of historicism is part of a philosophy of continuity. I once heard Gayatri Spivak call it "continuism," which is maybe as good as anything else. Continuism is a kind of ideology, but little by little, people turn away from it. They want to know *when* things changed, not even *what* has changed. I would say the modern efforts of periodization turn on that question: When? If you look at them carefully, you'll see that that is their secret question: Where is the break?

The name given to the biggest of these changes is modernity itself. The swindle here is that the break they call "modernity" will be treated as a period in the old style. Then they'll ask: What is modernity? What are its values? What are its structures? Modernity is not the name of a period; it is the name of a break. There are all kinds of breaks, and these Germans are always talking about them. Gadamer will talk about how hermeneutics is established when he is looking for a break with the Schleiermacher-Dilthey version of hermeneutics. I suppose the break always has to do with something new. That is how modernity will then be described. Bloch calls it the *novum*, though I don't think he means only "the new." The unexpected, the unknown-unknown—that is what the question of modernity involves, but it is wrong, it seems to me, to assign a substantive meaning to the notion of modernity. It is wrong to think of modernity as a period. If you do, then it turns out that what you're really talking about is capitalism. This is my view.

What Gadamer is concerned with here is the break, the beginning of a new hermeneutics. It is clear that this new hermeneutics is not simply an identification with the other. Rather, it will entail finding one's horizon of expectation. As we will see, in Koselleck, there are two basic domains of inquiry: the space of experience and the horizon of expectation.[4] It seems to me that one could also posit "a horizon of experience," beyond which one somehow cannot know anything. As one of you has pointed out, the horizon of experience involves foregrounding. That which falls within the horizon, the situation, is not an objective thing either. A horizon sounds fairly objective, but, in fact, it is constructed just as much as the situation within it is constructed, and, for this reason, in the long run, it is collectively produced. One of the questions one has to pose to Gadamer's hermeneutics is whether this is a horizon shared by a whole collectivity or whether it is unique to a particular writer. Even in the latter case, the individual's horizon must bear some relationship to the horizon of the collectivity, and the writer will have had to work on themes that are already given, to modify them in some unique way.

Frankly, we are not given very much in Gadamer. He is a philosopher, so he will not illustrate his ideas with literary works, meaning a literary use of Gadamer still needs to be filled out. I don't think the Constance thinkers do this satisfactorily enough, although they are very useful in their own way. The question is how we who possess horizons of our own relate our horizons to some larger horizon. Of course, that question results in the famous fusion of horizons. But what can that mean? How do horizons fuse? I think it certainly doesn't mean that we project ourselves into the past, that we project our own situation into the past, but rather that some continuity is found between the two. This is the sense in which Gadamer is a "continuist," tending to pose these issues in terms of nonhistorical permanence. Fusing horizons is not simply making the past relevant,

4 Reinhart Koselleck, *Futures Past: On the Semantics of Historical Time* (Cambridge: MIT Press, 2004).

although we know there are moments when bits of the past are suddenly revived. Hölderlin's insanity meant nothing to the nineteenth century, but all of a sudden, from the early twentieth century up until the present, everyone quotes his idea that where danger is, salvation also grows. Every single one of these Germans quotes that sentence. Why does Hölderlin suddenly provide some kind of an answer to their questions? It is obvious that there is a wish-fulfilling aspect to Hölderlin's newfound relevance: It can't get any worse, so there must be some possibility of salvation in our hopeless situation. There is no way out, and yet one is not to be worried.

What form would the fusion of horizons take? When Gadamer talks about "application," he means it as a rhetorical term. Let me illustrate something for those of us who would like something more concrete. "We must place ourselves in the other situation in order to understand it." But

> the historical movement of human life consists in the fact that it is never absolutely bound to any one standpoint, and hence can never have a truly closed horizon. The horizon is, rather, something into which we move and that moves with us. Horizons change for a person who is moving. Thus the horizon of the past, out of which all human life lives, and which exists in the form of tradition, is always in motion. The surrounding horizon is not set in motion by historical consciousness. But in it this motion becomes aware of itself.
>
> When our historical consciousness transposes itself into historical horizons, this does not entail passing into alien worlds unconnected in any way with our own; instead, they together constitute the one great horizon that moves from within and that, beyond the frontiers of the present, embraces the historical depths of our self-consciousness. Everything contained in historical consciousness is in fact restrained by a single historical horizon.[5]

Okay, but here is the horrible expression of Rorty, "the great conversation of the West," a loathsome and condescending expression. Does it mean there is some fundamentally human essence which is always present and which we can reach through seemingly different situations? In a way, the idea presented here resembles Hegel's dialectic of identity and difference. The situation has to appear identical to ours, but then we have to draw back and see its radical difference from us; these would seem to be two

5 Gadamer, *Truth and Method*, p. 303.

different moments of the same thing. The emphasis is, first of all, on the situation of the horizon and not on that of the self, but, somehow, there has to be a relationship between these horizons. Is it simply imaginary that we can place ourselves in other situations?

I thought I would try to illustrate Gadamer's fusion of horizons through our relationship to Dante. Dante presents us with a proto-psychoanalytic inquiry into sexuality, sublimation, and their relationship to theology. The troubadours established a first kind of poetic investigation of sublimation, how desire could coexist with the absence of its fulfillment. In the *Dolce Stil Novo*, the Italians turn this investigation into an avant-garde of sorts. How would such an investigation of sublimation be related to contemporaneous theological understandings of the universe and the various levels of sin? Indeed, you have here a kind of Freudo-Marxist riddle: What is the relationship between the psyche's passions and the structure of the world, class structure, power, and so on? That is one of the questions that Dante's work poses. Does he answer it?

Much like Collingwood, Gadamer is very intent on the idea that the experience of the past is one of question and answer. It seems to me that only when we turn the answer back into the question, and the question back into the answer, can we achieve some kind of fusion of horizons. But Gadamer goes further than that. It's not that we question the earlier text, he says. The text questions us. In fact, I have gone so far, although it may be a little rash, as to say that, in an act of interpreting the past, there are four positions: the situation of the writer, the articulator of that situation, our situation, and our articulation of that past text. Here we have a fourfold—not that of Heidegger, which is not between two human beings, the writer and the interpreter, but between two systems. In fact, it is a matter of one system judging the other, in some sense. It is as though the past is judging us, or, at least, to say so would be to move closer to the way I want to understand Gadamer's fusion of horizons.

So the fusion of horizons is not a moment of identification, and yet it involves identity in a certain way. It is not radical difference either, not in the sense of archaeological distance. It is not psychological either. But, he says, it is an event. This is a very important point: The fusion of horizons is not a structural fact but, rather, an event, a contact of some kind that might be considered anthropologically, just as the other situations of hermeneutics—those of the legal system, for example—involve interpretation as an act of understanding, if you like, and as a displacement of the self. What is presented in the fusion of horizons is a kind of experience, but not a purely psychological one. It modifies our horizons in some way that alters this contact, if it really is one. Gadamer's addition to the notion of question and answer is that there are some questions which are dead and whose answer is no longer interesting or even possible. Maybe that means that occasionally a question can revive itself and become of significance again. "Problem" is a bad word for him, because it tends to generalize the structure of this relationship, which again, is a unique event and not a generalizable form. I would say the question as to whether the notion of a problem is useful or not depends precisely on the situation, so I take it less seriously.

These ideas of experience are not unlike what you find in Benjamin. *Erlebnis* is a shock experience, whereas *Erfahrung* is the wisdom that you distill from an experience. While Gadamer is not using this kind of opposition, he does say, in a rather shocking formulation, that experience is always negative. What does it mean to say that experience is negative? Just as one's horizon is important not for what it contains but for what is not there—what remains on the other side of it—so any real experience will be a shock, because it will show us something that we didn't know before and that was not included in our previously accumulated experience. If it's something we know already, then it isn't an experience, just a repetition of something we are already familiar with. So, the new has to be something that is, in some sense, a shock, a shock of the unknown, if you like. Everything depends on discovering our own historicity.

I don't want to complicate what we have discussed so far too much by adding Blumenberg to the mix, but his work on secularization makes for a very odd but generative supplement to Gadamer and Koselleck.[6] Blumenberg argues that secularization is a faulty concept. It is said that Marx has secularized religion, but this makes no sense. According to Blumenberg, as a matter of fact, religion itself had already confronted an opposition between the authentic and the secular. In the centuries after Christ, the end of the world was expected. Then, little by little, people had to get used to the fact that the end was being indefinitely postponed, so they themselves had to secularize parts of their religion. Blumenberg

6 Hans Blumenberg, "'Secularization': Critique of a Category of Historical Illegitimacy" (1964), in *History, Metaphors, Fables: A Hans Blumenberg Reader*, ed. and trans. Hannes Bajohr, Florian Fuchs, and Joe Paul Kroll (Ithaca, NY: Cornell University Press, 2020), pp. 53–82.

therefore seems to say the opposite of what he said before insofar as he now uses secularization as an instrument of understanding. It is a very curious and dazzling demonstration, and it is certainly a marvelous exercise in historicity, but it is like a firework: When it dies down, you don't quite know what to take from it. I think his view of these historical moments contravenes continuism to such an extent that it ultimately becomes nominalistic. So, in Blumenberg, you have another lesson in discontinuity.

Finally, we come to something in Gadamer which is quite unexpected and unexplored: the foreconception of completeness. This is the secret kicker. We have to think that this moment in the past, this text which is a horizon and which is an experience of some kind, is complete. What kind of a requirement is completeness? If a text or a horizon isn't complete, then it can't really be interpreted. Following Collingwood, whom Gadamer cites, you can only understand historical actors if they are presumed to have acted rationally, in which case you can understand their role in history by reconstructing their rational decisions.[7] But if the decisions are irrational, and every instance of the irrational is uniquely incomprehensible to reason, how can you possibly understand the history which those decisions touch upon? At a certain point, A. J. P. Taylor, whom we won't call a traditional historian of Austrian history only because he was something of a scandal to his colleagues, suddenly proposed that we cannot understand World War II unless we are able to think of Hitler as a rational statesman.[8] If he was irrational, then, as with Collingwood, there is nothing to understand. There is a lot that we can know, but we can't understand Hitler's own decisions. In the later, unpublished volume of *Mein Kampf*, Hitler makes a decision about globalization; Hitler understood that Germany was threatened by the two great superpowers and had either itself to become a superpower or become minor. Therefore, he begins a convulsive struggle to make Germany into a superpower. A certain rationality lies behind that project. Obviously, what it leaves out is his maniacal anti-Semitism, although there are ways of fitting that into the reason which is posited for explaining his decisions: He wants Germany to be a superpower, and this is his way of making Germany German. But Taylor's idea is scandalous because nobody wants to think of Hitler as a rational statesman.

---

7 See Gadamer, *Truth and Method*, p. 364.

8 A. J. P. Taylor, *The Origins of the Second World War* (New York: Penguin, 1991).

What about fragments? What can be done with fragmentary texts in Gadamer's hermeneutics? I suppose we can reconstruct them to figure out how they fit into something larger. On this idea of foreconception, he uses Heidegger's notions.

> But this, too, is obviously a formal condition of all understanding. It states that only what really constitutes a unity of meaning is intelligible. So when we read a text we always assume its completeness, and only when this assumption proves mistaken—i.e., the text is not intelligible —do we begin to suspect the text and try to discover how it can be remedied. The rules of such textual criticism can be left aside, for the important thing to note is that applying them properly depends on understanding the content. The fore-conception of completeness that guides all our understanding is, then, always determined by the specific content.[9]

Suddenly we are confronted with something very peculiar, which has been smuggled in here. Like Heidegger, Gadamer's tastes incline towards traditional works, especially the Greeks, but you could think of it another way. If you're trying to understand modernism, you look at *Tender Buttons* by Gertrude Stein, and you say it's gibberish. You try to do a hermeneutic reading of it, but what could possibly be the experience that these crazy words express? In a funny way—I find rather obscene what she talks about sometimes—it is not libidinal language like that of the Surrealists. It is a funny kind of flat American language. How could you possibly find completeness or rationality in a work like *Tender Buttons*?

Let's say you wanted to hear in language only its sounds. Therefore, you listen to Hindi, Hungarian, German, English, purely for their sound values. I think a person doing that, perhaps a philologist, would not be listening to something incomplete but, rather, would have been isolating a single dimension which has a certain meaningfulness, namely the sound values of the way the language is constructed. So, it would be possible to posit a position from which, in reading *Tender Buttons*, you could hear only the dimensions that Gertrude Stein saw and used in her language, and you would therefore be leaving out traditional questions of meaning. Those questions would be bracketed. It wouldn't bother you that it was gibberish or that it was nonsense, because you would be listening only

9 Gadamer, *Truth and Method*, p. 294.

for that dimension of language which Stein herself was elaborating. Why she would do that is another question. She was a great theorist of what it meant to be American and what the distinctiveness of Americanism was. One would have to reconstruct the situation of Stein's writing and to explore it in such a way as to understand that its other features were of no significance for her to see how it is meaningful in an entirely different sense. It seems to me this is a useful set of problems to struggle with.

We don't have time to discuss Koselleck deeply enough. His case is rather different. Instead of a return to philosophy, it is a return to history. We read along and think, "This is fine. This is a historian who has written about the moment of modernity in Prussia, and this is certainly an interesting statement for historians, but what does it have for us?" Then, suddenly, we reach a climax, and I must say, it is stunning. Here we have the very embodiment of Enlightenment reason. Diderot wrote a wonderful dialogue, *Rameau's Nephew*, which was translated into German, but the French was subsequently lost. The original French text was only found after World War II in a chateau in Normandy. Goethe had translated it, so it is almost a text of Goethe's. Among the other papers is this one in Koselleck about despotism, history, the moment of revolution, confusion, and finally, some thought that Diderot scribbled on a piece of paper: commotion, plotting, conspiracy, mass … "The nation now is merely an entity dependent on a collection of criminals and corrupt persons. In this situation, only one man and a suitable moment are needed for an entirely unexpected moment to emerge." This is before Napoleon, before the French Revolution! "If the moment comes, the man emerges. He speaks to the people, who until this moment believe themselves to be all. He says, 'You are nothing,' and they speak as if out of one mouth, 'You are the lord.' And he says to them, 'Here are the conditions under which I have prepared to subject you.' And they say, 'We accept them.'"[10] This is amazing. Contained in this one passage is an analysis of the appearance of fascism.

Koselleck knows how to write an essay. This thing goes somewhere. It is essentially about three ways of looking at the future. The first and oldest one is prophecy, in which a really different future will arrive, and

10 Guillaume Thomas François Raynal, *Histoire philosophique et politique des établissements et du commerce des Européens dans les deux Indes* (Geneva, 1780), IV, pp. 488 ff.; qtd. in Reinhart Koselleck, *Futures Past*, p. 24. Koselleck notes that Diderot is now believed to be the author of this passage, which was added to the 1780 edition of Raynal's encyclopedia.

it implies the end of the world. The second, after prophecy, is prognosis. Prognosis characterizes a society ruled by a small group of people who are essentially the same in all countries: the court, the monarch, someone like Frederick the Great, a dictator, a statesman. Prognosis means the future is conceived as a set of situations that have the same elements, which themselves can be moved around like chess pieces. The smart one, beginning with Machiavelli, is the one who takes these pieces, puts them in a certain position, and says, "This is what's going to happen." Of course, Machiavelli was never right about anything except the truth of his political philosophy. Bismarck knows how to move the pieces around so that France will be pushed aside and Germany can emerge. But then there comes a point when, with a new stage of mass democracy in the late nineteenth century, leaders associate themselves with masses and movements. At that point, the elements of the future are no longer available as chess-like tokens, and prognosis goes out the window. What do you have then? Then we have modernity, a term with its own set of problems, as I've said. Where is the future in modernity? Is it cyclical? Koselleck outlines a cyclical movement from reaction to revolution, back and forth. There are no other categories. Diderot shows us a situation in which both prophecy and prognosis are no longer valid ways of dealing with the future. Lacan said this to the students in the '60s: *Vous voulez un maître, vous l'aurez.* "If you're looking for a master, you'll get one." Maybe he knew this part of Diderot. Under what conditions am I prepared for you to be my subjects? At the end of the war, Hitler said, "I'm wondering whether the German people are really worthy of my great ideals. Why aren't they winning this war? Are they really the master race after all? Let's destroy everything." That is the destructive emergence with which Koselleck ends his analysis.

We'll go on with this next time. The main point is that Koselleck is practicing a new kind of history, not the history of ideas but the history of concepts. I would also like to call it "critical lexicology." This is a history of words that are concepts, not ideas. Nobody has ever had an idea. What would an idea be? How could you write a history of it? There are a limited number of these little things we call ideas. You can move them around, but you can't add any new ones, and the game can't take on contours that have not been determined in advance. Next time we will see what his way of dealing with concepts has to tell us.

October 28, 2021

18

Gadamer, Koselleck, Jauss, Iser

We began with the Frankfurt School on one hand and Heidegger on the other. All the Marxist theoretical work that we are reading stems in one way or another from the Frankfurt School. Their students carried their work in different directions: *Öffentlichkeit*, action, a Marx revival. If you want to say that the Marx revival came out of Adorno's seminars, that would be alright. But we haven't really seen what comes out of Heidegger's work. Our aim today will be to examine his legacy further through Gadamer, who is not exactly a disciple of Heidegger but who, nonetheless, has come to represent one strand of Heideggerian thought. We may also get a better sense of how these two legacies are related, insofar as, in one way or another, they are both answering the needs of a reemergent Germany. Although we are not pursuing this history chronologically, we are getting an idea of how these trajectories progress at different rates of speed, competing with each other even as they draw on each other.

It would be helpful to go on with the example of Dante. On the one hand, Dante presents us with eros, sublimation, the tradition of the lyric, and on the other hand, the authority of the pope, the emperor, and political theory. Dante is seeking to unite those two problems, if you like. That is what the *Commedia* tries to do from our standpoint. Yet his solutions are not in any way contemporary. We don't want to turn them back into contemporary issues. Is it simply that our problems are analogous and can therefore be applied? What does "application" mean in the hermeneutic sense? Would it mean turning Dante into a precursor of all of our modern problems?

Would it mean projecting our modern questions into the past? God knows, if you were a Thomist, you might adopt Dante and bring Dante's whole language into the present! The orthodoxy of Dante certainly worked with T. S. Eliot's would-be system. Eliot said something very pertinent, which we can recall here, in an essay on Blake.[1] After praising the extraordinary power of Blake, he worries that Blake had to spend too much time making up a private mythology. Had Blake had a ready-made philosophical system, he wouldn't have had to exhaust himself creating something new. Blake is like somebody who had to make all the furniture in their room themselves. Eliot proposes that some kind of orthodoxy, something that you accept beforehand, facilitates the creation of poetry, because it allows you to work within a preexisting system that you don't have to invent from scratch. I would say that most of the people we think of as modern, even where they lay claim to orthodoxy, spend a lot of energy making up their own systems. However, the other side should be looked at too.

These postwar Germans don't necessarily have Eliot's imagined choice between orthodoxies. Or rather, they have too many choices. All of these systems, whether American "democracy," in quotation marks—I use that term as a shorthand for the interests of American foreign policy—or the Soviet system that Ulbricht insisted on, are foreign impositions. I won't use the language of coloniality, but they are the systems of power of the invaders, so to speak. Therefore, these two opposing systems of the Frankfurt School and of Heidegger would seem to stand in for a kind of orthodoxy that you could build on or work within.

We know that the Frankfurt School had its canon, its Hegelianism and Marxism, which it modified. But how can Heidegger be seen as providing something equivalent? Where would Heidegger fit into a modification of tradition, since certainly for his followers there was no option to go back to a Nazism that he didn't exactly represent, even though he thought for a moment that he could realize something in it? I would suggest that they go back to his notion of time, particularly as Gadamer understands it. That the problem of time is an ancient and quite unsolvable philosophical problem can be demonstrated by returning to Aristotle's very strange definition, which has to do with number, measurement, and movement. But the first postclassical thinker, if I can put it that way, who

1 T. S. Eliot, "William Blake," *Selected Essays* (London: Faber and Faber, 1934), pp. 317–22.

has something interesting to say about time—indeed, who has everything to say about time, and nobody has really ever said more than he did—is Saint Augustine. You will find Augustine's major statement about time in Book XI of the *Confessions*. Everyone should read it. It provides a literary example, a temporal analysis of a poem, a psalm, and it raises all kinds of questions about the inner temporality of such a work, the beats, the prosody. But it begins in a much more general way. It begins with the famous sentence, which everyone quotes because it's impossible to go much further than this: "What then *is* time? If no one asks me, I know; if I want to explain it to a questioner, I do not know."[2] At once you have a phenomenological distance between experience and language. This is going to be the case throughout the history of theories of time. We seem to have three words for time—past, present, and future—but how are they related to experience? If you're going to deal in experience, then you have to say that the past is not, that the future is not. Are you thereby led to the classical position, Parmenides's position, that there is only the present, only being, such that there can't be nonbeing? That is not very satisfying or exhaustive of human experience. So, how does one deal with these notions of time? Saint Augustine's solution is that there are not three separate realms. Each one has its own trinity. The past has its own past, present, and future. The same for the other present and the future. Each moment brings with it its own past and its own future. Husserl revives this solution, which is then taken up by Heidegger—nobody gives you Husserl, only Heidegger's version of Husserl, but that's alright—and it would be very important for working out some version of time that satisfies what Gadamer calls hermeneutics.

Indeed, when Gadamer picks up the redoubled notion of temporality from Heidegger, it is given a different language, but it is still the Augustinian, Husserlian solution. For Gadamer, too, the three dimensions of time, if I can call them that, are somehow inseparable, insofar as there cannot be a present without a past or future; each one has its past, its present, and its future; and as we move forward in time, those categories change in relation to one another, so that what was once a future in our past is what Sartre calls a "dead future," something that had the meaning of a real future, and although I can look back on it as a real future, it is no longer my future. In the same way, I suppose you could talk about dead pasts.

2 Saint Augustine, *Confessions*, trans. F. J. Sheed (New York: Hackett, 2006), p. 242.

Something once was a real past for me, and now it may no longer be my past. Of course, the past can be modified by our present acts—as Sartre says—but so can the future. To modify any one of those dimensions is to modify all of them. However, we must somehow try to separate them in order to do justice to their unity. In a dialectical way, we can't affirm them as unified without having separated them, and we can't separate them unless we have adequately recognized their unity.

In Heidegger's notion of *Vorverständnis*, "fore-understanding"—or what Gadamer calls "prejudice," *Vorurteil*, which is the idea that, when we approach a text, we bring with us all sorts of baggage—there are no beginnings. That is to say, we cannot leap into the world anew. There is no blank slate of human consciousness. Everything has a past and a future. No one can imagine being born, except of course Salvador Dalí, who described his own birth as a red screen, but the rest of us are "always-already," in the expression of the Althusserians. There is always-already a future. So *Vorverständnis* has its own three dimensions: *Vorhabe*, *Vorsicht*, and *Vorgriff*. Forehaving, foresight, and—like *Begriff*, the word for "concept," with its connotation of gripping—foreconception. Those concepts could be temporal. *Vorhabe* is what I bring with me. *Vorsicht* is what I see in front of me. *Vorgriff* is what I want to make out of these conditions. These are all parts of my *Vormeinung*, my forethought, the way in which I break out of the hermeneutic circle, which names precisely the impossibility of figuring out how you could ever understand something unless you had already understood it in advance. The hermeneutic circle, seen in this way, is the conversion of a mass of opinions or ideological positions into some form of knowledge (or, to use a distinction which runs throughout post-Heideggerian work, the transformation of *doxa*, or opinion, into episteme, or knowledge).

But things are not quite that simple. I want to stage the problem of hermeneutics in the moment in which the collectivity of the German nation, lacking identity, is meditating on what it is to become. This meditation involves figuring out what it should do with a national past that seems completely unusable. To do so, I want to look very quickly at Koselleck again, because Koselleck introduces a distinctive set of problems. He is dealing not with the history of ideas, as I said the other day, but the history of concepts. Is that any better? In Koselleck, there is a very sharp divide between having words for something and not having words for something. There are situations in which you have words and names for experiences which come from the past, but you are confronted with something new for which those words are inadequate. The new epitomizes this problem, because the new is precisely that for which you don't have words. If you can say what it is, it means you already have names for it, and therefore it isn't really new. All the avant-gardes have struggled with this question.

What interests me is the way in which a new word suddenly appears. It makes things visible which weren't visible before. The great example comes from Sartre, quoting *The Charterhouse of Parma*. In the novel a young man is in love, in fact, with his aunt. This all takes place on the level of the court politics of the town of Parma, where her official lover is a statesman. At a certain point, the nephew and the aunt drive off for one reason or another. The statesman says to himself, in effect: "If the word 'love' comes up between them, I'm lost." In other words: "They don't know what they're feeling right now, but if they suddenly name it then they will have brought it into being, and I'm no longer in the position I was with respect to them." The minute a feeling is named, the name and the feeling will congeal in a way that changes reality itself. For Koselleck, this is the way in which one can imagine a limited history, in which the appearance of new words signals a change in our conception of reality.

Koselleck is working with a Gadamerian opposition here: the space of experience versus the horizon of expectation. This will follow us down through the Constance School, and, of course, it is present in Negt and Kluge. You may say this is just a matter of words and literature, but we don't have anything else from the past. In that sense, the past is not. Even if you are talking about shirts, a certain form of vase construction, anything—those are also languages. Koselleck's examples have to do with war monuments, monuments to the dead of the world wars. Those are also ways of crystalizing the past, but, at the same time, they show the limits we are working within when we are trying to think that past. His examples are close to Blumenberg's historical concerns, namely the passage out of the Christian world. These periods turn on the fate of the end times. Already, we know that the believers of the first generation after Christ's execution had a conception of the end times which had to be constantly postponed because it never happened; the notion of the end had to take various other forms. It gets institutionalized in the church. It is integrated into, among other things, political theory. Amid such a sublimated belief in the end of the world, there exists a form of thinking and speaking which doesn't precede it or follow it: prophecy. Prophecy is giving a language to the vision of the end. There may be limits to it. It seems to me that Koselleck assumes that all of Christianity can be subsumed under this belief in a certain end of the world, and all of theology testifies that there is a lot more involved than simple eschatology. But his demonstration is interesting. When, in secularity, the end times seem imminent—this is not an infrequent experience—and when that experience withdraws, another relationship to the future emerges. That was a relationship in which a very well-defined catastrophic future sets certain kinds of limits to the experience of the present and of the past. The existence of prophecy as a political discourse testifies to that historical reality. To me, it seems impossible to draw conclusions from this history without the concept of secularization. A foreshadowing of the end of a dynasty, for example, mirrors the experience of Christianity in its earliest period and gives rise to analogous kinds of historical experience.

What is interesting now is that Koselleck proposes a second historical moment. This is the moment of the courts, the postfeudal era of absolutism. He is a historian of this moment in Prussia. He suggests the possibility of something generally called "late feudalism," even though it doesn't have much to do with feudalism. Louis XIV domesticated the aristocracy and the various provincial courts, which couldn't extend their influence as far as they did in a kingdom like Prussia under Frederick the Great. From Koselleck's standpoint, this transition out of feudal authority produces an altogether different experience of history. Historicity is the new concept that comes into being around the late nineteenth century to characterize the sense that modernity is different in its relationship to what it will call history. History is not just a set of dead facts. It is something inside of you that has to do with the way everything is changing. So, the emergence of the word "historicity," eventually launched by Heidegger, signals a change in our notion of history.

The absolutist courts, ranging from that of Louis XIV himself all the way down to the nobles, are the political units whose squabbling constitutes a certain level of historical change. For them, the European world is essentially a world of known quantities. For each of these courts, there are known social positions, classes, which persist for generations. Because all the elements are known, the great statesmen and political theorists of this period can deal with the future in terms that differ from those of prophecy. It is not a prediction so much as it is a diagnosis. Koselleck will call it "prognosis." I didn't like that word very much, but maybe the medical side of it is appropriate in the sense that, if several symptoms arise together, a disease can be identified whose outcome you can predict. After prophecy, prognosis allows the statesman to look at the various nation-states, foresee how their interactions will turn out, and to strategize on the basis of those interactions. His great example is Frederick the Great's wars with Russia and Austria. In those cases, there is a kind of wisdom to be learned, like in chess, by gaining a familiarity with the various positions on the board. I would add that this kind of thinking—I'm not sure what to call it—transfers the political knowledge of strategic prognoses to the individual realm. The paradigmatic strategic thinker would be Machiavelli, but he is followed by people for whom he provides a guide to individual struggles and relationships, in which, in a bounded field of individuals, they are able to deduce ways of acting and of gaining influence.

What happens when that period ends? I think everybody would agree that it ends with the French Revolution and the discovery of what we now call history. It is partly a matter of industrialization. Koselleck picks up two features of this moment. The first is its newness—such that one can't any longer use prognoses—and the second is its acceleration. Things now go faster, apparently. There is no simple generational rhythm, as there was in agricultural life, the rhythm of the seasons, as it existed before the French Revolution. Now, suddenly, a new kind of nonrhythm comes into being: speed itself. Everything rushes forward. We'll see when we get to Sloterdijk that, for him, the twentieth century was the abominable age of impatience. All of the great ideologies are based on impatience. That is what he calls utopia: The utopianism of both Stalin and Hitler was based on the impatience of wanting their vision right now. Let's not wait for it; let's do it right now. That is Sloterdijk's conservative—I would call it reactionary, but let's leave that aside—denunciation of ideological absolutism.

How else to describe this historical period? Is there a new kind of temporal analysis that we can invent for this new period of historicity? How is the future conceived? It seems to me that all of these various notions of history have their own responses to these questions. The one that I think is the most interesting is described by Koselleck as he is identifying the outcome of the French Revolution as republicanism.

> Republicanism indicated the principle of historical movement, and it was a moral dictate for political action to press it forward. Whatever constitution might be in force, it was necessary in the long run

> to displace the rule of men by men with the rule of men by law; i.e., to realize the republic. Republicanism was therefore a concept of movement which did for political action what "progress" promised to do for the whole of history.[3]

I suppose "progress" is the name for the historicity of this new period. But what he suggests is that, since this notion has no real content, it opens the door to a whole variety of possibilities.

> The temporal difference between all previously experienced forms of rule and the constitution that was to be expected and toward which one should strive was in this way embodied in a concept that had a direct influence on political life. This provides the outline of the temporal structure of a concept and recurs in numerous concepts that followed it, whose designs for the future have since then sought to overtake and outbid. "Republicanism" was followed by "democracy," "liberalism," "socialism," "communism," and "fascism," to name only the most influential.[4]

Another way of approaching the movement of this new temporality would be to say that it simply moves back and forth between reaction and revolution. But, here, we are really getting into conjecture. Are we still in one or another of these pendular swings? That is the point at which Koselleck leaves us. That is to say, despite the idea that he is a historian claiming simply to be noting certain patterns, there is always an ideology underneath what he notes, an ideology of modernity. As I said before, modernity is the catchphrase for the moment of change, the moment of transition to … to what?

I'm not going to spend much time on the emergence of the Constance School out of the Gadamerian idea that interpretation is an event, but I do want you to know how they propose to use these ideas of the space of experience and the horizon of expectation. Hans Robert Jauss was a medievalist, and he put forward what you could loosely call reception theory. Wolfgang Iser is the other one of this pair. What he proposes is a phenomenology of reading, and he begins with phenomenological

---

3 Koselleck, *Futures Past*, p. 273.
4 Ibid., p. 273.

predecessors like Roman Ingarden, a Polish phenomenologist. Both Jauss and Iser start from the principle that interpretation is something that isn't imposed from the outside but rather emerges from inside the work, which is a way of addressing a public.[5] So, if you wanted to speak as I did last week of Dante, you would have to ask what the horizon of expectation of his readers at the time would have been. What was their relationship to this text? What did they expect? What kinds of experiences did they bring to it? Such an approach could, in the long run, end up in a kind of objectivism, in which you simply try to reconstruct a reading past. But to do so would leave out Gadamer's sense that interpretation is an *act*, that it is the act in which the present somehow confronts the past, and in which the past is part of the present, such that the text from the past addresses us, rather than us addressing it. I don't think that either Iser or Jauss get that far. They are arguing on two fronts. They are arguing against older objectivist notions of interpretation, against notions of meaning of the old kind and, on the other hand, against the Marxists, who, on the other side of the border, in East Germany, are busy trying to reconstruct a purely objective historical criticism, that is to say, to ask how social class informs interpretation. Both of these alternatives, according to them, are, ultimately, positivistic.

Iser is particularly interested in how readers interpret a text. His idea is that there are blanks or absences which a text obliges you to fill in. Therefore, your interpretations flow from these blanks, which are the products of either primary or secondary repression. The primary set of blanks would be, let's say, traditional realism, eighteenth-century figures like Fielding. But then there is the question of modernism, Joyce and Beckett. There would have to be a differentiation of your relationship to what is now left out of such texts, which place the burden on you, as a reader, to restore in order to make it meaningful. But it remains unclear where to locate the interpretive act in this approach. For Jauss, to know something about a text you have to know the contemporary reception of it. I see this much more at work in art criticism than in literary criticism. For example, when the two most distinguished art critics, I would say, of our time—T. J. Clark and Michael Fried—are dealing with an impressionist painter, they provide

5 See Hans Robert Jauss, "Literary History as a Challenge to Literary Theory," trans. Elizabeth Benzinger, *New Literary History* 2, no. 1 (1970), pp. 7–37; and Wolfgang Iser, "The Reading Process: A Phenomenological Approach," *New Literary History* 3, no. 2 (1972), pp. 279–99.

long quotes from the newspaper reviews of these artists (since, in those days, there were official salons, a place for an elevated public criticism of the arts). In other words, to understand that past, you need the written reactions of their contemporaries. But the problem is that those reactions *also* have to be interpreted. They are written in nineteenth-century language, with nineteenth-century concerns, so they are as far from us as the painting is. We are back in the vicious circle of hermeneutics, in which we can't understand how they were reacting unless we understand the language of the whole period, and the language of the whole period is lost to us unless we can understand the particular reactions which constitute it. There isn't really a place for us to stand in that notion of reception.

I think we can conclude there. We will go on to Negt and Kluge next time.

November 2, 2021

19

Negt and Kluge

I'm not giving you anything in this course that I don't have some kind of respect for. Jauss and Iser, well, in life they were a very annoying pair, but, nonetheless, both left considerable work, much of which is of value. I would say that Jauss, in particular, was responsible for a lot of polemics, which are fine. I don't pay much attention to those now. But his contribution was to point to the moment at which history enters literary study, something that happens a century before the French Revolution with the *Querelle des Anciens et des Modernes*, the quarrel of the ancients and the moderns. This is the first full-blown debate about the nature of historical value. It involves a very naive question: Who is better, Sophocles and Aeschylus or Racine and Corneille? It is evident that Racine in particular has a perfection that no ancient work could ever aspire to, but, on the other hand, the Greeks not only came first but had a power and an invention that the moderns can't attain. So, it goes back and forth—some defend the ancients, some the moderns—in a debate that lasts from the 1680s until the 1720s. The conclusion is simply that one was not better than the other; they're just different. Suddenly, with that seemingly complete evacuation of the question, you are faced with history. That is to say, the ancient and the modern are two different historical epochs characterized by two different kinds of works, which you can't compare as if they were in some kind of competition. Each has its own characteristics and demands its own philology, let's say. The conclusion of difference, the disappearance of the question of value, and I would say, of beauty, means the emergence of philology as a historical discipline. Philology, in this period, is not yet completed. It seems to me that we have now arrived at a philology of the present, of the contemporary, and that really is a very complicated and difficult thing. The original philologists had no conception of a philology of the present. What they were aware of was the historicity of the past. So, to mix the languages of our various writers, one should attend to the *Begriffsgeschichte*, the Koselleck-type history of this neologism, "historicity," to understand what it means for the modern interpreter gradually to come to some awareness that he or she is also historical and that they are grappling with a two-way problem. I think Jauss deserves some credit for that insight, and as for Iser, his phenomenology of language can be very useful.

Let's say that this question of history and historicity leaves us with four different themes. One is the break itself. I told you that I thought the questions about periods are productive for a description, for an early stage in this process. You have to be able to describe a period, but this requires a process of differentiation, in which you identify how this period is different from some other period. The underlying question is: Where is the break? Every one of these works is subtended by some kind of belief in the modern. We have never been modern, says Bruno Latour, but, for Latour, the realization that we have never been modern is itself a historical break, so he has an idea of a break even if he doesn't want to say so. The existence of capitalism also implies a break, after which, suddenly, it becomes possible to speak of a specifically capitalist mode of production. So, I suggest that this movement from history to historicity is our old friend the question of modernity disguised as a conceptual event.

Negt and Kluge share a certain number of these concerns, including the question of the otherness of the past, or more generally, otherness as such. Does the projection of otherness require a call for empathy? Can we understand the other? Is there something beyond the relationship of one other to another, as in Hegel's master and slave? Is it possible or desirable to move beyond the duality of otherness? Do we consider the other as an object or as a subject for whom we are the object? We are told we must give up the subject-object relationship. The position of the interpreter, of hermeneutics, addresses the other as a situation. There is an other there who is demanding to be the object of my understanding. With Dilthey and the theorists of history in the late nineteenth century, the hermeneutic process is all about *Verstehen*, understanding the other, which gives rise to a new concern, namely empathy. The word comes into English in the early twentieth century, but it emerges from these theories in late nineteenth-century Europe. It remains problematical. What is this other? Or, as Negt and Kluge will sometimes say, isn't the other constructed? And if we have to construct otherness ourselves before we try to understand it, is any encounter with otherness bound to be an encounter with ourselves, with what we already know?

Many of you have said—and they say so themselves, in so many words—that Negt and Kluge's *History and Obstinacy* is rhizomatic. I personally don't happen to have a physical attachment to books the way a bibliophile would, but this one is really remarkable. It is published by Kluge's own publishing house, 2001. The date of the first publication is 1981, so the name comes from a future 2001, a publishing house of a future which hadn't yet arrived. It's full of pictures. You can always attribute the presence of the pictures to Kluge. Maybe you have a philosophical argument from Negt, but the pictures will be Kluge's wink at you. They are often paradoxical, or rather they don't necessarily illustrate the argument. They provoke problems, or they suggest solutions that the argument itself doesn't propose.

One that I particularly like is about the emergence of beaten paths.[1] In the rubble of a city, clearly right after the war, we have a milkman. I don't think we have those anymore. He has a white coat. He's carrying an old-fashioned holder for milk bottles, seven or eight milk bottles. This figure is striding very calmly through a landscape that is completely destroyed. Are not beaten paths the way that habits are formed? The emergence of beaten paths would be both the cause and the effect of habit. Here is the rubble. How do you make your way through it? If you cross it often enough, like a milkman would—who is he bringing his milk to?—then a path is made in a place in which there are no longer any streets.

In what sense is this book a rhizome? The notion of rhizome is an attack on the conceptual schema of the tree, which you find all the way back in Aristotle's logic. A concept has its dependencies, its origin, its base, and its direction. It has its branches and its roots. It can be parsed analytically. In that sense, it brings an order to what it names. For Deleuze, it is a royal schema, a schema of power, domination, and order. The rhizome is also something organic, but unlike a tree, it sends off its shoots in all directions,

1 Alexander Kluge and Oskar Negt, *History and Obstinacy*, trans. Richard Langston et al., ed. Devin Fore (New York: Zone Books, 2014), p. 112.

like a potato. Does a rhizome have a center? Eventually not, or, at least, that is what may be desirable in them. I think that this book is more of a rhizome, in a way, than Deleuze's own books, but it is, nonetheless, unfinished. There is a little epilogue, just a page or so, where Negt and Kluge say, in effect, "Look, we're exhausted. This is enough. We can't do any more right now, but maybe we'll come back to some of these things." The problem with the translation is that the translators, who are certainly to be praised for this effort, shouldn't have given this back to Negt and Kluge, because, obviously, Negt and Kluge cannot keep their hands off of anything. They have taken their own work apart, removed some things, added others. Of course, they are reworking the book primarily for an American public, while the original itself addresses a German history, a German public, as was the much more conventional-looking book on the proletarian public sphere.

It is even more difficult at this distance to know exactly what the original was doing, but we know it has something to do not just with the transformation of Germany but also with the reinvention of Germany. This is a reinvention of a certain kind of strange Marxism. It is a reinvention of the Left. It is a process of combining the analysis of the past and of tradition with the production of new learning processes. But it is a very different combination of the past and the future than that of the German '60s student movements, and, in that sense, it stands all by itself. You can't say it is a monument. You could say it is a collection of ruins, something like Stonehenge. It has a unity, no doubt, or a completeness, but in fact, up close, it turns out to have been composed of many separate parts. To discern its separate elements is part of the pleasure of reading it.

It is divided into three parts. The first part is about labor power. The second part in German is about *Öffentlichkeit*, that is, the public sphere, the transfer into the public sphere. And the third is about relationality. The question is: How to look at these separate parts? What we have lost in translation is their analysis of Germany in the second part. That loss is a great pity, but I can restore a little bit of it as we talk about this section. Let's begin with the notion of labor and labor power. In the 1850s, Marx writes to Engels and says, "Listen, I've just discovered something. We've gotten all this wrong. We've been talking about labor, but it's not labor that we're talking about. It's *labor power*." What does he mean by that? Why are they not talking about labor or work when they're talking about wage labor? To answer these questions, we have to return to the difference between quantity and quality, the difference between the concrete and the abstract. Any form of labor is concrete. It always has individual qualities and calls on individual capacities. It produces a certain effect. All of this, because it is already done. Labor is what has already been done. Marx says that, in a way, the capitalist is really in debt to the workers, who have worked the whole week without pay, only to be paid at the end. The workers are giving him their labor on credit. They have themselves created this thing that he then pretends to pay them for. Looking back at their work, they have done a specific task and produced a use-value. They built a road, let's say. A road has a use. But then they have to build a bridge. That would be a different kind of thing with different requirements. It involves a whole different set of problems than the laying of a foundation of a road. So, labor is not the word we want for both of these different activities. What the worker is, under capitalism, is his *capacity* to work. He hasn't done anything yet. He is selling his time. Time and labor power are the abstraction, exchange-value. Labor itself is use-value. Accordingly, Negt and Kluge talk about phenomena in terms of labor power, rather than commodification, labor, or any of these other codes.

But they don't only follow Marx's method of abstraction when discussing labor power. André Gide was asked in an interview with a little magazine why he writes. "Well," he says, "there are three answers. I write because I want to please you, because I want to pursue something, and because I have a good pen." The *why*, the various constituents that make up an act, can be separated. Let me give you an example of how Negt and Kluge do that. They're talking about the multiplicity that goes into a so-called self.

> It would be a gross simplification to assign a single personhood to every single person, as well as to every one of their internal representatives that feed off of strife and life. One characteristic shared by people ensnared in a fight and people who are happy, for example, is the fact that they are capable of expressing themselves rationally... We could break down both arguing and happy people into their actual characteristics, which themselves are individual persons; within a single divided person, these characteristics sit across from one another only extrinsically. Passion's eyes are different from its hands. The eyes of the objective remote senses are different from those of the immediate senses. The eyes involved in fleeing from another are different from the eyes involved in a person's

> appetite. In certain respects, the entire history of humanity—the society responsible for bringing these characteristics about—is present in a fight within the family or in the happy caresses between a few select people.[2]

I think this has a lot in common with affect theory. If you think of affects, as they do, as forms of labor power, then you can see how you could take apart a combination of affects and you could endow each one with its specific productive powers. In this regard, their work could rejoin the kinds of theory that they were doing in France at the time, in which everything is conceived as production (a very mannered way of intellectuals trying to be Marxists or trying to be political by using this word, "production"). Nonetheless, Negt and Kluge allow one to reimagine analysis in terms of production, or better still, in terms of the combination of labor powers, which requires us to see how the unskilled laborer is also a combination of skills, and how even the complete lack of skill would itself be a kind of skill, if you like.

There is also the question of the remnant of the production process. In other words, now I'm trying to answer the most problematic question about this whole book: What do Negt and Kluge mean by *Eigensinn*? *Geschichte und Eigensinn*, *History and Obstinacy*. What can obstinacy possibly mean here? Clearly—although maybe it isn't clear—it has to do with something beyond the various capacities of labor power. Maybe you could call it self-preservation or the Spinozan *conatus*. It is what keeps something in being. Obstinacy is this insistence on continuing to be. It is also a resistance to training. Labor power requires training. You have to train these various impulses so as to put them together in some way, to make them function. That is a form of discipline which nobody particularly enjoys, so obstinacy would be the resistance against it.

One of the nice features of this argument, if we can call it that, is its use of a pair of concepts: ontogenesis and phylogenesis. What things have to come together in an individual? And what has to come together for a community? Going back to the past is not just a question of history. It is a question of finding the underlying impulses that have constituted an individual and a society. That is why the book is marked by the presence of fairy tales, the Grimm brothers being among the first to discover and collect what remained of the storytelling past.

2 Ibid., p. 362.

Here is a story from the Grimm brothers about obstinacy. It is quite hideous:

> Once upon a time there was a stubborn child who never did what his mother told him to do. The dear Lord, therefore, did not look kindly upon him and let him become sick. No doctor could cure him, and in a short time, he lay on his deathbed. After he was lowered into his grave and was covered over with earth, one of his little arms suddenly emerged and reached up into the air. They pushed it back down and covered the earth with fresh earth, but that did not help. The little arm kept popping out. So the child's mother had to go to the grave herself and smack the little arm with a switch. After she had done that, the arm withdrew, and then, for the first time, the child had peace beneath the earth.[3]

I think this is a particularly hideous story, and I hope you all agree. Is this a horror story, the return from beyond the grave? Certainly, the ghosts are figures for some form of obstinacy, not in death but in life. The mother and God himself clearly stand for order, for the disciplining of the primal impulse to life, and yet the narrative seems somehow to endow them with something more positive. There is something horribly puritanical about this story. They draw on Horkheimer's essay on authority in the family, which allows them to draw a direct line from the notion of the family, the paternal ogre or disciplinary figure, to the authoritarian personality. And yet somehow the child exceeds the power these figures exert over him, at least until the final punishment allows it "peace," an odd name for this dystopia in which all living impulses are repressed.

Obstinacy, as this story illustrates so well, is what constantly resists discipline. It is the source of disobedience, and it is life itself. What is the role of obstinacy in capitalism? Nobody wants to work under a wage labor

3 "The Obstinate Child," *Children's and Household Tales*, qtd. in Negt and Kluge, *History and Obstinacy*, p. 292. In a footnote to the story, the editor, Devin Fore, provides the following quote from Negt: "In *History and Obstinacy* we are always looking for the aspect that has been covered up, for what is burrowing around under the surface, which is why our favorite animal is the mole that works *sous terre*, as Hegel says. That is precisely where, within man, the concealed, buried, and distorted characteristics are located—protest energies, which we try to straighten out in our writings; but this is also where certain needs are located in the form of concrete" (pp. 459–60; citing Negt, *Der Maulwurfkennt kein System*, p. 12).

system. The question of productive and unproductive labor is perennially posed, but it can be quite misleading here. Given the nature of our society, of course, everybody thinks that to be productive is good. Marx lay around on his couch, dozed, covered himself with the ashes from his cigarettes and cigars. Okay, well, that is surely unproductive. But Marx says at some point: No, productivity is making surplus value for the boss, the owner. Who wants to do that? There is no virtue in laboring productively. Are we, in the university, laboring productively or unproductively? Supposedly, in the immense collection of notes called *Theories of Surplus Value*, Marx says that only someone working for a private university is doing productive labor. I haven't found this myself, but this is a very interesting thought for all of us to consider, whether or not Marx said it.

Obstinacy under capitalism is the refusal to produce surplus value. But it is not necessarily a good thing. Would we say, for example, that warfare is the ultimate example of obstinacy? I think not, since warfare implies a certain kind of coordinated effort or construction. Kluge wrote a little book on Stalingrad, which is, again, filled with all kinds of interesting things, including notes from a manual handed out to the soldiers.[4] How was this disaster for the Germans constructed? It's as though someone set out to imagine the worst possible catastrophe, and then asked: How can I possibly bring it about? What elements do I need? What kind of labor power do I have to acquire and combine in order to produce this absolute disaster, the battle of Stalingrad?

We'll end with one more example, although there is much more to see in this text. Long before Stalingrad, there is another disaster, which is at the source of the uniqueness of German history according to Negt and Kluge. Because they use the fate of the peasantry as a leitmotif for their exploration of social history—and indeed they draw on Bahro's discussion of modes of production—they are aware of the various ways in which societies are built on the labor of the earth. At what point do we find our way out of the relationship to the earth which is unique to the peasantry and into a different, capitalist, extractive relationship to the earth? And what becomes of the peasants? Negt and Kluge discuss English, French, and Italian versions of the peasantry's path into capitalism. These new societies emerge from the peasantry which they encounter as a first form of obstinacy. How, in these different cultures, is the resistance of the

4 Alexander Kluge, *The Battle*, trans. Leila Vennewitz (New York: Hill-McGraw, 1967).

peasantry managed or maintained? In Germany, the peasant wars are the catastrophe that prevents Germany from modernizing—the barbarity of the massacre of the peasants in 1517 with Thomas Müntzer, as opposed to Luther and his soldiers of the princes. This is the primal trauma in German history, which is repeated over and over again, surfacing as a nightmare in the Thirty Years' War, which is only ended by a treaty, which is largely responsible for the formation of modern nation-states. You can't say that Negt and Kluge are making an argument for the peasant wars as an original national trauma, because they don't make arguments in that way, but the peasant wars are certainly their primal source of obstinacy in German history, as if finally Luther's princes and their noble armies have beaten back this hand that keeps coming out of the grave, having put this power of obstinacy to rest in some ultimately unproductive way.

We'll go on with Negt and Kluge next time.

November 4, 2021

20

Negt and Kluge, Weiss

What can we do with Negt and Kluge? I confess I'm at a loss, because there is so much in here that it can be difficult to organize. After all, it is about organization for them—their production of this book is a formal and organization problem—and, in that sense, it is a medium which is its own message. But what I think we need to retain from the first section as we move into the other two is the notion of *Trennung*, "separation." They want to insist that there are two dimensions to their problem: the formation of tradition and the individual subject. Those dimensions are not the same, and yet, obviously, they have a relationship to each other. This is a book about that relationship.

I want to say more about the *Trennung* idea, but I'll do so by giving you a personal reaction rather than an explication of their actual theory. One of the fundamental dialectics that are of importance to us in such theoretical investigations is the dialectic between identity and difference: Identity turns into difference and difference turns back into identity, so that, really, they are a pair that imply each other and thus imply that we must take a position wherever we find them. When you try to identify a thing, you end up identifying all the things it's not. When you want to talk about the difference of things from each other, you end up talking about their identity. This plays its role, I think, in the question of unity in the history of literature. It seems to me that unity is always the result of an act of unification. There isn't any unity. Bits of the world must always be put together. Sometimes, they are put together under the aegis of common sense, which is also an ideology of unity. Common sense tells us that the world is composed of separate objects which are all arranged together in some separate space. So, if you want a version of realism—in the novel, too—then it would be the construction of those continuities. With the modernist break—to stick with the novel—it seems to me that you have the emergence of radical differences which are still dealt with in the spirit of a possible unification. I would say that one of the fundamental units in the modern movement is that of the ideogram—in Pound and Eisenstein—different images or signs which can be brought together such that their difference becomes a kind of unity. Postmodernism, I think, relaxes this tension in the elements of modernist construction so that an ideology of difference can preside over them.

I tried to invent a slogan—"difference relates"—which would be useful in understanding how elements that seem to have no relationship to each other nonetheless determine each other.[1] This is what the concept of *Trennung* names and provides with historical specificity. It is at the origin of Marx's notion of alienation in the early writings, which are very much organized around separation. This was something Hegel could not have seen. The first real labor strikes take place in Lyon in the early 1830s. Hegel died in 1831. This was one of Marcuse's arguments in his book on Hegel: Hegel could not be accused of failing to theorize class adequately because class was not something that he had experienced in its modern form. So, with Marx, we can see that alienation is the worker's separation from his product, his tools, his fellow workers, and, finally, from his life or his species-being. For Negt and Kluge, then, reunification is only possible on the basis of this preliminary separation on the level of the individual psyche as well as on the level of the collectivity. The histories of each level depend on this cycle of separation and the construction of relationships between what is separated (and that is indeed a special word for Negt and Kluge: "relationship" or "connection," *Zusammenhang*). Obstinacy is then what has been left over after these separations. It is what can't be captured by any of these forces and therefore remains in an inchoate state that resists everything.

As for the collective, it is the mode of production which is crucial. The obstinacies of older modes of production are those that do not fit into the new order, the new capitalist system as it emerges. What do we mean by

1 See Fredric Jameson, *Valences of the Dialectic* (London: Verso, 2009).

the emergence of capitalism? The traditional category for this emergence is so-called primitive accumulation. Primitive accumulation is always a version of the break or separation, if you like, which a pre-capitalist society has to undergo in order to become capitalist. If you think of the difference between what happens in England, where the legal process of enclosure throws the peasants into the road, so to speak, where they become the reserve army of the factories to come, and what happens in Peru or Mexico, where Spanish invaders force the native inhabitants to work essentially as slaves in the mines, gathering gold and silver to send back to Spain, then you find that there are two basic forms of the emergence of capital, of primitive accumulation. This is not something that Marx insists on, since he is dealing directly with England, but he provides a conceptual vocabulary for characterizing various capitalisms, the ways capitalism strikes each of these societies differently depending on how it has been absorbed into what would soon be a world-wide system. In the original book, Negt and Kluge include a section on the path of each country in question into capitalism, but, in the translation, these are reduced to a single section.

They locate the actuality of this way of thinking in the Frankfurt School. "As of 1932, the thinkers of Critical Theory practiced by the Frankfurt School no longer considered the proletariat as the historical subject of emancipation." Why? Because the workers voted for Hitler.

> They observed how Communist unions and National Socialist organized labor joined forces in the Berlin transportation strike of 1932. How could it have happened that workers possessed no immunity to fascism? Since then, the adherents of Critical Theory—along with the authors of the book before you—have discontinued investigating the emancipatory potentials within entire social groups and instead have turned to consider the raw material of these potentials, the ruptured, yet still lively INDIVIDUAL CHARACTERISTICS located beneath the level of the whole person.[2]

These modes of adaptation, so to speak, of the existing populations are going to essentially bear on peasants, agricultural laborers in the earlier mode of production. How have peasants been absorbed into the new system? In each of these places it takes a different form. "In England, the

2 Negt and Kluge, *History and Obstinacy*, p. 220.

expulsion of peasants and the burning of their cottages were carried out almost completely." And then we have some questions. "Does the particular talent of Britons—be it forming working lower classes, being a 'British subject' at every point within the colonial empire, or operating under the umbrella of FINANCE CAPITALISM—derive from this historical fate"—this fate of the English peasantry, as well as the Scottish, Welsh, and so on? "How does French CAPITALIST PRODUCTION—its techniques, forms of life, and values are easily differentiated from Britain's—relate to the peasant uprisings there and the equilibrium of power established thereafter, the expropriation of nobility and the churches, as well as the fates of the peasant class and urban cultures of France? What occurred differently in Italy? What was different in Islamic countries?" And, since this is a book about Germany, what happened in Germany? What happened was the peasant wars, and they "ended in bitter disappointment, not only for peasants, but also for the cities in league with them. Did this lead to the fact that in this region later called Germany, a revolution like France's never succeeded, and instead, a 'National Socialist revolution' was realized?"[3]

Later, when they look at fairy tales, they will compare Greek and German. In reply to Adorno's analysis of the *Odyssey* in *Dialectic of Enlightenment*, they use a later Greek poem, *Argonautica*, the search for the golden fleece, Jason and Medea, as their object of study. What they note in both these examples is that labor is what must be controlled or suppressed. Odysseus's oarsmen have their ears stopped, while he is able to hear the sirens. Their analysis of the golden fleece, meanwhile, makes much of the fact that, as the legend tells us, one side of it is gold, but on the other side is a map, the map of the Mediterranean that Jason wants. It is the key to the imperialism of the seaborn society, whereas, in Germany, which is landlocked, everything will turn around the house. In these fairy tales, you have the defense of the house against the wolf. In Germany, the stories of trauma turn around the protection of the house against outside forces. "The fact also comes into view that on account of the specific relations of German history, it was initially difficult to determine whom Germans let in with Hitler. There were couriers bearing nourishment, flour-covered paws, and voices both falsetto and wolflike. The man privately called himself Wolf"—Hitler's own name for himself—"but actually was Adolf.

3 Ibid., pp. 221–2.

He kissed women's hands, issued criminal commands, was a vegetarian, cared for both a chicken in every pot and equality, eliminated an entire people in the cruelest of ways, and brought about unity."[4]

The wolf dresses up as a grandmother, as you recall. How are the Germans to identify this thing that they have let inside the house? This is one of the upshots of the narratives which they consider to be a source of information about how a peasant culture resists an emerging society whose existence is predicated on the absorption and elimination of the peasantry itself. My sense is that, in a way, the peasantry, even in its reduced form today—when the actual peasantry, even in countries where it survives and has not been transformed into a mass of agricultural workers, is reduced to less than 10 percent of the workforce—has protected a relationship to culture which doesn't exist in countries in which the peasantry has been completely assimilated to capitalism. You have two examples of countries in which the government has deliberately kept the peasantry alive by subsidies and in which the payoff is the existence of a culture that has not been completely destroyed by a globalized capitalism into which these countries have otherwise been absorbed: Japan and France. It does seem to me that this is Negt and Kluge's point of view: The peasantry is this ultimate force which embodies the authentic obstinacy of a people.

The story of Jason and the Argonauts is also a parable of separation. The inhabitants of Colchis, where the Argonauts have stopped to look for the golden fleece, are terrified of these beings, a little like the inhabitants of the so-called New World were of Spaniards when they arrived. So, they lay out a number of items on the beach to propitiate the gods. In the night, the sailors from the *Argo* take all those items. The inhabitants then assume that the gods have been satisfied and accepted their offerings, but, of course, for the people on the ship, this is an exchange relationship, not a gift, so they get out of their end of the deal by laying much of the village to waste. Gradually, Negt and Kluge tell us, these inhabitants learn what an exchange society is. They undergo a learning process whereby they come to understand that their items are involved in a reciprocal process of exchange.

I wanted to illustrate the way in which the form of the past will give the labor power of the present its quality or workability. There is a brilliant example from Karl Korsch, whose book *Marxism and Philosophy* was one

4 Ibid., p. 282.

of the basic texts of the '20s. He was Brecht's teacher of Marxism, so to speak, and he broke with the party at some point. He wrote an analysis of the blitzkrieg. The blitzkrieg was, of course, the most successful feature of National Socialist warfare. It was the reaction in strategy to the immobilization of trench warfare. Of course, every war is the last, so the general staffs of all these countries assumed that it would be another version of earlier wars, only bigger. But the blitzkrieg was the way in which the superiority of Nazi armies was at first to be demonstrated: the liquidation of Poland within a few weeks, and finally the lightning attack on the low countries and on France a few months later.

It has always been assumed that it was because Hitler was smart enough to draw the lessons of mechanized warfare and to allow free rein to his generals, who were really intelligently aware of how mechanized warfare could be used, that the blitzkrieg was possible. In France, General de Gaulle insisted on a reconstruction of the French army along mechanized lines. He was unsuccessful. Later, the most famous American general to have adopted this strategy was Patton. Korsch asks: Is this new type of warfare simply a matter of technology? Is this simply the obvious advantage of mobile technology? The modern form of warfare poses all kinds of logistical problems. For an army to outrun its supply of oil, for example, is a big problem. Is the solution to the oil problem the initial secret of success?

Negt and Kluge reference this essay of Korsch, who analyzed the blitzkrieg as he was in exile in Boston. He could not believe that the fascist enemy had mastered such an intelligent military strategy. Where did it come from?

> In his analysis, he established that in their civilian life, the majority of the tank crews of the German divisions were car mechanics or engineers (that is, industrial workers with practical experience). Many of them came from the German provinces that had experienced bloody massacres at the hands of the authorities in the Peasant Wars (1524–1526). According to Korsch, they had good reason to avoid direct contact with their superiors. Almost all of them could also vividly remember the positional warfare of 1916, again a result of the actions of their superiors, in whom they had little faith thereafter. In this way, Korsch continues, a readied and focused motive emerged from the spirit of the balance economy: it is advantageous to have as little contact as possible with the adversary, and therefore he must be outflanked once he is cut

> off in a confined space. At the same time, it is also advantageous when advancing to switch off any radio equipment enabling communication with your own commanders. According to Korsch, it thereby became possible for the troops to invent for themselves the blitzkrieg spontaneously, out of historical motives at hand. Orders alone would not have been sufficient to achieve such a thing.[5]

That the soldiers who were involved in the blitzkrieg were already laborers of a specific kind is what gave the blitzkrieg its power. That is what gave them the ability to improvise, to prevent certain breakdowns. As you remember, the famous Schlieffen Plan of World War I was the German plan to go through Belgium, strike downwards into the center of France and take Paris. They failed in the Battle of the Marne, when the French, government seized all of the taxis in Paris and sent the troops out to meet the German armies at the river. But, in 1940, this plan succeeds, and its success is based on a certain kind of labor power.

That is how I wanted to finish with this mammoth work of Negt and Kluge. I want to very rapidly go on to Peter Weiss. Husserl talked about *Abschattungen*, the aspects or nuances of the work that cannot be made into a unity but that each offer a kind of semiautonomy. I want to show you how that would work in Weiss's *Aesthetics of Resistance*. It can even give us a different view of the famous fusion of horizons. Here you have something like a reception of a reception.

"The populace, when trudging by on solemn days, scarcely dared to glance up at the effigy of its own history." Why "effigy"? Because this phrase is already the picture of a popular revolt which is put down by superior force. What is being described is the Pergamon Altar, which depicts the revolt of Gaia, the earth, and her children against the Olympians. The whole thing is a horrible, nightmarish scare-picture warning the underclasses of what will happen to them if they rise and revolt, which later they do. That could be a veiled allusion to the famous revolt in East Germany in 1953, which included workers who were constructing the new Stalinallee, now Karl-Marx-Allee. I won't say Peter Weiss was very close to the East German regime, but he went there frequently and had friends there. This is one of the few works to be published simultaneously on both sides of the Wall, the Iron Curtain. I have a friend who was teaching a seminar

5 Ibid., p. 330.

on it after Reunification in Humboldt, and he said the West German students got nothing out of it, whereas the East German students were very excited by this work that was so central during the West German student movement in the '70s.

"The populace, when trudging by on solemn days, scarcely dared to glance up at the effigy of its own history, while—along with the priests—the philosophers and poets, the artists from elsewhere, all full of factual knowledge, had long since walked around the temple; and that which, for the ignorant, lay in magical darkness was, for the informed, a handicraft to be soberly assessed."[6] Now, we get a multiplicity of viewpoints, the viewpoint of the intellectual, so to speak, the priests, the slaves, the populace, and so on. Already there is a fusion of horizons in that original reaction to the work with which our horizon of expectation can presumably coincide.

But what I really wanted to show you was how this novel works. One of the features of this opening scene is the stone which has to be dragged by slaves from its quarry and brought to the center. "In the marble quarries on the mountain slopes north of the castle, the master sculptors had pointed their long sticks at the best blocks while eying the Gallic captives toiling in the sultry heat." Here is one plateau, if you like: the hidden labor that has been covered over by the final product. In the final product we see nothing of nonaesthetic labor, the sweat of just bringing these stones in. But then: "Shielded and fanned by palm branches, squinting in the blinding sun, the sculptors took in the rippling of the muscles, the bending and stretching of the sweating bodies."[7] So now you have not only the use of the slaves in bringing the stone, but you have the slaves themselves serving as models for the figures that are to be carved into this stone, that is, the bodies which are to be reproduced in the form of the myth being portrayed here, the struggle between these various kinds of bodies. There is a very strange separation of form and content here, but it is a separation that also allows them to be recombined. If we assume that it is the slaves who are the physical models, their bodies, that takes us in one direction. If we are to concentrate on how this stone is brought out of the earth, what kinds of social relations were involved, then we are moved in another direction. This whole narrative is constantly finding,

6 Peter Weiss, *The Aesthetics of Resistance, Volume 1*, trans. Joachim Neugroschel (Durham, NC: Duke University Press, 2005), p. 5.

7 Ibid., p. 10.

over and over again, different aspects of a historical process that it suggests can never be exhausted.

The novel turns into a history of Pergamon. The hero will end up in Spain during the Spanish Civil War, where he finds traces of the Pergamon empire of the Hellenistic period in settlements in Spain. So, it is a history that doesn't leave him. It follows him all over, this exploration of the very epitome of subjection, of civil war, of oppression and resistance:

> Heilmann asked whether we had noticed that inside, in the altar room, a spatial function had been inverted, so that exterior surfaces had become interior walls. In facing the western perron, he said, we had our backs to the eastern side, the rear of the temple, that is, in its merely rudimentary reconstruction, and the unfolded southern frieze stretched out to the right while the relief on the northern cornice ran to the left. Something the viewer was to grasp by slowly circling it was now surrounding him instead.[8]

Instead of a purely aesthetic appreciation of this thing it becomes something inside of which we are caught, a work which, by virtue of these multiple aspects and our exploration of these rhizomatic sides is going to include us in it in some way. I think that would be a way of thinking through the fusion of horizons somewhat differently than has normally been put forward. Whether Gadamer would accept that or not, I don't know.

Two more things and then we'll have to finish. It seems to me that these three students are going to represent different tendencies. Heilmann is already a member of the party, and he will be caught and executed in the third volume. The narrator represents the idea of the unification of the Left, that is, the Socialist Party and the Communist Party. In this earlier period, before the Popular Front, there is the so-called Third Period of Communist strategy in which any connections with the Socialist Party are to be broken. The Popular Front will be an attempt to recombine those factions. After the war, in the East, what is left of the Socialist Party is at least technically allied with the Communist Party, but is, in fact, swallowed up by it. Anyway, the whole work is a plea for the unification of these forces, represented by a figure who we don't really see, Münzenberg, who

---

8 Ibid., 10.

was the historical figure who tried to keep the Comintern alive as a synthesis between all of these left movements, a cultural synthesis in fact, an insistence on the value of superstructures in the struggle. One must also consider the doctor, Max Hodann, a part of this insistence; he is based on a real person, operating in the tendency of Wilhelm Reich, who argues that the revolution would have to be a psychic one—I don't say sexual in the sense of Reich's sexual politics, though it is related—as opposed to the revolutionary puritanism that was maintained in the Communist Party. The first two volumes are composed of long discussions between the narrator and his father, between other historical figures, and, particularly in this initial part, between Heilmann, who has a sense of utopia, and Coppe, who insists that there has to be a dictatorship of the proletariat. So, the sympathetic rendering of contradictions is hard enough to solve. The whole thing will take a form not of unification but of the difficulty of giving a picture of the entire Left and its defeat during this period.

The other way to look at this novel is by noting that it tries to give a picture of the contradictions of its own internationalism. We have a name for what the most elaborated form of collectivity is: "nation" or "nation-state." Beyond that, we don't have anything that works. We use words like "globalization" to name larger relations between elements that were earlier confined to the nation. We have various idealistic pictures, like that of a federation or, of course, the Soviet Union itself, with its notion of a union; Yugoslavia was the other place in which something like a federation was attempted until the civil war. But we don't yet have any sense of what a larger political unit should be called. We still call the United States a nation-state, for example, which it isn't exactly. When you read the essay of Perry Anderson on the European Union you will see this problem at work: Europe is only apparently a unified kind of a nation-state.[9] But, in Weiss, the form that this problem takes is the old idea of socialism in one country. Whereas it would be desirable for the Left to have a unified politics, the actual unified politics of the '30s and '40s turned out to be the defense of a single nation-state, a single socialism, that is, the Soviet Union.

These political discussions become very complicated over the course of Weiss's novel. Instead of being able to argue out the situation of the Left in a given country, they also have to add a consideration of whether it will be

9 Perry Anderson, "The European Coup," *London Review of Books*, December 17, 2020.

good for the Soviet Union or not. Sometimes what is good for the Soviet Union is not good for the Hitler–Stalin Pact or, in fact, destroys national communist parties, because their strength depends on a resistance to the Germans. I want you to see this as a formal problem, that is, the problem of an international view of left politics—since this is certainly a political novel and a historical novel—which lacks a concept of internationalism. I think that is a problem which Weiss solves in some ways, but which is still very much with us. I think we have to break off here.

November 9, 2021

21

Bohrer, Kittler

After the war, when nobody is a fascist anymore, as Adorno put it in his letter to Thomas Mann, and even conservatives disguise themselves, there arrives a moment when it is again possible to express an anti-left conservatism. Something like that is certainly happening with Karl Heinz Bohrer. Bohrer is not a fascist, but let's put it this way: He is antipolitical, which entails anti-leftism as much as conservatism. As for the fascists themselves, we are seeing how it can become possible again to claim even a fascist position in mainstream discourse. After the war, a distinguished French film and literary scholar, Maurice Bardèche, who was certainly a collaborator, wrote a little book called *What Is Fascism?* in which he says that Hitler gave fascism a bad name. At the beginning of the student movement in France—at that point a left-wing student movement, nothing like the right-wing student movements of the '30s—he said that, if the students really knew what fascism was, and if it hadn't been distorted by propaganda, then they would realize that they were, in fact, a fascist rather than a left-wing movement. We are certainly entering a period in which it is allowed to take an extreme right-wing position.

One of the writers whom Bohrer and others in this tendency draw on is Ernst Jünger, who was a decorated soldier in World War I, born around the turn of the century. He was well known for his novel *Storm of Steel*. He was never a Nazi and did not participate in the Nazi movement, but he eventually rejoined the army and had a distinguished army career. This brings us to the myth of the aristocracy of the general staff and of the Wehrmacht, the army, as opposed to the SS. Quite a bit of propaganda went into making that distinction, because we know that the Wehrmacht in Eastern Europe certainly participated in the SS atrocities, but there remained a myth that the German army itself had traditions which were completely different from those of the Nazis, as, indeed, the Stauffenberg attempt on Hitler's life in 1944 demonstrated. But those people weren't leftists, of course. They were conservatives, military conservatives and aristocratic conservatives. The term *Junker* signifies the aristocratic land-owning class of Prussia, but, by extension, since Germany was reunited with Prussia by Bismarck, it is linked with the army. During the war, however, some of these distinctions begin to reemerge.

With Bohrer, we have a phenomenological analysis which begins with the surface phenomenon and then probes for its deeper meaning. In the text I've assigned, we begin with an abstract idea—suddenness—and then we work out towards all of its manifestations.[1] In both cases, Bohrer's method raises the question of what theory is. I think it would be worth dwelling on that question for a moment, because we will have to face it much more intensely when we come to Kittler. Theory, as it was used in the '60s and thereafter, is an attempt to philosophize in a situation in which philosophy is no longer possible. Philosophy, it seems to me, is based on the idea of a system, and the last real system was Hegel's. In Hegel's system, there is a series of three approaches to the Absolute: religion, then art, and then finally, at the famous end of art, the torch passes to philosophy itself. You see that in the *Aesthetics*. My own reading of this sequence is that Hegel was both right and wrong: It actually did not fall to philosophy to express the Absolute; it fell to a new kind of art, modernism, and that art has been the domain in which to seek the Absolute ever since. The works that we now consider classical in the modernist canon are precisely ones which don't so much express the religion of art as they do approach a kind of religion in their very attempt to convey or to approach the Absolute. Heidegger's Being is an attempt at something similar. It is very easy to transfer all of those languages back into the language of religion, and they give themselves as a substitute for religion, whether they are explicit attempts at secularization or not.

But then the problem becomes, if you can't do philosophy anymore, what does it mean to do theory? It seems to me that Bohrer gives us an

1 Karl Heinz Bohrer, *Suddenness: On the Moment of Aesthetic Appearance*, trans. Ruth Crowley (New York: Columbia University Press, 1994). Jameson assigned chapter 3, "The Prehistory of the Sudden: The Generation of the Dangerous Moment," pp. 39–69.

example of that problem by abstracting and analyzing a single element of a general situation. His is a thesis about temporality, but it is not integrated into a philosophy of temporality or even a history of it. That is why the word "modernity" is so helpful and so dangerous: It allows you to get away with anything. You can simply say that modernity begins with this phenomenon of suddenness, and then he shows us how suddenness is everywhere. It is, indeed, the way in which a present somehow secedes from the other temporalities and establishes itself as an absolute novelty. I do not mean to dismiss Bohrer's method entirely. I think it is very impressive, and I think one would be tempted to follow him in this. We used to talk in English-language studies of Joyce's epiphanies, and Bohrer's suddenness seems to be a similar but much more interesting phenomenon, at least to the degree that it is less familiar and can be dealt with independently from philosophical systems. He doesn't have to appeal back to Heidegger or to the philosophical analyses of temporality for some rationale for this secession of the present, and, yet, this notion of suddenness could very well function in the context of Heidegger's philosophy insofar as, like so many other things, it tries to overcome a vulgar temporality—"vulgar" meaning "everyday"—in the service of a deeper temporality characterized by these moments of breakthrough.

Bohrer's notion of suddenness, *Plötzlichkeit*, comes out of a famous definition by Goethe of what a story is: *unerhörte Begebenheit*, an unheard-of, scandalous, unexpected, astonishing, and unforeseen event. That is what one tells when one tells a story. Something radically new happens. You can see that this is going to fit into a modernist aesthetic, in which each new moment in the development of modernism is the emergence of something both radically unforeseen and logically adherent to the previous formation. So, one could talk about Adorno and Horkheimer's notion of stages of rationality, in a sense, in which each scientific discovery reconstructs a history behind it, so that the previous history before it came into existence suddenly falls into place as its preparation. This is what suddenness is used for, but it seems to me that one can't authentically fit suddenness into a philosophy of temporality or modernity, or indeed a politics, because to do so would be to reabsorb the concept into a system, making of suddenness something which is in fact foreseen. The very attempt to find a place for suddenness in a system deprives it of everything that gives it its authentic meaning.

The references here are very interesting. I mentioned Ernst Jünger. In the '30s he writes a book called *The Worker*, *Der Arbeiter*, which foresees phenomena like the Tiller Girls, except in society and the army, the total mobilization of society such as the Nazis carry out, though Jünger himself is too aristocratic to be interested in Hitler. During World War II, he is stationed in Paris, and his journals from the time are very interesting for chronicling the life of the intellectuals in occupied Paris. After the war, *Der Arbeiter* has a tremendous impact. Heidegger gives a seminar on it. They exchange letters. Jünger becomes, if not a philosopher, then a theorist. In his own career, Bohrer began by writing a dissertation on Jünger and the poetics of horror in his war novels.

I should say that Bohrer became a major figure in the Bundesrepublik. He wrote columns for the *Frankfurter Allgemeine Zeitung*, and he took over the editing of the *Merkur*, which was the most distinguished of the nonpolitical literary journals. What about Bohrer's politics? I would say the most important connection for understanding his politics is with another major conservative figure from an earlier generation, Carl Schmitt, to whom we owe a theory of the political as such and a certain idea of sovereignty. Sovereignty, for Schmitt, is exercised by whoever controls the state of exception. Obviously, this notion of sovereignty is a critique of representative democracy and is played out in the Nazi seizure of power. The whole notion of the state of exception is a kind of political version of suddenness, at least in the sense that it destroys the legitimacy of the past. It is imagined that this set of successions in representative government also legitimate it; the rulers are legitimated by these events codified in constitutions, and that legitimacy is passed on in much the same way a dynasty would pass on legitimacy in many older societies. In a sense, the theory of the state of exception says there is no legitimacy. Legitimacy is a false doctrine whose true power and existence only comes from people's belief in it. The minute the state of exception is declared, it becomes clear that true power is exercised in the state of exception itself.

I do not say that Bohrer endorses Schmitt, only that it would be very interesting to situate this doctrine of suddenness with respect to the state of exception. It seems to me that you could see Schmitt's doctrine as an embodiment of Bohrer's form, if that is what you want to call this notion of suddenness, or vice versa: If the reality of legitimation is such as Schmitt describes it, then the state of exception also supplies the meaning of Bohrer's criticism, namely that the modernist telos is nothing but an ideology. The modernist work has no relationship of legitimation to anything but itself. *Ulysses* or *The Waste Land* establishes its own legitimacy by a kind of *coup d'état* and again is reified by the academy or some other institution. These are the ways in which Bohrer's idea can really gain in momentum.

We can take Bohrer as a sign of the breakdown of the learning process of postwar Germany, of the idea that new subjectivities can be constructed in this new situation following year zero, the destruction of Germany. This is not the affirmation of tradition in Gadamer's sense, but it is, somehow, the acknowledgement and even concretization of the impossibility of creating the new. It signals a new which doesn't lead anywhere, which is an experience in its own right but does not construct a tradition or a culture or a subjectivity.

One should be aware of and look for the degeneration of these theories into what I would call culture critiques, in which one identifies something which is original in the present and then turns it into the defining feature of a psychology, psychologizing the people or the collectivity for which this has been a formative experience. Simply calling this formative experience "modernity" is the ultimate cop-out in my mind. Nobody knows what modernity is except that it isn't the past and might be the future. Modernity can, then, be a form of suddenness. Here is a generation that has now learned that real, authentic time is a revolution of suddenness. Okay, how do you explain that? It's modernity. Or you choose something else. Communication, for example. Suddenly, we might decide that what gives our time its reflexivity is the problem of the other, intersubjectivity, and the matter of language. Our society, then, would be one in which communication is recognized as the supreme reality. And so on. As interesting as that move may be, it marks the fatal slippage of these analyses into some psychological picture of society. If anybody took Bohrer's notion of suddenness seriously as a social or historical diagnosis, it would ultimately fall into that group.

We don't have very much time to start on Kittler, but I will outline my positions so that we can talk about him more next time.[2] This is the way I'm using Kittler for us: Kittler represents an absolute break with all that we've read. Yes, he quotes Heidegger at some point, but not in any serious

2 Jameson discusses other works by Kittler in more detail in the next lecture, but the assigned readings for this lecture, along with the Bohrer book, include Friedrich Kittler, *Optical Media: Berlin Lectures, 1999*, trans. Anthony Enns (Cambridge: Polity Press, 2010), pp. 1–46 (the introduction by John Durham Peters, Kittler's preface, and chapter 1, "Theoretical Presuppositions"); and Tom McCarthy, "Kittler and the Sirens," *LRB Blog*, November 9, 2011.

way. This is not philosophy anymore. Having failed to put together a real notion of history or historical situations, he decides to specialize in a more objective kind of cultural artifact. In earlier work, this objective form could have been a specific medium—in Kracauer's case, film. In a course I taught on French theory last year, people resisted the inclusion of film theory on the syllabus, because they felt that film theory was not French theory, that it was a specialized domain. This is actually quite false. But film theory, nonetheless, seemed to be some kind of science and thus not part of the speculations that make up theory. Here, even more, we find this to be the case. Kittler's is not just *a* media theory but *the* media theory, in which everything is a medium. With this expansion of the media concept, thought disappears. That is one of his philosophical positions, if you like.

What is the status of media theory? Is it a philosophy? Can it or should it be a philosophy? Should it not be something separate from theory in general? It seems to me that its object has moved from notions of writing, from Plato to Derrida, to technology. *Tekhne* in Greek was connected to *poiesis*. It was an art of using objects, but of course the objects that they used are not at all like ours, so suddenly media theory evolves, just as engineering split off from a general, everyday understanding of measurement into something at once far more specialized and far more objective. It seems to me that here you have a split not unlike that of manual and intellectual labor. Media theory returns to some deep kind of manual labor, writing as a use of the hand, the instrument; finally writing becomes a paradigm of technology, itself a domain of communication. With people like Habermas, the partially abandoned aspects of communication get sucked back into philosophy. The distance between problems of media and the general problems of communication autonomizes itself and then, in some of these thinkers, turns back into something like an ideology of media.

Kittler is, I think, the ultimate example of this. He is the first German writer—I exaggerate a little bit, but it can be useful to identify what is specific about him—to have felt the impact of the French. With Kittler, we are talking about the late '80s, largely. Before the break of the '80s, Germany remains—despite the influence of American sociology and systems theory—a culture whose principal source is German idealism, from Kant to Hegel. There is a relationship to thought in that tradition, even in Heidegger and phenomenology, which allows us to talk about a German philosophical culture which is suddenly broken by French theory, Foucault, and all the rest of it. Habermas makes attempts to talk to these people, since he is of course imperialistic and interested in subsuming or solving the problems raised by Derrida and others. But French theory is understood to be alien to German thought. This is a prolongation of—I won't call them "nationalisms"—the older geopolitical relationships.

In Thomas Mann's *Doctor Faustus*, there is a scene with the *Wandervogel*, the youth movement before the First World War in which the youth would take hikes into nature—not exactly like the Boy Scouts, since it is a very specific movement of German youth which goes back to the nineteenth century. In the novel, we hear some of the discussions among these students, who say, "The French, for us, have only form; the Russians and Slavs have only depth; but only we Germans have both together." Here, we see a way of thinking quasi-geographically about these different traditions, but it certainly relies on a feeling of national identity and a differentiation, above all, from the French. I won't say that it leads into the Nazis, but the Nazi movement is based on the resentment of the Versailles Treaty, which is really a French-imposed agreement. So, there is a constant tension with the French tradition.

This is the moment of the break after which the gates are open to French theory. First of all, French theory offered Kittler a persona. He was certainly an *enfant terrible*. He ended up having his own following. His colleagues detested him. He had a personality of a distinctive type, somebody like Foucault or Derrida. Kittler's followers called themselves the *Kittlerjugend*, like the Hitler Youth, not because they were fascists but because they idolized him, followed him around and encouraged his sense that he was a cult figure. We have to understand what kind of thought makes that idolization possible. If you can't ask whether media theory is possible, then you have to ask about the status with which he endows it. He certainly knows that he has a relationship to people like McLuhan or Virilio. I should mention his famous last words: "Shut off all the devices." *Alle Apparate abschalten*. This is a materialist view of life: Our life, our personalities, what we do, are all apparatuses. They are media. All of life is this cable on which signals are carried. When all of those signals shut down, life ends. An older notion of death itself is to be replaced by a shutting down of the apparatuses. As I say, he was a dramatic figure.

I'm not pushing these things on you, only taking them apart and seeing how they work. I think we can do some of that next time with Luhmann as well.

November 11, 2021

22

Kittler, Luhmann, Habermas

Regarding the shape of the course and our return to Habermas, I'm very anxious—although this is a powerful, energetic figure in many ways, whose students have had a lot of power in the West German establishment—that you not think this course reaches its climax with Habermas. He has certainly accompanied us throughout, from the end of the war. We are coming now to his masterwork from 1985, *The Theory of Communicative Action*. Habermas considers reason to be a matter of arguments, and he has entered into many of them, which we are not necessarily going to follow. But one of them is worth mentioning, an argument with a number of historians about the origins of Nazism. A famous historian, Ernst Nolte, took it upon himself to defend the thesis that the Soviets had already invented the kind of mass murder committed by the Nazis, and that the right-wing movement in Germany is thus to be explained by this previous fact of the Soviet revolution. Obviously, this is not what the Left has thought since the war. Habermas was offended by this thesis and entered into a fierce debate with its advocates, a move which is characteristic of the position he has held as the public intellectual of West Germany.

The work we are considering today is a systematic study of communicative reason. I admire it as a construction, but I don't want you to end this course with a belief that everything proceeds to Habermas—even though he has arranged the history of German thought that way—or that I am myself in profound sympathy with his views. He is, however, the public intellectual of the representative situation of West Germany, a role that he has filled better than anybody I can think of in any of the other so-called Western democracies.

I want then to put Habermas into historical perspective. It seems to me that, while the political development of West Germany is quite different from that of the other countries, it has been exemplary in many other ways. Something happens to Germany, something which happens to the other Western countries, too, and it is with this sudden historical transformation that I would end this story. With the early 1980s, there is a shift from Keynesianism and classical liberalism to free market practices and privatization. West Germany had been exemplary in its construction of a welfare state, and Habermas himself gained his influence as the spokesman of this welfare state. But, since the onset of neoliberalism and a certain kind of conservative statecraft, the welfare state has been not only under ideological attack but is also being actively dismantled. Privatization has been the major current of this turn. We have only to consider the fact that the socialist prime minister of France, Lionel Jospin, privatized more industries than any of the right-wing ministers before him. In many ways, the spread of privatization has brought with it a diminution in cultural and intellectual activity, but in the German context, these developments have to be connected with the emergence of Europe itself.

That is why I give you the article by Perry Anderson, whose description of the implementation of the various soft coups, let's say, I follow very closely.[1] Broadly speaking, Anderson tells the story of how the European political framework has overtaken the national states by a host of financial and legal limitations, which rule out certain kinds of national economic initiatives, including all the initiatives pursued by the Left. Maastricht would mark the principal but certainly not the only moment in this process. The Left, but not only the Left, reacted very strongly to Brussels's attempt at a constitution. It was turned down by the Danes, first of all. It seems to me that such attempts at continental legislation tend to be very bland and human-rights-friendly documents which completely rule out, as I say, any kind of national control over state initiatives. You may say, after reading Anderson's article, that he makes a very strong case for Brexit, and indeed, in a sense, Brexit represents a certain roadblock—the Greek crisis was another one—to this new political formation. It was felt

1 Perry Anderson, "The European Coup," *London Review of Books*, December 17, 2020.

that to accede to this new Europe was to lose a whole set of national possibilities. Anderson's subsequent articles, however, mount a devastating critique of Brexit.[2]

Together, Anderson's articles provide a description of how a supernational formation, which is not yet completely theorized, has relegated the possibilities of the nation-state to the past. I wanted to bring this up when we were talking about Peter Weiss, because it seems to me that Stalinism initiated another, though altogether different, version of that process: the various national communist movements as opposed to the Popular Front itself, an attempt to reestablish a connection between the communist and socialist parties. The international, in other words, turned into more of an obligation than a possibility: At every turn, when these national leftist movements had a chance at developing something new, a supernational obligation was imposed on them, namely, to defend the Soviet Union. In the rest of Weiss's novel, he goes through all the moments at which leftist initiatives are blocked by this supernational obligation, because, of course, they depend on the Soviet Union, and if the Soviet Union is destroyed, either by Hitler or by some other enemy, then the communist parties wither on the vine, as you have been able to see since 1989.

This is a situation for which we don't yet have a political language. Federalism is the only concept that has emerged to name something larger than the nation-state, but it is not a workable concept, I think. The tragedy of Yugoslavia is the acting out of its problems. There isn't an analogous tragedy in the Soviet Union because its federalization was recontrolled in many ways, and therefore met a different set of limitations. But one must understand that in the Yugoslav case, as I think most reasonable explanations of all this agree, it is not some ancient rivalry between Serbians and Croatians that stands to blame, but, rather, the fact that, little by little, the International Monetary Fund and other organizations began to favor the individual Yugoslav republics over the whole. It is not insignificant for us that Helmut Kohl, one of the longest-serving German prime ministers, was one of the first to recognize the break-off republics. The end of the twentieth century, therefore, should not be understood as marking the failure of federalism but, on the contrary, as the sign that some supernational concept is emerging that doesn't yet function politically. Globalization has taken a negative meaning in no small part because it has taken the path set

2 See Perry Anderson, *Ever Closer Union? Europe in the West* (London: Verso, 2021).

by Europe in forging a softly repressive apparatus to pull together different states in the service of social reproduction. What I'm trying to say is that, in the situation of globalism today, the ultimate limit we reach in thinking and conceptualizing political collectivities is the nation-state, even when supernational entities like the EU have been formed and that this limit is itself the tragedy of globalization, because it is obvious to anyone aware of the problems facing us that there will have to be larger collectivities. The Right fantasizes about the black helicopters of the United Nations moving into the United States, but the broader presence of similar anxieties shows that there is an empty spot in the collective imagination itself, waiting to be filled by something beyond the nation-state.

All of this has been epitomized by the idea that the nation-states have been replaced by member-states. The European states are now member-states. What does that mean? This is a place in which the word "autonomy" could be used with reference both to their political and their cultural independence, because they can no longer entertain the kinds of experiments that the older nation-states could. I'm not saying that it was possible to go on with the earlier geopolitical arrangement, which produced two or even three world wars, if you want to count the Franco-Prussian War. But one need only look at the various statesmen who represent stabilization to see the effects of becoming a member-state. Mrs. Merkel's genius, until she faced the immigration crisis, was to be able to control all of these situations. She continued the path of Kohl in this, with Brandt being the last symbolic figure of Germany's autonomy.

Likewise, it seems to me that, after the German '60s and '70s, the intellectual scene sees a greater tendency toward specialization, less in the way of daring theory, with a few exceptions, among them Kittler; by way of his audacity and his scandalousness as an individual, he epitomizes what was required for somebody to break through the conformity that settled down over West Germany with Habermas, not least of all because the left professors were all fired with the *Berufsverbot*. Enzensberger said it was time for the Germans to be mediocre, average, boring. Kittler didn't do that, so whatever one thinks of his work, one has to recognize that a place was ready for him in this new situation. I've said that he is the first German to introduce French theory into his thought, but he is also the first to take what is emerging as media theory in Canada and then in other places—film theory in France, for example—and make an antihumanist theory of the role of mechanisms in thought. This he did with great flair and wit.

Now, the problem that we have here with media theory in general is whether there can be a philosophy of media. It is related to the problem of film theory. As I say, I was surprised that, last semester, when I tried to do something analogous to this study of postwar German thought for the French situation, the film-theoretical moment somehow didn't seem to fit in for many people. I think that was because there is a foreign body in film theory: the camera. The camera is, of course, the apparatus, the solution to humanism. Suddenly, we don't need people anymore, because we have the apparatus to think for us. Perhaps you know Slavoj Žižek's joke. You want to copy a film? Okay. Once you copy it, you don't have to see it anymore, because your VCR has had the *jouissance*. It is not necessary for a human being to do so; the VCR has seen the film, and that's quite enough. The point in Lacan, in any case, is that it doesn't matter who has the *jouissance*. What matters is that the *jouissance* is there. Well, it is there in the apparatus.

The philosophy of apparatuses takes leave of the tricky problems involved in subjectivity, so as to end up only with things, machines. Media theory, in general, sets itself the problem that it is impossible to philosophize the thing that remains there at the center of it, the media object. You can transport this problematic back into the past, as Derrida does, with Plato and say that it was always there as a problem, in the middle of which is writing itself, the pen, this foreign body. There is always this material piece of machinery in the middle of your philosophy that you can't get away from unless you reduce it to the material supplement of thought. It is the mind-body problem again. You think you are dealing with the mind and its contemplation of meanings, and suddenly you stumble across the body in the middle of it all. What do you do with the body and other material things in the realm of thought? You allegorize them. Material things are turned in one way or another into some allegory of subjectivity.

The major French meditation on this problem we owe to the late Bernard Stiegler, who used the notion that the various media apparatuses can be thought of like prostheses. In the old days, when human beings were post-hominids, it would not be a terrible scandal for something to be the prosthesis of the hand. To have the hand be the prosthesis of the conscious body—that is the first prosthesis, in a sense. Then we can make tools that are an extension of it. But, once you get to things like writing, prosthesis becomes a doubtful concept. Is it really a philosophical concept. Isn't media theory a halfway point between the ideal and the material? Isn't it a study of the place where you try to stick the two together and find that you can't? The body is not meaningful. Evolution is not meaningful. Life is not meaningful. Nature is not meaningful, unless you make it meaningful through the allegories of religion. Of course, the mind is meaningful, but it isn't the body. It isn't real, in a sense. So, media theory and film theory operate at that scandalous impasse, which we can't seem to overcome unless we make some fast moves to conceal this scandal and to turn it into something useful. That's what Kittler does. Life is meaningless, okay. Life is the fiber-optic cable. It is just a material thing, even if there are ways you can turn it into something else.

In Kittler's other book, *Gramophone, Film, Typewriter*, he lays out another aspect of the prosthesis problem. Amid the continuities of life, he tells us, it is impossible to make sense of anything without some kind of discontinuity; we have to stop the clock and identify the present to make it meaningful. Each of these apparatuses—the gramophone, film, and typewriter—each overcome this continuity in time and stamp it into something retrievable, but in doing so, they also make it possible to overcome space. The gramophone and the radio are mechanisms which are disjointed and which therefore, by virtue of their disjointedness, are able to produce acoustic or visual images; and in a sense the typewriter becomes the supreme example of this process, because it spatializes and breaks up speech—a continuity of sound, however dissectable that sound may be—into reproducible letters. Until you get apparatuses for performing this operation, you won't be able to register them in quite the same way. The typewriter brings this phenomenon out into the open and says that not only are there gaps between the words; there are gaps between the letters, which are themselves a kind of a fiction for sounds. A divisibility, a set of discontinuities, is precisely what the apparatus will then, in another moment, pull back together into a fictive continuity. But this apparatus will also allow us at a metalevel suddenly to see that what we thought were unities are only the artificial reassembling of produced and reproduced discontinuities, which represent the impossibility of making a meaning of the original continuity of life as much as of the fiber-optic cable.

He draws heavily on Lacan, but it may not be immediately obvious why Lacan's notion of the mirror stage, for instance, would be useful in this analysis. In the beginning, does the child have the illusion of continuity? Not really, because, to know that something is continuous, you have to first see it against the background of discontinuity. The child lives in continuity but only insofar as it experiences its as-yet meaningless body, meaningless as far as the child is concerned. It has its various discomforts, its hungers, its itchings, and there isn't any central consciousness to be aware that all these things are its own. So, when does the child discover itself? In the mythical so-called mirror stage, the child discovers itself when it recognizes itself in the mirror and thus, from the mirror, sees itself as a unity. Suddenly, all those feelings then belong to it and are the experiences of a unified body. From there, the child enters Lacan's stage of the Imaginary.

Kittler astonishingly uses Lacan's entry into the Imaginary to develop his philosophy of media. The Imaginary is the stage in which you are able to put together an illusion of continuity out of these fragmented things.

> The imaginary, however, comes about as the mirror image of a body that appears to be, in terms of motor control, more perfect than the infant's own body, for in the real everything begins with coldness, dizziness, and shortness of breath. Thus, the imaginary implements precisely those optical illusions that were being researched in the early days of cinema. A dismembered or (in the case of film) cut-up body is faced with the illusionary continuity of movements in the mirror or on screen. It is no coincidence that Lacan recorded infants' jubilant reactions to their mirror images in the form of documentary footage.[3]

This is an allegory in which the mechanisms of media reproduce the processes whereby our false identities as human beings come together, but, Kittler says, if we stand back from those processes, if we observe their mediation, it is possible to understand how these false identities are a humanist ideology. The attack on humanism, the attack on the centrality of the mind, of consciousness, of the self, is obviously, in France, the domain of Foucault, and certainly Kittler models himself on Foucault in many ways. Foucault's famous attack on the construction of Man is the operation that he wants to reproduce here. In language, an analogous operation will be at work with the various texts, beginning with the gramophone and its grooves, which have to be somehow unified into something intelligible. Meanwhile, language, because it is a separate set of words, of phonemes, is the domain of Lacan's Symbolic, and a relationship between the Imaginary and Symbolic is transposed onto that of external media themselves. We

3 Friedrich Kittler, *Gramophone, Film, Typewriter*, trans. Geoffrey Winthrop-Young and Michael Wutz (Stanford, CA: Stanford University Press, 1999), p. 15.

have to exceed ourselves into the Symbolic to develop the illusion that we are unified beings. As for the Real: "Finally, of the real nothing more can be brought to light than what Lacan presupposed—that is, nothing. It forms the waste or residue that neither the mirror of the imaginary nor the grid of the symbolic can catch: the physiological accidents and stochastic disorder of bodies."[4] The Real is that which cannot be put into words. All of this falls back very nicely into Kittler's version of media studies. I think this is quite a remarkable performance, which climaxes in his own famous last words. And one must recognize this as a significant moment in the thinking of the period and in the richness and invention of it.

With Niklas Luhmann, I can go into even less detail, given how little time we have left.[5] One could ask: Aren't we moving away from philosophy? German philosophy under the sign of Hegel always affirmed that it was a matter of consciousness. Hegel's *Begriff* is a phenomenon of absolute consciousness, absolute unity. In a sense, the Frankfurt School tried desperately both to adopt and repudiate Hegel's heritage by turning his insight into a negative diagnosis. That is, they are not Hegelians in the sense in which they look forward to the arrival of Absolute Spirit, but they are able to criticize the Real in the absence of that unification. They are negative Hegelians in that sense—particularly Adorno, but even later figures like Habermas, to an extent. In France, the atmosphere of philosophical work is that of a constant rebuke to the philosophy of the subject. The Germans are not quite so dramatic about this, since, in a way, Marx and the Frankfurt School seem to represent some positive outcome of the Hegelian moment which in France is so stridently refused. Nonetheless I think both traditions follow the same pattern, and I agree with its general impetus. We don't want psychology, the last outcome of a philosophy of subjectivity as a normative procedure that we cannot finally accept. Our problem is collective subjectivity—which at this time has also been sought through the philosophy of the concept—but that is not something we can so easily point to; it is a very difficult problem.

Both Luhmann and Habermas in effect choose sociology as a way out of this dilemma. The same is true in France of Bourdieu. The position of the sociologist is cleaner than that of the philosopher. The philosopher makes us ideologies—even if that ideology is the rejection of ideologies—whereas

4 Ibid., pp. 15–16.

5 From Luhmann, Jameson assigned "Differentiation of Society," *Canadian Journal of Sociology / Cahiers canadiens de sociologie* 2, no. 1 (Winter, 1977), pp. 29–53.

the sociologist simply observes in a tragic spirit, according to Bourdieu in his defense of this last place of critique. Luhmann certainly goes on to do just that, but in a very special way. He doesn't reinvent sociology but continues it. Sociology begins with Max Weber, and with Durkheim to a certain degree. Habermas's two volumes can be taken as a vast and very lucid introduction to sociology itself. Goffman, Piaget—all of these side alleys of modern thought are put together in this supreme defense of sociology, as distinct as it is from Luhmann's.

The other thing that comes out of Weber, whose main theme is of course modernity, is systems theory. His American translator, Talcott Parsons, invents on the basis of much of Weber's work an account of systematicity: Everything is a system or a connecting up of the various systems with each other. I won't go into systems theory here, because it can be a repulsive thing, but, certainly, Luhmann, in his later years, made an enormous contribution to it by applying systems theory to practically everything. There is also a little book on love, which represents a systems theory analysis of newly emergent emotions or affects.[6] I think it is not completely successful, but you should know that it exists. As far as art goes, there is a huge volume called *Art as a Social System*, and it begins with a theory of perception. After all, Baumgarten's original aesthetic derived from the Greek word for perception. Differentiation comes in when we consider how to take something which is just part of everyday life, as we perceive our surroundings, and to make it an autonomous domain of experience and inquiry. Differentiation means to produce the autonomy of some such domain, to separate it off from others, and to produce a system for it. Art, in its modern form, makes perception as a worldly event somehow semiautonomous, in that now, when we enter a museum and look at a painting, we stop doing everything else; we leave the world, and we consider art to have left the world, too. Painting then has its own systematicity, an internal logic. The sociologists can deal with politics, power, economics, emotions, maybe even the physiological, but art is constantly, as with Adorno, wanting to be autonomous and independent—it makes itself a system—and in this respect, it also plays Luhmann's game. The question then becomes how art can establish a new connection with the other systems. This is a word that Habermas is going to keep, as

6 Niklas Luhmann, *Love as Passion: The Codification of Intimacy*, trans. Jeremy Gaines and Doris L. Jones (Stanford, CA: Stanford University Press, 1998).

well as this notion of the *system* as the object of sociological inquiry. And Luhmann certainly plays his role in Habermas, who is, in his own way, not only a great *bricoleur* but a conqueror of all these external theories, which he puts together for his own purposes in an admirable way, I must say, even if I don't ultimately endorse it.

Systems theory recommends itself for an analysis of modernity and is therefore subject to all the problems with this concept that I have already raised. Yes, societies are very complicated, so either you want to rely on a concept of modernity or some other vague, catchall but meaningful-sounding abstraction that you can put all that together under: Complexity or acceleration are two that we will see at work shortly. Luhmann, with the concept of differentiation, gives you the chance to do this. But where is the dialectical leap? You know that Hegel talks about the leap from quality to quantity, from quantity to quality. Enough stuff piles up that it suddenly changes character and jumps into a new phenomenon. I suppose Luhmann could turn around and make a dialectic of systems theory by saying there is a moment when differentiation itself becomes autonomous and a moment when traditional societies suddenly mutate into modern societies. At any rate, such a dialectic would not simply be a matter of knowing what is happening right now—that we could leave to the economists and bloggers and cultural critics—but we have to know what it came from so as to recognize what about it constitutes something new and what may come after it.

Differentiation is a very important tool for many German thinkers in this period. We've seen Kittler use it, and we've begun to see how Habermas and Luhmann use it, but how does it fit into a larger intellectual moment and how does it fit into a longer history of thought? Consider, for instance, our theme of separation, the central idea of Marx's theory of alienation. In a sense, Marx would be the inventor of this notion of differentiation. Differentiation begins with the separation of the worker from his tools, from his object, from his organic life, and from his fellow workers. This is the codification of an earlier notion of separation, which forms a part of our postmodern cognitive aesthetic. Most modernist history, it seems to me, insists on breaks and differences rather than continuities, and the emergence of systems theory is one formalization of that tendency.

That emergence—passing now into Habermas—is not new. You remember that, in the late nineteenth century, Dilthey begins to worry whether there is a radical difference between the sciences and the

Geisteswissenschaften, cultural and social forms of knowledge. Their difference is then codified as the difference between explanation and understanding, *Erklärung* and *Verstehen*. The sciences explain; they explain how the atom can be split, and how time varies but the speed of light is always the same. Science explains all those things without their having a meaning. There are laws, but they don't mean anything. What is the atom? Is it something that means something? What could it mean, unless you turn it into an allegory of something else? On the other hand, in *Geisteswissenschaften*, somehow, you come up against the other. Some of you have been startled that I use this expression. We sometimes may forget that what we experience is not just the struggle between the mind and the various conditions of matter but also a struggle between people. There is a third term here, which is the collectivity. Why have we neglected it? I think philosophers have neglected it. Just speaking as an outside observer, in philosophy, not ethics, it seems to me that the other does not truly appear until Hegel's *Phenomenology of Spirit*. Descartes looked out the window and wondered whether those creatures moving about in the street were not automatons. But the question about the other as an existence which puts us absolutely in question as individuals is a late discovery and maybe a Romantic one. It is hard to date these things. But the existence of other people is a simple way of stating what philosophy has to struggle with after Hegel, and it is at the core of Habermas's notion of communication.

Now we can think of a cloud that floats above everything, into which all of these separate, impossible subjectivities are submerged, who are all unique centers of something which is connected to all the others. What is this substance of connection itself? Language, of course. It gives us a set of philosophical alibis with which we cover over the scandal of otherness and the impossibility of conceptualizing collectivity, which, it seems to me, would be the closest thing we have to a nature. It seems to me that Habermas is trying to identify something like this cloud of connectivity, because he wants to figure out how consensus and norms are possible. Insofar as he is an ideologist for a certain kind of society, he is interested in showing how this society is possible, how it is normatively justified, and how it can be maintained on the basis of that justification. This is the sense in which Habermas is the philosopher of the welfare state. As I said, West Germany didn't have to have an army—they couldn't—and they didn't have to have much else that the Americans supplied, and therefore West Germany could create its own version of a capitalist utopia or welfare state. So, in a sense, it is the laboratory—and, in the context of the Cold War, it had to be the proving ground—of what capitalism or modernity has often promised without delivering.

Habermas's project is a complicated one. First of all, he has to deal with Europe. I don't mean the Europe that Perry Anderson was talking about. I mean what people attack when they critique Eurocentrism. It doesn't matter if you say that capitalism originated in Europe, and therefore all the other things that were unique to Europe followed from it, because there will always be the question: Why? Why did China not invent capitalism? Why is it that the richest country on earth in the eighteenth century suddenly became the victim of the Europeans in the Opium Wars and the Boxer Rebellion? Yes, Habermas is offering a defense of Europe, in some sense. Something original is claimed to have happened in Europe when it separated religion from the state, invented this thing called capitalism, and began to think in a secular way using what the Frankfurt School will denounce, namely rationalization. As a sociologist, Weber—as critical as he was of modern European culture—somehow had to defend the position that rationalization, rationality, is a norm for human societies. That is, he universalized a process which was, in fact, unique to Europe. It must not be relativized. People talk nowadays about all kinds of modernities, a modernity in Southeast Asia, in Latin America, and so on. Yes, but will such modernities also be Eurocentric? How will the very notion of modernity not be derived from this thing that happened to Europe? Habermas accordingly will show that European modernity is normative, that is, that all rationality must be the one that develops in Europe. Habermas's project is to fulfill that promise. He must refuse the Frankfurt School critique of Weber and their idea that rationality devolves into instrumental reason and reification, and he must show that all of the other cultures of the world are, in fact, moving towards this same rationality, which they attain only by virtue of its invention in Europe.

What Habermas has to show is the passage from the symbolic to the communicational. How is it that the rational communicational system of which Europeans are so proud is already there in the symbolic itself, in religion and theology, such that modern rationality doesn't come as a break with the past but rather as a process of drawing out what was already present? Habermas needs this continuity in order to universalize his version of rationality. We'll come back to this next time.

November 16, 2021

23

Luhmann, Habermas, Sloterdijk, Rosa

This is our last class. We will finish with Habermas before saying a word about Sloterdijk and Hartmut Rosa. To set the scene, let's go back to the nation-states in the '80s and '90s as they became member-states. As I said, they begin to lose their autonomy in the transformation of great powers into small powers. The European nation-states are no longer completely independent; however important they were as great powers, as some of them certainly were or strived to be, they can no longer be considered as such. In this respect I want to suggest something which ought to be meaningful to anyone in the so-called humanities or *Geisteswissenschaften*: Something is happening to language. One great, collective alienation is undermining the status of language. One aspect of that alienation has to do with the powerful languages of the member-states. Spain, in its undoing after 1898 and the loss of the empire, has regained part of its status as a great power. In a way, you could say that Spain reconquered Latin America in recent years and that its reconquering is secured by Spanish as a world language, or as the Germans say, a "culture language," a language in which there are writers whose works have become classics, so to speak, beyond their linguistic boundaries. Those languages are dependent on national power. During the Gorbachev period, a French history teacher said to me that every time something significant happens in another nation, the number of students learning its language goes up. With General de Gaulle's return to power in 1958, suddenly enrollment in French courses shot up. With the arrival of Gorbachev in the Soviet Union, suddenly the same happened in Russian courses. I think that is significant, but not for the obvious reasons. Look at it the other way around; consider the small powers with a less powerful language, like Holland or Hungary. I would like each of you to tell me who the greatest Hungarian poet is. I don't think any of you know. If I asked you who is considered the greatest Russian poet, you would say Pushkin. If I asked you about Germany, you would probably say Goethe. But every country has some kind of central writer of that kind, even if they don't circulate beyond their linguistic borders to the same extent as some of the other great national writers. Therefore, when I talk about a nation's cultural energy, the circulation of its language is part of what I mean: To write in this language means something world-historical. It is a kind of destiny. Sometimes it takes a different form. Hungarian is notoriously difficult to learn. Even if you were interested in Sándo Petőfi, who is the great Hungarian poet, or Lukács and the whole school around him, it wouldn't be very easy to learn their language. Dutch should be easier, but I have the feeling that they don't want us to learn their language. They react to this situation by affirming the fact that nobody can speak Dutch. So, there are ways in which small powers deal with this problem.

I'm saying all this not to belittle any of these traditions—far from it—but to emphasize the mingling of translation and political power. In the old days, the Comintern and the socialist countries certainly outperformed the United States in this arena. But it is hard to attract an international public to volumes of Hungarian poetry or Vietnamese literature. The politics of translation are determined by capitalist corporations, whereas, at other times and places, it has been run by the state. We are in a situation in which a great, world-power language, which produced some of the central ideas in philosophy and literature, has become a small-power language. How many people learn German anymore? This is a great trauma to a national culture. It affects cultural production, and it affects ambitions, determining anything from translation projects to immigration. And this is reflected in intellectual production. Just look at Habermas's footnotes. They are full of American sociologists.

There was a desperate attempt to create a new European culture. T. S. Eliot, in the '20s, from a conservative point of view, talked about the great European traditions. Later, after '89, Derrida, Bourdieu, and others were involved in an attempt, from a different point of view, to set up a European cultural diffusion whose great writer turned out to be Milan

Kundera, not to my mind equal to Virgil in Eliot's scheme of things. As for the empires, Russia and Britain yesterday, China and the United States today, I am reminded of a new history of the great Spanish Empire in the sixteenth and seventeenth centuries, a revisionist but definitive work in which the historian explains that, while we think that Shakespeare and the Elizabethans were the center of the world, England at the time was a tiny place that lived off of piracy. Even the pope had little interest in it. Spain was the great power, and all the Elizabethan plays are fascinated by Catholicism, the Mediterranean, the villains of Italian and Spanish origin. One can take a fresh look at those writings with that in mind. And modernity may as well begin in literature with Quixote. Spain's literature was translated all over Europe but not yet all over the world. Mario Vargas Llosa claims that in the new world it was forbidden to publish novels until the eighteenth century. I don't know if this is true. But at least in Europe, translations of Spanish writing flourished, while, in Spain itself, there were hardly any translations. They didn't care about the other languages of the continent—Dutch, English, French, German—because they were the center of the world. Their literature was the important one, not this stuff from the periphery. I tend to think that this is the implicit American position. "Yeah, we admit a few foreigners into our pantheon, but really we don't need to translate these things because we're the center of the world." In China, I can't say what the situation is. In an imperializing situation, a widely encompassing cultural strategy is necessary, so I suspect that it is the same. The Chinese Middle Kingdom has never had to be all too interested in anything outside of itself, even after the British arrive in the Opium Wars, at least for a time. Once China is reborn with the People's Republic, it can refocus on itself. Empires have no need to look elsewhere, because they are the world.

Returning now to Habermas, who is writing amid another great change in the cultural powers. Habermas is offering a communication-based proposal, not a linguistic one, but his idea is that language and gesture are all forms of action. The universal is not language, but it is somehow action. He himself might say that he must make the link between premodern and modern forms of universality. Most definitions of the modern claim a sharp break with the legitimating function of religion. He doesn't want to rely on such an easy story. He insists that the passage from the symbolic to the secular or the linguistic-communicational is simply a matter of the "linguistification," as he calls it, of the symbolic, such that these earlier symbolic forms are annexed by language, with its universalizing procedures. There is not a break but a continuity there.

For his diagnosis, he turns to the distinction between the lifeworld and the systems. This is his way of putting together two seemingly incompatible kinds of thinking: lifeworld—Heidegger and phenomenology—and systems—Weber and systems theory. He thinks that these systems are like two separate, incompatible languages. They work together, but they are not exactly translatable into each other. One is a matter of explanation—how does it work?—and the others are matters of understanding—how do I feel or imagine it? So, we still have a division here that can be traced back to Kant, who gives us a particularly egregious form of separation. The title of his late essays, *The Conflict of the Faculties*, is a joke, referring to two separate notions of "faculty." Kant believed in mental faculties: reason here, sensation over there, not unlike how contemporary brain sciences imagine the different parts of the brain. Hegel made fun of Kant's insistence on the faculties by calling his notion of the mind "the soul sack," a great sack in which you throw the various faculties that make up the human. Then you can carry it around as your identity. But "faculty" also means a university faculty: the law faculty, the theological faculty, and so on. Kant's joke suggests that those are in some way the same. We wouldn't have a separate law faculty if we didn't have some specific part of our mind that had to do with moral judgements, for example. We wouldn't have a department of physics if we didn't have a part of the mind that attempted to register sensations and forces and to measure them. So, here is your original set of differentiations, as Luhmann calls them. How do you put them back together again, if not in Hegel's soul sack? If you didn't have these separations, then you would find yourself back in something like animal existence. Every society has, presumably, differentiated these domains in one way or another, but the separations have to be somehow reunited.

Habermas is very pleased with this differentiation of domains, but he also realizes that all of our problems come from this differentiation, that is, the uncoupling of the systems from the lifeworld. Economics, for instance, becomes uncoupled from the lifeworld with money and eventually capitalism. Habermas's project strives towards putting them back together again. That project is based on argumentation and the possibility of persuading people. If someone is lying—perhaps a politician—then you don't have to persuade them, because you know that these politicians have their conniving strategies. I keep quoting his muttering back in that debate: We have our laws. Laws are the last defense. So, rationality is the crucial thing here, enshrined in the *Grundgesetz* or otherwise. I think this ends up as a description rather than as a politics, because, as we well know nowadays, laws themselves are very fragile written things.

With that we pass to the *enfant terrible* Sloterdijk. He is some twenty years younger than Habermas. He first emerged in the '70s with his thesis on Weimar culture called *The Critique of Cynical Reason*. The whole notion of cynicism was, for him, the central fact of the Weimar Republic. The Germans, having been a very youthful republic, having failed to make their republic in 1848, having destroyed themselves in the First World War, had no illusions, so to speak. They had formed no real, usable traditions of the type that Gadamer and others were seeking to reestablish. So, they emerged without illusions into the Weimar period and were immediately confronted by a second catastrophe, which is the famous inflation crisis of the '20s, when what could formerly buy a loaf of bread became essentially worthless. There are famous examples of people wheeling wheelbarrows full of this worthless paper to the grocery store. This disaster is partly caused by the reparations demanded by the Treaty of Versailles, in which the French very stupidly exacted revenge not only for World War I but also for the Franco-Prussian War and the loss of two of their provinces. American bankers underpinned the Weimar Republic and saved it from this crisis, but not quickly enough to efface the memories of World War I or the stab in the back of Versailles.

If you recall now that the central figure of Weimar was Brecht, you immediately recognize the importance not only of having no illusions but also of having proposals, so to speak. Brecht wrote his own epitaph: "He made proposals. We carried them out." I was told by friends of his that when he came back to East Germany he had proposals for everything: street lighting, garbage collecting, everything. Of course, he only lived a year or two longer. The combination of Brecht's productivity, energy, and cynicism is what makes for the flavor of *The Threepenny Opera*. Nonetheless, for Sloterdijk, cynicism is a corrosive mindset, especially if you don't share Brecht's ambitions. You cannot attack cynicism for its will to see through everything, as it were. Yes, understanding must entail seeing through everything, as though everything is a facade, and we must know what goes on behind it. At the same time, to see through all the pieties of social life, to say that human beings are worthless and incapable of any kind of honesty, is to wind up in a situation beyond politics, a situation which can be claimed neither by the Left nor the Right, although I suppose it would be more aligned with the Right, because the next steps towards organizing this kind of society are the Hobbesian steps toward mitigating the havoc which the human animal wreaks on itself.

So, for Sloterdijk, cynical reason, epitomized by the collapse of Weimar, "letting the wolf into the house," as Negt and Kluge put it, means that, in order to preserve the right kind of cynicism—which comes from the word for "dog" in Greek, and dog philosophy comes from Diogenes, who was looking for the one honest man—it is necessary to know what a real, active cynicism could be. Does this mean that Sloterdijk is a cynic because he analyzes cynicism with this end in mind? I think it would be better to ask: Is cynical reason not without its uses? We're all cynics today. Each country has gone through the experience of a disillusionment which leaves its belief in legitimacy and the legitimation of its forms very much in question. So, what is the proper use of cynicism after that disillusionment?

Sloterdijk believes he has an answer to that question. He wishes to go through the negative, the cynicism of this disillusioned world, and to find some kind of positive solution in negativity itself. Does this remind you of Adorno? Could you call Adorno a cynic? I think Adorno was certainly willing to see through anything, as was Brecht. I think Adorno did not draw back from seeing the weaknesses and the vices of the world, or at least of other philosophers. But I would rather compare Sloterdijk to Enzensberger, although he doesn't have Enzensberger's corrosive wit. He is not a man of the Left, but not a fascist or a conservative either.

How did Sloterdijk end up? He ended up not as a theorist or a philosopher exactly but rather blossomed, essentially, into a blogger. He entered into this blissful state for public intellectuals, which they borrowed from France. In France, there are intellectual celebrities, not like our Hollywood celebrities. France is one country in which being an intellectual is not a lowly condition and an offense, as it is in the United States, where intellectuals don't exactly have a good name. Like *Apostrophes*, the TV show in France, Sloterdijk's TV program was popular and lasted for about fifteen years. But a TV host cannot be the source of creative conceptual production, because if you're running a discussion, you can't constantly intervene to hit your guests over the head with your own ideas. In some way, you have to give them room for debate, so it was not the most productive for his own ideas.

When he came out of his TV phase, he became something like an encyclopedist. In the Middle Ages, from Isidore of Seville onward, there were books which gathered all that had been said about certain topics in other books. On this point, Foucault is very intelligent. People say that Isidore's encyclopedia was a collection of superstitions, reproducing all the alchemical stuff, the weirdest beliefs of people. No, Foucault says, it is not a question of belief or truth. Rather, it is that what people had said or written was interesting in itself. It is not a question of finding out whether this kind of stone cures leprosy. It is rather a question simply of knowing that, in certain parts of the world, people *believed* that a stone cured leprosy. In any case, these are immense collecting operations. I think that art has in some sense returned to this function of collecting. I think that you could call it the passage from the artist or the philosopher to the curator. A lot of contemporary theory is simply collecting, arranging, and mounting an exhibit. The French are thinking X, Y, and Z, so let's put all the interesting ones together, since there is no absolute framework for their work anyway, and what is needed is only a place in which we can try to transcode all those theories and make some kind of more general approach out of them.

The later Sloterdijk introduces his so-called *Hauptwerk*, these three volumes on spheres, in which he has collected and curated all the various ways in which people think, for example, of the world.[1] Do they think of it geographically? Is it a ball, like the earth? What were their pictures of this sphere? What he collects is not quite a set of worldviews, which would mean selecting a few basic categories. This is a matter of representations, I think, rather than of truths. But it is a project which no longer strikes us who have now read Adorno and Deleuze and Negt and Kluge, since it comes to us less as a statement of position than as a collection of various things, on which he takes positions, to be sure, but whose ideological interventions are not negative, as in the other theories we've read which point to fragmentation, alienation, or acceleration. He likes to have happy endings, I think, so he doesn't quite do that, and instead he proposes a kind of solution which he calls ecological Calvinism.

1 Peter Sloterdijk, *Bubbles: Spheres Volume 1: Microspherology*, trans. Wielan Hoban (Los Angeles: Semiotext(e), 2011); *Globes: Spheres Volume 2: Macrospherology*, trans. Wielan Hoban (Los Angeles: Semiotext(e), 2014); *Foams: Spheres Volume 3: Plural Spherology*, trans. Wielan Hoban (Los Angeles: Semiotext(e), 2016). For an overview, Jameson recommends Bárbara Freitag Rouanet, "The Trilogy Spheres of Peter Sloterdijk," *IOP Journal*, Volume 21 (2011), pp. 73–84.

What is ecological Calvinism? I go back to a period in which everybody was worried about images. Back in the '50s and '60s, it was very concerning that, in this modernity of the image, the individual was said to be bombarded by 10,000 images a day. In our time, in the 2020s, this number would be greatly increased, to the point that we can imagine our philosophers telling us that, in fact, everything is an image to which there is no corresponding reality. But this anxiety about images mutated instead into a worry about algorithms and manipulation by technology. To be sure, this technology involves images and advertising, the selling of objects via their images. A car is sold not for its intrinsic powers but because it looks good, has sexual overtones, is streamlined, can be associated with certain people. What is bought is an image. So, what were the solutions? Susan Sontag and Jean Baudrillard independently came up with the idea of the diet cure of images: Let's decide to see fewer images. Like most diets, this is a pious hope, and nobody is actually going to do it for very long. Sloterdijk is proposing something similar: Let's cut down on all the environmental factors which are harming us and which culminate for him in a form of accelerating complexity. So, ecological Calvinism is another way of grappling with this buzzword: complexity.

Sloterdijk says that the twentieth century was an age of impatience.[2] Why is it, he asks, that Heidegger defines the human being as a being-unto-death? Why are we, like Montaigne, supposed to think of death at every moment? The existential future, he says, induces a kind of desire for acceleration. Death is the end of it, so let's jump ahead. Let's not wait for it. Let's be aware of it right now. I think it is a marvelous diagnosis of Heidegger, but it can be extended far beyond his philosophy. If something is worthwhile, this ideology states, let's do it right now. Hitler says the world will be better if he conquers it, so let's do it right now. In the sciences, there ought to be a certain solution to a certain problem, so let's work it out now. If socialism is good, let's kill all the peasants and do it right away. Let's not fool around. All acceleration is this impatience to get to the end of a plan. This is not the apocalyptic end of the world one finds in medieval Christian eschatology, but it has something in common with that premodern form of temporal expectation, because it reasons that, if the end of the world is a good thing, because it names the moment when

2 Peter Sloterdijk, *What Happened in the Twentieth Century?*, trans. Christopher Turner (Cambridge: Polity Press, 2018).

Christ will return and with him the kingdom of heaven, then let's do it right now! I think that can serve as a productive diagnosis of the meaning of acceleration. But what would the solution be? Don't be impatient? Be patient? That isn't a very exciting solution, is it? Nobody who has any kind of impatience in them wants to be told to be patient, to cut down on their intake of images, to stop pushing forward, to go back to a simpler world, to reduce complexity. So, Sloterdijk himself is exhibiting a kind of impatience when he says we must learn to tolerate our condition.

There are certainly ways of connecting the diagnosis of impatience to the nature of capitalism, as Rosa does, but it is not necessarily a good solution. So, let's turn to Rosa. He is from another generation, born in 1965. Rosa very cleverly connects sociology back to ethics to say that this experience of impatience must be diagnosed, rather than merely described. But the central questions that the Greeks asked about ethics must also be revived alongside this diagnosis. Those questions are about what was called "the good life." Aristotle said that the good life was the life of the mind. Why? Because, for the Greeks, to practice the life of the mind required one to be a man and to be wealthy. It is a matter of having the money and the time for contemplation.

In Rosa, it is more a question of doing away with the constant push to increase the speed of social development.[3] But what does it mean to seek an increase in "speed"? Speed, in this case, is the rate at which subjects are released from economic compulsions. Rosa goes on to do something with this idea of a release from the economic that I think Habermas—who otherwise may be considered quite close to this position—knows but doesn't insist on or pursue very much, namely that this problem derives from the specific economic structure of capitalism and that capitalism is essentially a matter of growth. All of that is in Marx, but if you want a more accessible version of this, then you should turn to *The Long Twentieth Century* by Giovanni Arrighi, where you find his description of the various moments of capitalism and the way in which its central point of accumulation jumps from area to area. Arrighi begins in the Italian city-states, which are found to be too small, the terrain of capitalism exhausted, whereafter the Genoese have to become the bankers of Spain, a bigger empire in which to invest, though Spain is hobbled by the extension of its empire and a

3 Hartmut Rosa, *Acceleration: A New Theory of Modernity*, trans. Jonathan Trejo-Mathys (New York: Columbia University Press, 2015).

number of other political and economic factors, including the wars in the low countries, first a principality of Spain and then divided into what we call Belgium and Holland, where a different kind of capitalism emerges, a new imperial variety which will later become the model for the East India Company, England being the inheritor of this new company-form when it becomes the center of the industrial world, whose limits it reaches before handing it over to America. At each transition, a similar question arises: At what point does your field of operation and your market become saturated? Arrighi notes a very interesting corollary: The final stage of each of these capitalisms is a financial stage. When finance becomes a dominant part of the economy, capitalism has entered its autumn, a term he borrows from Braudel, something that has been happening in the United States recently. At that point, capitalism can only continue expanding by shifting its center of accumulation to a new place. He thought for a time that the most likely candidate for the next center was Japan, then he came to realize it was China.

One of the deductions that you can make here, which is already in Marx, is that capitalism can only overcome its contradictions by expanding. A contradiction cannot be solved. It can only be expanded, creating new contradictions. Capital must grow, increase, and multiply. We understand this is not a new problem, but it shows us that growth and acceleration are the same, as Rosa describes them, and the term "globalization" has been used to mean approximately the same thing. Any of these loosely defined terms can identify the enemy of the theory that uses them.

Along with acceleration, I think, something happens to space. This book is over a decade old, so maybe Rosa didn't see that at the time. But most discussions of postmodernity, which is, of course, what he is talking about, have insisted on the importance of its spatial aspect. I would simply invite you to imagine the most probable future of the globe, which is to say, a Canada populated by Spanish-speakers, a Scandinavia populated by Arabic- and Farsi-speakers, a Siberia populated by Vietnamese-speakers and maybe some Australians. You can see that these movements of populations and migration are not just the result of some desire to get to some other place—of course, it is a desire to get to a place where a job can be found—but it is also the warming of the earth that makes people move to cooler climes and to places which still have a yield, where you can still grow things. So, there are certainly ways to reintroduce space into this problem. But he limits his discussion to temporality, which is fine because he does it very well.

Let me now say what is the matter with all of this. I think it is very elegant and intelligent, but what it amounts to—for me, at least, despite what he says about capitalism—is what I call a culture critique. That means taking a population, probably your own, and describing its psychology. What does one do with that? One can salute it, of course—as in accelerationism—and say, "Good! Let's go even farther in this direction." But that is a different kind of choice and an acceptance of your destiny, in a way, rather than a political proposal. And it seems to me that, if a diagnosis of a culture and of the diseases of the culture—in this case, temporal diseases, let's say—is not followed by some kind of infrastructural strategy, then it remains caught in a purely cultural sphere. One can think of Lasch on America's culture of narcissism. These culture critiques can be useful for seeing the relationship between a range of symptoms that wouldn't otherwise be so obviously connected. But are we then simply to psychoanalyze a collectivity? What next? This is today, I think, how the opposition between idealism and materialism is still valid. These are idealistic critiques. They are not wrong—they are in many cases very illuminating—but something is lacking, namely the problem of infrastructure itself, even if, as in this description of capitalism and growth, an infrastructure has been borrowed and turned into cultural terms, which is no solution either. Anyway, it is with this that we conclude, rightly or wrongly.

November 18, 2021

Index